REPRESENTING THE OTHER

REPRESENTING THE OTHER

A *Feminism & Psychology* Reader

edited by

Sue Wilkinson and Celia Kitzinger

SAGE Publications
London · Thousand Oaks · New Delhi

First published 1996

SAGE Publications Ltd
6 Bonhill Street
London EC2A 4PU

SAGE Publications Inc
2455 Teller Road
Thousand Oaks, California 91320

SAGE Publications India Pvt Ltd
32, M-Block Market
Greater Kailash - I
New Delhi 110 048

British Library Cataloguing in Publication data

A catalogue record for this book is
available from the British Library

ISBN 0 7619 5228 4
ISBN 0 7619 5229 2 (pbk)

Library of Congress catalog record available

Typeset by Regent Typesetting, London
Printed in Great Britain by The Cromwell Press Ltd, Broughton Gifford,
Melksham, Wiltshire

Contents

Contributors

Magdalene Ang-Lygate is a PhD student in the Department of Government, University of Strathclyde, Glasgow, Scotland.

Diane Bell is Henry Luce Professor of Religion, Economic Development and Social Justice at the College of the Holy Cross, Worcester, Massachusetts, USA.

Manjit Bola is a PhD student in the Department of Human Sciences, Brunel University, UK.

Brown is based at Aston University, Birmingham, UK.

Erica Burman is Senior Lecturer in Developmental and Educational Psychology and Women's Studies at Manchester Metropolitan University, UK.

Amparo Bonilla Campos is a PhD student and a Lecturer in Psychology at the Facultad de Psicologia, University of Valencia, Spain.

Jean Carabine is a Lecturer in Social Policy in the Department of Social Sciences, Loughborough University, UK.

Becky Chasey is based at the Department of Clinical and Community Psychology, Exeter District Community Health Service, UK.

Joan C. Chrisler is at the Department of Psychology, Connecticut College, Connecticut, USA.

Adrian Coyle is based at the Department of Psychology, University of Surrey, Guildford, Surrey, UK.

Kathy Doherty is a Lecturer in Social Psychology in the Department of Communication Studies, Sheffield Hallam University, UK.

Rosalind Edwards is a Senior Research Fellow at South Bank University, London, UK.

Hannah Frith is a PhD student in the Department of Social Sciences, Loughborough University, UK.

Mike Gane is based at the Department of Social Sciences, Loughborough University, UK.

Christine Griffin is at the School of Psychology, University of Birmingham, Edgbaston, Birmingham, UK.

Gabriele Griffin is Professor of Women's Studies at Leeds Metropolitan University, UK.

Anita Harris is at the Department of Political Science, University of Melbourne, Australia.

Beth Humphries is based at Manchester Metropolitan University, UK.

Tracey L. Hurd is a Postdoctoral Research Fellow at the Department of Education, Brown University, Rhode Island, USA, and Visiting Scholar at the Center for the Study of Human Development.

Sheila Jeffreys is at the Department of Political Science, University of Melbourne, Australia.

Celia Kitzinger is Senior Lecturer in Social Psychology and Director of Women's Studies in the Department of Social Sciences, Loughborough University, UK.

Amanda Kottler is based at the Child Guidance Clinic, University of Cape Town, South Africa.

Anna Livia is a novelist/short-story writer and linguist, based at the Department of French, University of Illinois at Urbana-Champaign, USA.

Alice McIntyre is Adjunct Assistant Professor, Department of Counselling, Developmental Psychology and Research Methods, Boston College School of Education, Massachusetts, USA.

Katie MacMillan is a doctoral student in the Department of Social Sciences at Loughborough University, UK.

Ann McNulty is Coordinator of the Northern Initiative on Women and Eating, Newcastle upon Tyne, UK.

Anna Madill is at the Department of Psychology, University of Leeds, UK.

Deborah Marks is at the Centre for Psychotherapeutic Studies, Department of Psychiatry, Sheffield University, UK.

Marion Martin is at the School of Education, Centre for Adult and Higher Education, University of Manchester, UK.

Kate Paulin is based at the Department of Psychology, University of Auckland, New Zealand.

Jackie Reilly is a PhD student in the School of Psychology, Queens University, Belfast, Northern Ireland.

Diane Richardson is Senior Lecturer in the Department of Sociological Studies at the University of Sheffield, UK.

Barbara Katz Rothman is Professor of Sociology at Baruch College and the Graduate Center, City University of New York, USA.

Diana E.H. Russell is Emerita Professor of Sociology at Mills College, Oakland, California, USA.

Liz Stanley is based at the Department of Sociology, University of Manchester, UK.

Marian Titley is at the Department of Clinical and Community Psychology, Exeter District Community Health Service, Exeter, UK.

Sue Wilkinson is Senior Lecturer in Social Psychology in the Department of Social Sciences, Loughborough University, UK.

Jan Winn is a PhD student in the Department of Sociological Studies, University of Sheffield, UK.

Anne Woollett is based at the Psychology Department, University of East London, UK.

Acknowledgements

Items by the contributors listed below appear in print for the first time in this Collection:

Celia Kitzinger and Sue Wilkinson
Marian Titley and Becky Chasey
Anita Harris
Mike Gane
Anna Madill
Jean Carabine
Gabriele Griffin

All other items appeared first in *Feminism & Psychology* as listed below:

Feminism & Psychology (1995) 5(2): *Observations and Commentaries* (ed. Celia Kitzinger)

Manjit Bola

Feminism & Psychology (1995) 5(4): *Observations and Commentaries* (ed. Celia Kitzinger)

Brown
Sheila Jeffreys
Erica Burman
Katie MacMillan

Feminism & Psychology (1996) 6(1):

Special Feature: 'Representing the Other – Part One' (ed. Sue Wilkinson)
Anna Livia
Liz Stanley
Barbara Katz Rothman
Magdalene Ang-Lygate
Amanda Kottler
Deborah Marks
Anne Woollett
Adrian Coyle
Tracey L. Hurd and Alice McIntyre

Feminism & Psychology (1996) 6(2):

Special Feature: 'Representing the Other – Part Two' (ed. Sue Wilkinson)
Rosalind Edwards
Diana E.H. Russell
Joan C. Chrisler
Christine Griffin
Diane Richardson
Diane Bell
Kate Paulin
Marion Martin and Beth Humphries

The Spoken Word: 'Speaking of Representing the Other' (ed. Celia Kitzinger)
Celia Kitzinger *in conversation with* Manjit Bola, Amparo Bonilla Campos, Jean
Carabine, Kathy Doherty, Hannah Frith, Ann McNulty, Jackie Reilly and Jan
Winn

Thanks to Hannah Frith for assistance with the index.

PART I
ARTICLES

1
Theorizing Representing the Other

Celia Kitzinger and Sue Wilkinson

> No one should ever 'speak for' or assume another's voice . . . it becomes a form of colonisation.
>
> *(Sinister Wisdom* Collective, 1990: 4)

> We must take on the whole world; we cannot afford 'no go areas' of the imagination; we cannot afford to refuse an opinion on any subject.
>
> (Anna Livia)[1]

This book, the third in the series of *Feminism & Psychology* Readers,[2] highlights a key issue in contemporary feminist theory and practice: whether, and how, we should represent members of groups to which we do not ourselves belong – in particular, members of groups oppressed in ways we are not. The 'Call for Short Contributions' which juxtaposed the two contradictory extracts above, asked for papers addressing questions of representation and difference, and suggested a range of possible dimensions of Otherness, including 'race' and ethnicity, class, age, sexual identity, (dis)ability and motherhood status.[3]

The issue of Othering obviously struck a chord in feminist imaginations, and we received more than 80 formal submissions from across a wide range of disciplines, including (among those published in this volume) contributions from sociology, social policy, political science, women's studies, linguistics and anthropology, as well as from psychology.[4] The book's 39 contributors draw on their personal experiences of speaking 'for' and 'about' Others in their research, professional practice, academic or fictional writing, and in their political activism. Together they make an important intervention in scholarly discussion of Othering across the disciplines.

The concept of the Other has been developed predominantly in relation to Woman as Other (de Beauvoir, 1949/53), and in relation to anthropological representations of race and ethnicity (e.g. Clifford and Marcus, 1986; Fowler and Hardesty, 1994; Said, 1978, 1989). In this volume, two male contributors discuss the theoretical issues involved in representing women (Brown[5] and Mike Gane), but it is contributions discussing the problems of representing Others with different 'racial', ethnic or national backgrounds which are a particularly strong feature of the book. These include chapters reflecting upon the theoretical and political issues involved in representations of: black South Africans by white South Africans (Diana E.H. Russell, Amanda Kottler); Aboriginal women by white Australian feminists (Diane Bell); Maori women by white feminists in Aotearoa/New Zealand (Kate Paulin); Chinese women by a Malaysian Chinese Nonya woman (Magdalene Ang-Lygate); and black women living in the UK by white British feminists (Rosalind Edwards). Two chapters (by Diane Bell and by Marion Martin and Beth Humphries) address the difficulties consequent upon the authors' decisions, as white women, to work collaboratively with Aboriginal/black colleagues: both have unhappy endings because of the social and institutional contexts in which their research was conducted. Conversely, the problems of white-on-white research are discussed in the chapter by Tracey L. Hurd and Alice McIntyre; and Manjit Bola, both in her chapter and in her contribution to The Spoken Word (Part III), reflects upon the consequences for her, as a black woman researching white women, of the debates in this area.[6]

This book extends discussion of Othering beyond the confines of gender and ethnicity to embrace issues of disability (Deborah Marks), weight (Joan C. Chrisler), sexual identity (Christine Griffin, Kate Paulin), age (Marian Titley and Becky Chasey, Anita Harris), HIV status (Adrian Coyle), and more! The diversity of feminisms means that, as Diane Richardson argues, some feminists position other feminists as Other simply on the basis of their feminism. Although contributions on social class were specifically requested in the Call for Short Contributions, none of the chapters makes this its focus, although class is among the issues discussed by Liz Stanley, and by Jan Winn, Kathy Doherty and Jean Carabine in The Spoken Word. Issues relating to social class more generally are addressed in the 1996 Special Issue of *Feminism & Psychology*, edited by Valerie Walkerdine, and we would like to encourage future submissions to the journal on this topic, especially (but not exclusively) as it connects with questions of Othering. We are aware that this volume does not (and indeed *could* not) include chapters addressing every possible form of Othering: notable omissions, in addition to the paucity of coverage on social class, include research by childless feminists on motherhood, research by adults on childhood, and research by 'sane' women on madness. We are sure there are many more! However, the key contribution of this book lies not so much in the 'topics' covered (important as these are), as in the way in which, through their engagement with these topics under the rubric of 'Othering', authors have developed feminist theory and politics around this issue.

A central contribution of this volume is the extent to which it illustrates that the issues involved in representing Others are not simple questions of method, susceptible to 'quick fix' solutions. Whereas some social scientific writing suggests that the 'answers' lie in (for example) a white researcher hiring a black research assistant to enable the 'inclusion' of black research subjects; or in developing 'empathy' and gaining the 'trust' of research participants Other to the researcher (see, for example, Andersen, 1993), the contributions in this volume shatter any such notions. Discussing a wide range of different Others, the authors as a group draw the attention of the reader to a set of complex but vital questions. These questions include: who is the Other, and who are 'we'? Along what shifting lines of power and powerlessness is Otherness constructed? What are the costs and benefits of 'including' or of 'excluding' the Other from our research, and on what terms? Should we speak only for ourselves? Should we act simply as 'conduits' through which the voices of Others can be heard? How do we resolve disagreements between 'us' and the Other about the meanings and implications of what is said between us? In what ways can representations of Others create social change? How can we interrupt the process of Othering?

In the remainder of this chapter we perform two tasks. First, we offer an introductory overview of previous work on Othering ('Looking Back'). Secondly, in the section subheaded 'Moving Forward', we introduce the arguments of the various chapters of this book, illustrating the contributions they make in advancing our theories and understandings of what is involved in 'representing the Other'.

Looking Back: Previous Work on Othering

In this overview of previous work on Othering, we begin with early formulations of 'Woman as Other'; go on to discuss the implications, for feminists, of 'Other Others'; then summarize some of the main 'Theories of Othering'. Finally, we examine feminist approaches to 'Negotiating the Problems of Othering': by 'Speaking only for Ourselves', by 'Celebrating Otherness', by 'Destabilizing Otherness' and by 'Interrupting Othering'.

Woman as Other

Woman is defined as Other to a male norm. As Simone de Beauvoir wrote more than 40 years ago:

> Humanity is male and man defines woman not in herself but as relative to him; she is not regarded as an autonomous being . . . She is simply what man decrees . . . She is defined and differentiated with reference to man and not he with reference to her; she is the incidental, the inessential as opposed to the essential. He is the Subject, he is the Absolute – she is the Other. (1949/53: 18)

Despite trenchant feminist criticisms of many aspects of de Beauvoir's work (e.g. Evans, 1983; Felstiner, 1980), 'almost every feminist writer since 1949 acknowledg[es] a debt to her' (Spender, 1982: 712), and the notion of woman as Other has been thoroughly absorbed into contemporary feminism. As Dale Spender remarks:

> That women were made not born, that man and not nature is the maker, and that man sees himself as the norm, the positive and central reference point in reality, and thereby makes woman 'other' and 'wrong' are such accepted principles these days (within select circles) that they rarely promote excitement. (1982: 714)

In contemporary feminism, then, the concept of woman as Other (sometimes with a capital 'O', sometimes not; sometimes in scare quotes, sometimes not;

sometimes italicized, more often not) involves the central claim that Otherness is projected on to women by, and in the interests of, men, such that we are constructed as inferior or abnormal. In particular, contemporary feminist writers suggest that women's menstruating, lactating, gestating, birthing bodies – above all, our *sexual* bodies – act as a focal point for attributions of Otherness:

> A key aspect of women's 'otherness' from the perspective of masculine scientific discourse is our reproductive capacity . . . Once science and medicine had become established as masculine institutions and as masculine modes of knowledge, ever more sophisticated accounts of women's 'otherness' were produced.
> (Jackson et al., 1993: 363, 365)

Constructed as Others, women are relegated to the position of mere objects of male knowledge and our own knowledge and experience are routinely obliterated: 'women have been rendered as the silent Other' (Radway, 1986: 97). The feminist project of speaking out about women's experience, giving voice to women's versions of reality, discovering what women know, relies on the idea that women's voices are different from – fundamentally Other to – the hegemonic patriarchal discourse: 'Beginning from the point of view of the female "other", feminist theory assumes the fact of difference and asserts that if Truth rests on generalization, it must take into account experience that has previously been ignored, forgotten, ridiculed and devalued' (Personal Narratives Group, 1989: 262).

Within feminist psychology and the psychology of women, these ideas have taken a firm hold – and researchers typically do little more than restate Simone de Beauvoir's initial thesis of woman as Other, augmenting it with contemporary examples. For instance, feminist psychologist Jane Ussher (1991) repeatedly invokes the images of woman as Other throughout her book, *Women's Madness*. She seeks, she says, to expose the 'positioning of women as "Other" within the misogynistic discourse' (Ussher, 1991: 21) and she cites various ways in which women's Otherness is reinforced and maintained through 'phallocentric' discourses about menstruation ('our blood marks us as Other', p. 22); rape ('the fear of rape acts to control all women. It keep us as the Other', p. 32); media images ('images of women position us as the Other, as objects for the gaze of man', p. 300); and madness ('women are positioned as Other and labelled as mad, when they step out of line', p. 247). Despite adopting the concept of the Other as a recurrent motif, Ussher uses the term exclusively with reference to gender: it is always *women* (or particular subgroups of women, e.g. mad women, witches) who are Other. The concept is never used by Ussher to invoke those oppressed by class, race, sexual identity or other power divisions. This use is typical of the psychology of women as a whole. By continually drawing attention to the phallocentric power of the misogynistic male gaze in constructing woman as Other, by continually insisting on 'woman' as the Other and by reserving this term for those oppressed by the *gender* hierarchy, an implicit assumption is made that Otherness is a production only of gender. This assumption that Otherness is constructed only in terms of gender, that Otherness is conferred by femaleness alone, takes for granted the primacy of gender in women's lives, and obscures other dimensions of power and powerlessness.

Other Others

Within feminist theory, the 'innocent assumption that gender unites women more powerfully than race and class divides them' (Gluck and Patai, 1991: 2) has increasingly been challenged by women (and men) Othered because of (for example) their 'race', ethnicity, class, sexual identity, disability, or age. Women (*qua* women) do not have a monopoly on Otherness. Simone de Beauvoir drew attention to other Others in *The Second Sex*:

> No group ever sets itself up as the One without at once setting up the Other over against itself . . . [T]o the native of a country all who inhabit other countries are 'foreigners'; Jews are 'different' for the anti-Semite, Negroes are 'inferior' for American racists, aborigines are 'natives' for colonists, proletarians are the 'lower class' for the privileged. (1949/53: 52)

More recently, the oppression of women of colour (Afshar and Maynard, 1994; Fine, 1994; Hill Collins, 1990; Lorde, 1984; Morrison, 1992), and of non-western people (Aziz, 1992; Liddle and Rai, 1993; Patai, 1991), has been discussed in terms which draw upon the concept of the Other and its theoretical underpinnings. The challenges posed by black feminist writing are powerful critiques of feminism's universalism and imperialism. Acknowledgement of the diversity of ways in which women experience oppression (and oppress each other) has led to an awareness (at least in some quarters) of the non-homogeneity of the category 'women', emphasizing differences *between* women based upon 'race' and class, religion, culture and language, history and historical development (e.g. Riley, 1988; Spelman, 1988). Representations of 'women' which imply a homogenous category of Otherness render invisible the different experiences of women of varied ethnic, sexual and class locations.

Over the past decade or so, anthropologists critical of traditional anthropological theory and practice have been particularly vigilant in identifying the ways in which Otherness is constructed in non-western peoples and in exposing the domination and Othering encoded in anthropological texts. Otherness, according to Winzeler (1994), is what gets anthropology books published and sold: headhunting, cannibalism, human sacrifice and culturally sanctioned sexual promiscuity are among the best-known instances of 'ethnographic exotica' in anthropology. They symbolize savagery, and the idea of savage Otherness has been used 'to justify imperial expansion, warfare, Christian evangelism, colonial control . . . slavery and the appropriation of aboriginal lands, and genocide' (Winzeler, 1994: 82).

Crucially, according to these arguments, colonialism has not involved simply the use of physical force and military might; it has also involved the construction of representations or discourses of the oppressed which serve to justify and legitimate the oppressor. In his enormously influential book *Orientalism*, Edward Said (1978) argues that Europe came to terms with its colonies in the Orient by inventing a discourse of Otherness which involved the re-creation of a people's history by those 'outside' of it, and in so doing established hierarchies of knowledge and power. 'The bulk of colonial writing in India focused on demonstrating the peculiarities of Hindu civilisation, and the barbaric practices pertaining to women' (Said, 1978: 34), and this re-created history was used to explain the fall of oriental cultures, and to justify continued colonial rule. Some feminists (mostly outside psychology) have drawn extensively on Said's writings (described as: 'excellent', Aziz, 1992: 305; 'authoritative', Ganguly, 1992: 73; 'enormously productive and energising', Mani, 1990) in formulating theories of colonial Othering. Key to such approaches is the idea that oppressed and colonized peoples are represented as Others in ways which reinforce the power and purported superiority of those with control over the processes of representation:

> Slavery, conquest and colonialism created dominant and subject peoples within global structures of material exploitation and political subordination. They also involved the representation of the dominated peoples discursively – in language – as an inferior Other (as against the 'superior' white peoples of Europe and North America). (Aziz, 1992: 291)

> White supremacy can thus be conceptualised as a set of discourses and practices that subjugated non-European people and cast them in the position of subjected Others, while it advanced the interests of European nations. (Mama, 1995: 17)

Despite the heavy emphasis on woman as Other in much (white) feminist writing, then, Othering has been powerfully invoked to theorize 'race', ethnicity and colonialism, and to discuss the construction of third-world subjects as the objectified Others of North American or European imaginations.

In part, this Othering of non-western women has been possible within feminism because, as Mohanty (1988: 80) points out, the speaking subject of feminist theory is almost invariably a western woman: 'Third World women ... never rise above the debilitating generality of the "object" status.' In speaking 'about' or 'for' third-world women, white western academic feminists collude in Othering, reproducing orientalist discourse in a feminist guise (Amos and Parmar, 1984). For example, Joanna Liddle and Shirin Rai criticize Mary Daly's *Gyn/Ecology* (1978) for its embodiment of 'an Orientalist discourse' of the Hindu ritual of *suttee* (widow burning):

> *All* of the sources used by her in constructing the history of *suttee* in India and its justi- fication, and acceptance by the Hindu culture, are Western sources; furthermore, all except one are male. While Daly challenges the male version of cultural history, she does not do the same with the Orientalist construction of a religion and people. Indeed, she acquiesces in that construction and thus validates it. (1993: 17–18, emphasis in original)

(See also the similar criticisms raised by Helen Carr, 1988, of white feminist writing on the Mesquakie [Native American 'Fox Indian'] women.) This problem is not, of course, confined to the representational work of western white women. As Liddle and Rai (1993) point out, because of their participation in international hierarchies of knowledge and power, western black women have continued to speak for women from the 'third world' – indeed, have often been expected to do so by western white feminists, who have accepted token western black feminist voices as authentically representing all indigenous women from their countries (or even continents) of origin. In this way, western feminism has conveniently been able to ignore or to overlook the non-participation of non-western women in feminist dialogues.

In sum, then, women are not the only Others, and the non-western Other has been extensively discussed in the critical anthropology literature and in the writings of postcolonial feminism. If dimensions of power and powerlessness are taken as constituting the Other, then there are multiple fissures across lines of 'race', class, disability, sexual identity, age, and so on, in relation to which questions of Othering might legitimately be explored. As Lennon and Whitford (1994: 3) point out, the theoretical and political developments which have led to the framing of questions in terms of Othering mean that western academic feminists, committed to the articulation of what is Other in relation to patriarchal male values, now have also to confront the challenge of other Others for whom they themselves constitute a new hegemony, and in relation to whom they stand in positions of power and domination.

Theories of Othering

Feminists have inherited the concept of the Other from several different and distinctive perspectives: the existential philosophy of Simone de Beauvoir (1949/53) and the anthropological critique of Edward Said (1978) have already been mentioned as (hugely disparate and widely cited) sources for feminist thinking on this issue. Many feminists also express their indebtedness to the psychoanalytic work of Jacques Lacan (1977), who describes the unconscious mind of the subject as the discourse of the Other. Lacan's account of the development of subjectivity suggests that the infant develops a sense of self (during what he calls 'the looking-glass phase') through differentiating itself from Others. Lynne Segal offers one of the more cogent summaries of what she describes as Lacan's 'opaque, elliptical and sadistically "playful" prose':

> The reflection arises in the gaze of the mother, and in the infant's jubilant, but still illusory, sense of unity gained through the appropriation of its reflection in the mirror. However, this is not the beginning of a 'true self', but of an inevitably alienating and constraining ego, a self-for-others, always 'referential to the other' and therefore distanced from the infant's inner drives and desires. (1994: 131)

Many French-speaking feminists (and those French women writers influenced by feminism), such as Irigaray (1981), Cixous (1983/92) and Kristeva (1980), demonstrate in their writing the dual inheritance, however transformed, of both Lacan and de Beauvoir. Other feminists too, in reflecting on issues of the Other, make explicit their appropriation of Lacanian ideas (e.g. the feminist psychologists Burman, 1994; Hollway, 1995).

We do not intend, in this context, to overview or to critique the theories of de Beauvoir, Said, Lacan, or other theorists for whom notions of the Other have been important. Rather, we suggest only that in thinking about how, as feminists, we may address the various pressing questions raised by Othering, we need to be aware of the freight the term 'Other' carries with it. For feminist *psychologists*, this is especially so now that 'the Other' has begun to seep out of the contexts of existential feminism, critical anthropology and French psychoanalytic theory into the academic discipline of psychology itself. The publication of psychologist Edward Sampson's (1993) *Celebrating the Other* (like the publication, in anthropology, of Clifford and Marcus's, *Writing Culture*, 1986) marks a significant development in terms of (some) psychologists' growing recognition of the complicity of our discipline in constructing and perpetuating Otherness. As Nigerian-based psychologist Amina Mama (1995: 160) points out, 'psychology has generated scientific discourses which construe the Other in ways that have reproduced and legitimised white supremacy' – and, we would add, many other forms of oppression too. In addressing these oppressions from the perspective of feminists involved in psychology, we may usefully draw on aspects of theoretical and political approaches to Othering developed outside this discipline.

A key aspect of the various theoretical approaches to Othering (albeit differently treated by each), is the observation that the notion of who and what Others are (what they are like, the attributes assigned them, the sorts of lives they are supposed to lead) is intimately related to 'our' notion of who and what 'we' are. That is, 'we' use the Other to define ourselves: 'we' understand ourselves in relation to what 'we' are *not*. Writing about the changing characteristics of racist ideology over time, Guillaumin describes as 'altero-referential racism' the racism which asserts the difference of Others as a way of defining itself:

> Enter the Others, who will act as a mirror, an inverted image, for this bourgeoisie anxiously seeking its own identity. Since the bourgeoisie did not know what it was, unlike the nobility which had a very clear view of itself, it wanted at least to know what it was not. The era of positive definition was therefore followed by a time of definition by negation, and auto-reference by altero-reference: the bourgeoisie is not black, nor Jewish, nor proletarian. (1972/95: 56)

Similarly, critical anthropologists have illustrated the way in which, in early ethnography, 'the author's ethnographic report is a reversed mirror image of his own ethnocultural ideal' (Vidich and Lyman, 1994: 26). Early ethnography 'discovered' primitive tribes and hence demonstrated the steady march of progress in the West; it revealed the idol-worshipping rituals of pagans and hence illustrated the godliness of good Christians: 'a culture which "discovers" that which is alien to itself also thereby fundamentally reveals that which it is to itself' (McGrane, 1989: ix). The imperative to know oneself through the construction of the Other means that 'if there were no other, one would invent it' (Cixous and Clement, 1975/86: 71). This notion that Othering functions as a self-aggrandizing device for those in charge of systems of discourse and representation runs through much of the literature, and different approaches to Othering converge to underscore this point.

For many commentators, this observation is not simply a claim about broad trends in representation observable at a cultural or institutional level. It is also (or instead) a fundamentally *psychological* claim, a claim about the nature of human identity and self-understanding which, at its most stark, portrays Othering as a psychological *necessity* for the development of human subjectivity. Drawing on Lacanian notions to explore discourses of heterosexual desire, Wendy Hollway (1995: 94), for example, claims that: 'Throughout an individual's history, meaning has been achieved, consciously and unconsciously in relation to others. Since infancy, we have used significant others as vehicles for containing some of the ambivalent feelings which it is difficult to acknowledge in ourselves.'

From a different theoretical perspective, but with the same emphasis on the *psychological* issue of Othering, Naomi Scheman (1993) draws on Alice Miller's (1984: 91) suggestion that 'children who have grown up being assailed for qualities the parents hate in themselves can hardly wait to assign those qualities to someone else so they can once again regard themselves as good, "moral", noble and altruistic'. The apparently unitary self of the privileged, suggests Scheman (1993: 166)[3] is 'bought at the price of the projection onto stigmatized Others of the split-off parts of themselves that they were taught to despise'. Although this claim is commonplace – and variants of it even appear in the classics of mainstream psychology as theories of prejudice and stereotyping (e.g. Adorno et al., 1950; Allport, 1954) – it is important to remember that this is *only* a theory, albeit one with an immediate appeal and plausibility for many people in modern, individualistic and psychologized cultures. It is, moreover, a theory which focuses on *individualistic* rather than cultural reasons for Othering, and can be read as leading to the pathologization of individuals, at the cost of broader sociopolitical critique (see Kitzinger and Perkins, 1993, for a discussion of this point in relation to theories of 'homophobia').

One corollary of this general observation that the Other is a construction or a set of discourses through which the dominant group defines itself, is that the Other is silenced or delegitimized. Others' representations (of themselves or of 'us') are threatening to the dominant groups. As Edward Sampson says:

> We know that the self needs the other in order to be a self at all. We know that when those selves are dominant in a given society, they can construct the other so as to affirm a particular kind of self for themselves . . . If I find myself in and through you, but no longer control the you that grants me my self, then I am forced to deal with a self that is beyond my control, and I may not enjoy this self with which I must now contend. (1993: 153)

An important form of the 'control' exerted by dominant or hegemonic groups over Others is control over their processes of representation. Others' representations of themselves (and certainly their representations of 'us') are routinely 'de-authorized', dismissed as neither credible nor coherent: see, for example, Kimberle Crenshaw's (1992) analysis of the de-authorization of Anita Hill's testimony (as that of a black woman), and Anna Marie Smith's (1995) analysis of the de-authorization of Jennifer Saunder's testimony (as that of a young working-class lesbian). As Smith argues, because both Hill and Saunders are (in different ways) Others, their speech is de-authorized not simply because of what they say but because there is no legitimate position from which they can say it:

> Hegemony does not take the form of brute domination; it entails instead the delimita-tion of the intelligible . . . To fail to achieve an adequate 'fit' within an officially recognized position is to be de-authorized – to be denied recognition as an author of a text, and to have one's text dismissed from the start as incoherent, illegitimate, or unbelievable. (1995: 169)

In sum, Others are not accorded expert status either on their own lives or on that of the dominant group.

A second corollary of this idea, that the dominant group defines itself through its representations of the Other, is that representations of Otherness can be read as inverted representations of those doing the Othering. As Vidich and Lyman (1994: 26) point out, 'early ethnographies reveal as much about the West as about their objects of study.' Amina Mama makes the same point about psychology's representations of black people: 'Psychological constructions of "the African" in the colonies and "the Negro" in Britain and North America also tell us more about the subjectivity of Europeans than about what it meant to be black and Other under a colonial or racist order' (Mama, 1995: 160). Instead of reading accounts of Others as transparent texts which more or less adequately reveal information about those Others, such texts can be inverted and read as being 'about' their authors – that is, as reflecting and revealing the strategies by which those with the power of representation construct themselves. One way of knowing what 'white' people are like (how they construct themselves) may be to look at their representations of black people; one way of knowing what 'heterosexual' women are like may be to look at their representations of lesbians – and so on. Toni Morrison (1992), for example, analyses white Americans' fictional representations of African-Americans and describes how white Americans created what she calls 'serviceable' African-Americans, i.e. African-Americans whose constructed characteristics were essential, says Morrison, to the definition of the white-American character.

As feminists and as psychologists confronting this unsettling and disturbing legacy of Othering, how can we proceed? Claims to objectivity and universality of representation have been shown to be the alibis of the powerful – the powerful among women as much as the powerful among men.

Negotiating the Problems of Othering

The following pages explore various ways in which feminists have attempted to negotiate the problems of Othering: by speaking only for ourselves; by speaking of Otherness only to celebrate it; by attempting to destabilize Otherness; and by interrupting Othering.

Speaking only for Ourselves   Contemplating the problems consequent upon representing Others, some feminists suggest that the solution is to refuse to be drawn into representing Others at all. Speaking only for *ourselves*, we leave Others to represent *themselves*. Instead of speaking for Others, we maintain a respectful silence, and work to create the social and political conditions which might enable Others to speak (and to be heard) on their own terms.

The idea that we should speak only for ourselves, and eschew speaking for Others, derives in part from a sense that the Others have been too much spoken for and about already. It comes from the belief that it might be more appropriate to silence the cacophony of dominant voices busily regulating, explaining, justifying, exonerating or celebrating Others in favour of simply pointing to the silence of those Others and thereby helping to create space for them to speak for themselves. However well intentioned our speech on behalf of an Other, it acts to reinforce precisely that Otherness which speaking may be intended to undermine. The Other is silenced *because* she is Other, and the speech of the dominant group on her behalf reinscribes her Otherness simply through the fact of its being spoken, and irrespective of its content:

> A conversation of 'us' with 'us' about 'them' is a conversation in which 'them' is silenced. 'Them' always stands on the other side of the hill, naked and speechless, barely present in its absence. Subject of discussion, 'them' is only admitted among an 'us', the discussing subjects, when accompanied or introduced by an 'us', member, hence the dependency of 'them'. (Trinh, 1989: 65)

A similar point about the way in which the dominant group's speech about Others continues to legitimate and reinforce their own authority and dominance is made by bell hooks:

> I am waiting for them to stop talking about the 'Other', to stop even describing how important it is to be able to speak about difference. It is not just important what we speak about, but how and why we speak . . . Often this speech about the 'Other' annihilates, erases: 'no need to hear your voice when I can talk about you better than you can speak about yourself. No need to hear your voice. Only tell me about your pain. I want to know your story. And then I will tell it back to you in a new way. Tell it back to you in such a way that it has become mine, my own. Re-writing you, I write myself anew. I am still author, authority. I am still the colonizer, the speaking subject, and you are now at the center of my talk.' (1990: 151–2)

The final injunction of hooks is simply 'Stop'.

This position of speaking only for oneself is in direct contradistinction to the conventional practice of the social sciences, within which speaking 'for' or 'about' Others has been the norm. Indeed, the methodological and epistemological assumptions expressed in traditional psychology give the clear impression that the scientific psychologist's 'subject' bears more than a passing resemblance to Edward Said's (1978) 'oriental', who must be represented and spoken for by the 'expert'. The traditional 'objectivity' of the social sciences (especially psychology), in pursuit of which a rigid detachment is maintained between researcher and 'subject', has been replaced, in much contemporary feminist research, by an ethic of involvement. Pointing out that men's representations of their Other (women) have been self-interested and inadequate 'science', much feminist research (especially in psychology), eschews any attempt at objective distance, emphasizing instead the shared experience of researcher and researched. 'We' research 'ourselves'. The contemporary feminist researcher is likely to construct herself as sharing personal experience and/or identity with the people she is researching and to use this as warrant for her 'findings'; she is speaking, 'for herself' and for her 'community'. The titles and subtitles of much feminist writing reflect this preoccupation with 'speaking for ourselves' (e.g. Seifer, 1976; White, 1990).

One problem for feminists who take this position lies in defining who, exactly, 'we' are, and what constitutes 'our community'. In much of this work, 'we' are, of course, 'women'. As Daphne Patai points out, in attempting to 'include' Other women, while making gender primary, 'the new, ostensibly feminist scenario substitutes the claim of identity, our identity as women, while often straining to disregard ethnic, racial, class, and other distinctions' (Patai, 1991: 144). The claim that 'there's nobody here but us women' results in 'a homogenizing of "women's experience" and an obliteration of the full range of oppressions to which we are subject, the diversity of communities from which we draw our strengths' (Kitzinger and Wilkinson, 1993: 8–12). But attempts to define 'us' with more precision inevitably become reductionist: can we (the authors) speak on behalf of *all* women, or only all white women, all white middle-class women, all white middle-class childless lesbian women, all white middle-class childless lesbian British women? . . . and so on. As Linda Alcoff (1994: 287) has pointed out, 'the complexity and multiplicity of group identifications could result in "communities" composed of single individuals.'

A second problem with 'speaking only for ourselves' lies in the peculiar com-position of the group 'academic feminists', such that to do this would result (indeed, has resulted) in a massive over-representation of the views of white, middle-class, western women. Speaking only from, about, and in relation to our own (untheorized) positions of relative privilege has, in fact, been part of the *problem* of feminism, contributing to its false universalizing and imperializing tendencies to the extent that it is hard to reconceptualize 'speaking only for oneself' as part of the *solution*.

Thirdly, there is the problem of the continued silencing and exclusion of Others in feminist theory and practice. Although it is clear that *speaking on behalf of Others* serves to reinscribe their silence and their Otherness, it is equally the case that feminist insistence on '*speaking only for ourselves*' can serve the same function. If 'we' are prevented from representing Others, those Others are equally barred from theorizing 'us', and so excluded from the process of develop-ing feminist theory and method which interrupts dominant assumptions. For example, in relation to the hegemony of heterosexuality, speaking only for oneself, while authorizing lesbians to speak *qua* lesbians *on lesbianism*, serves equally to *dis*authorize lesbian theories of heterosexuality. Lesbian theories of heterosexuality can be challenged as not being based in (current) identity or experience (only heterosexuals can speak of heterosexuality); and, conversely, heterosexual feminists are relieved of the burden of theorizing lesbianism (see Kitzinger, 1994a, for an extended discussion of these problems). In relation to women internationally, as Joanna Liddle and Shirin Rai illustrate:

> The choice seemed to lie between *being* the same and speaking for the women of 'other' cultures or to be disengaged from the 'others'' experience, languages, and, therefore, logically from their struggles. This disengagement is disempowering of Third World women in two ways. First, politically, it does not given them the option to represent their own lived experience in a self-written text while at the same time linking up in resistance with an informed, sympathetic support base outside that experience. Second, the likelihood of Third World women making any intellectual and theoretical contribu-tion to debates within feminism – which continue to be dominated by Western dis-courses – is greatly reduced in such a context. (1993: 20)

In sum, whatever the intentions, the *effects* of speaking only for ourselves are often the silencing of Others, the erasure of their experience, and the reinscription of power relations.

Celebrating Otherness   Others, by definition, are oppressed and marginalized by the dominant culture: consequently, their cultures and traditions are typically represented as inferior or pathological. A common representational strategy of some feminists is to seek to refute this dominant representation by documenting and celebrating the survival skills, the inherent strengths, and the positive cultures and traditions of Others. The celebration of woman's Otherness is familiar from the work of some of the French-speaking feminists (e.g. Cixous, 1983/92; Irigaray, 1981), and has been described as characterizing the writings of psychologists committed to revealing women's 'different voice' (Gilligan, 1982) or different 'ways of knowing' (Belenky et al., 1986). Jacquelyn Zita (1994: 6) expresses the same idea in lauding lesbian philosopher Jeffner Allen for her manifestation of a 'personal and intellectual preoccupation with deliverance from the Same and a desire for an "Otherness" that truly evades the grasp of power'. This is an important corrective to the traditional focus on the weakness and suffering of the Other.

However, one of the problems endemic to 'studying down' (Olson and Shopes, 1991: 198) is 'the temptation to exaggerate the exotic, the heroic, or the tragic aspects of the lives of people with little power'. The danger lies in romanticizing Others and in using our representation of them to delineate 'our' vision of the Good Life. Some early ethnographers saw in 'primitive' cultures the nobility of the 'savage', the healing rituals and harmonies of the 'natural' life, and the pure essence of the precolonial (Van Maanen, 1995). In 'reclaiming' the lives of Others for feminism, we run the risk of representing in their lives what we would like to see in our own. Heterosexual women, for example, when not expressing overtly anti-lesbian views, often represent lesbian lives in extraordinarily romanticized terms: lesbians are supposed to enjoy the 'luxury' of 'doing away with men' (Yuval-Davis, 1993: 52), and it is to lesbians 'that heterosexual feminists look in the hope of finding a model of equality which can eventually be applied to our relationships with men' (Croghan, 1993: 244). Similarly, white western women, when not expressing overtly racist views, often idealize and romanticize the lives and traditions of black women, and/or women from other cultures. Reflecting on the North American white feminist romance with Native American women's lives, for example, Helen Carr points out:

> The correlation of Indian otherness with dangerous (often female) sexuality has been part of the discourse of dispossession since the seventeenth century, just as the present idealization of Native American women's lives by some white feminists is an extension of the primitivist tradition that in its own way equally denies the human complexity of Native Americans. (1988: 142)

Part of the feminist 'celebration' or 'romanticization' of Other women's lives often involves the claim that Other women are always aware of, and actively acting to resist, their oppression (cf. Salazar, 1991). In part, this is a reaction against the notion of 'false consciousness', whereby 'we' saw the truth and Other women were enmeshed in patriarchal ideologies from which it was 'our' duty to rescue them. Instead, Other women are now often assumed to possess their own (often implicit) critique of gender (and other power) relations. This critique is often suspiciously similar to that of the feminist representing them. For example, Helen Carr (1988) describes the transformation of the autobiography of a

Mesquaki (or Fox Indian) woman (published under the name of her ethnographer, Michelson 1925, cited in Carr, 1988) into a feminist-authored novel for teenage girls (Irwin, 1984, cited in Carr, 1988). Of the novel, she says: 'painted with a sentimentalizing feminist-separatist gloss, it presents an unproblematic solidarity among Fox women, who happily accept the distinctiveness of women's role' (Carr, 1988: 142). Similarly, oral historian, Katherine Borland (1991) reflects on the problems of interpretation and analysis of an interview she conducted with her grandmother, whom she represented as a proto-feminist heroine, courageously claiming her rights as a woman within a male-dominated society. Her grandmother, Beatrice Hanson, 'expressed strong disagreement with my conclusions' (Borland, 1991) in a 14-page letter:

> So your interpretation of the story as a female struggle for autonomy within a hostile male environment is entirely YOUR interpretation. You've read into the story what you wished to – what pleases YOU. That it was never – by any wildest stretch of the imagination – the concern of the originator of the story makes such an interpretation a definite and complete distortion, and in this respect I question its authenticity. The story is no longer MY story at all. The skeleton remains, but it has become your story. (Hanson, quoted in Borland, 1991: 70)

Women's solidarity among the Mesquaki as represented in a feminist novel may or may not be 'fact', but clearly owes a great deal to the contemporary politics and pedagogic concerns of its (white) author. Bea Hanson's disputed 'feminist consciousness', as attributed to her by her granddaughter, obviously owes more to the need of the feminist oral historian to discover and celebrate feminist heroines than it does to Bea Hanson herself. Similarly, the allegedly oppositional politics of the masses has become a commonplace of feminist cultural theory, as 'left-wing academics are busy picking out strands of "subversion" in every piece of pop culture from Street Style to Soap Opera' (Williamson, 1986: 14). All of these examples illustrate the projection, on to the oppressed Other, of the political and social ideals of the person representing them.

There is no possibility of completely evading the grasp of power: power is deeply implicated in constructing the discourse of the Other. As Linda Alcoff (1994: 200) points out, 'the speech of the oppressed is not necessarily either liberatory or reflective of their true interests.' In choosing to represent Others as always resisting, undermining or subverting the dominant order, feminists, in our anxiety to avoid apparent criticism of Others, fall into the opposite trap of romanticizing them. In sum, celebrating Others, as much as derogating them, may project onto those Others our own political agenda, appropriating them to our own 'cause'.

Destabilizing Otherness As strategies for dealing with the problems of Othering, 'speaking only for ourselves' and 'celebrating Otherness' share some epistemological assumptions both about the nature of Otherness, and about the meaning of 'representation'. Feminists writing from a range of perspectives, but particularly those influenced by postmodernism, have challenged these assumptions and have attempted to destabilize the entire problem.

First, in both the strategies already discussed, the Other is conceptualized as a member of an oppressed group in relation to which the person doing, or refusing to do, representational work is a dominant group member. We have, however, already alluded to the fact that there are many dimensions of power and power-lessness along which Otherness can be constructed, and it is clear that these multiple intersecting discourses of Otherness can position researcher and researched in shifting ways. Kum-Kum Bhavnani has described how, as a black woman interviewing young white men:

> my role as a student researcher, my age, and my assumed class affiliation may have been taken as sources of potential domination. However, my racialised and gender ascriptions suggested the opposite. That is, in this instance, the interviewees and myself were inscribed within multi-faceted power relations which had structural dominance *and* structural subordination in play on both sides. (1993: 101)

June Jordan (1989) powerfully evokes the same shifting power dynamics in her moving discussion of the contradictory relationship between her class, 'race', and gender as a middle-class African-American woman on holiday in the Bahamas. Both examples point to the dangers of thinking simply in terms of dualities (male versus female; black versus white; heterosexual versus lesbian, etc.) as though people were 'fixed' in binary locations and could speak only from these positions. More than this, using these identity markers, and reinscribing them in discussions of Othering, means that we run the risk of fetishizing Otherness, simply revers-ing the hierarchies of the original categories, attributing spurious homogeneity to patriarchally defined categories, and keeping the binary structure intact. No theoretical discussion of 'representing the Other' can fail to take up the question of the category itself. We cannot write about the Other as if some totalizable intelligible object simply 'exists' out there, waiting to be represented. Others are *constructed* – by those who do the Othering, by those who reflect upon that Othering, and by the Others' own representations of themselves.

Secondly, postmodern and postcolonial critics have insisted upon the need to shift debates on representation from the terrain of 'truth' or transparency to a consideration of 'regimes' of representation – that is: 'to a specification of the machineries and discourses that constitute both the possibility of representing an "other" and the criteria by which such representations function in the field of knowledge' (Ganguly, 1992: 71). Most feminist research in psychology con-tinues to be governed by the norms of representational realism. Feminist social psychologists (like many feminists across the social sciences) attempt in their work to present their female research participants 'as they really are' (as opposed to the way men have presented them) and 'in their own voices' (as opposed to the authoritative voice of the researcher–interpreter). Sceptical of the possibility of any such presentation of women's experience in direct, 'pure' or authentic form, Spivak (among others) recommends that feminists should proliferate no more accounts of the sort entitled '-- Speak', where the Other is simply a name that provides the alibi for erasing the investigator's intervention into the construction and representation of the narrative (Spivak, 1986: 229). Representation is never merely descriptive: it serves also a constitutive and regulatory function which is obscured in (but not absent from) accounts relying upon the conventions of representational realism.

Interrupting Othering   The problem, then, is how to go on conversing about, theorizing and attempting to challenge structural power, while recognizing the multiple intersecting forms of power and powerlessness; how to think about our own and/or others' Otherness without fixing it as an essential attribute; how to speak without our words serving to disempower Others; and when to remain silent. For feminist psychologists engaged in empirical research, these problems raise potentially intractable questions. Whom shall we include in our samples? In what ways will they be the same as, and in what ways different from, us? How will we represent their views? As feminist researchers, we are 'chronically and uncomfortably engaged in ethical decisions about how deeply to work with/for/despite those cast as Others' (Fine, 1994: 75).

Wrestling with problems of Othering, feminists and other critical social scientists have suggested ways out of the apparent impasse. Linda Alcoff (1994: 301–2), for example, who writes powerfully and passionately on issues of Othering, recommends four 'interrogatory practices' to evaluate instances of 'speaking for Others': firstly, she suggests that we should analyse, and perhaps resist, the impulse to speak at all; secondly, she asks us to engage in a critical interrogation of the relevance of our autobiographies (e.g. as white, heterosexual, etc.) on what we say – and not simply as a disclaimer against ignorance or errors; thirdly, she suggests that we maintain an openness to criticism; and fourthly, she asks us to analyse the actual *effects* of speaking on the discursive and material context. These concerns are increasingly incorporated (in a variety of forms) into contemporary feminist social science practice – with the aim of interrupting the process of Othering. Feminist psychologist Michelle Fine, to whose sophisticated and sensitively argued writing we owe an important debt in thinking about these issues here, suggests that we can interrupt Othering by 'working the hyphen' in the Self-Other equation:

> Self and Other are knottily entangled. This relationship, as lived between researchers and informants, is typically obscured in social science texts, protecting privilege, securing distance, and laminating the contradictions. Despite denials, qualitative researchers are always implicated at the hyphen. When we opt, as has been the tradition, simply to write *about* those who have been Othered, we deny the hyphen . . . When we opt, instead, to engage in social struggles *with* those who have been exploited and subjugated, we work the hyphen, revealing far more about ourselves, and far more about the structures of Othering . . . By *working the hyphen*, I mean to suggest that researchers probe how we are in relation with the contexts we study and with our informants, understanding that we are multiple in all those relations. (1994: 72)

In practice, 'working the hyphen' seems to include the following approaches (here our taxonomy overlaps with, and extends Fine's, 1994, classification): (a) checking out with Others the validity of one's representations of them; (b) listening to Other's accounts of 'us' as a way of exposing the operation of Othering; (c) listening to members of the powerful group to hear the ways in which they construct Others; and (d) finally (perhaps more in hope than with any sense of current possibility) developing opportunities for *dialogue* between 'us' and Others. We now (briefly) discuss each of these in turn.

First, an approach not unfamiliar to feminist social psychologists is to give representations back to the represented for comment, feedback and evaluation; the idea is that the researcher should negotiate representations with those represented and, in some versions of this, they are described not as 'subjects' or even 'research participants' but as 'co-researchers'. As the story of Katherine Borland's interpretative conflict with her grandmother illustrates, however, it is not clear what the researcher can do if she and those researched disagree, and a number of dubious 'quick fixes' are frequently used to take care of this problem (see Kitzinger and Wilkinson, 1995). (We return to this question later in this chapter, as it is raised by several contributors to this book.)

Secondly, many feminists emphasize *listening* to Others – creating conditions under which it is possible to hear the voices of Others 'talking back': to 'us', over 'us', regardless of 'us', to each other, or to other Others. As we have seen, Others' representations of themselves, and certainly their representations of 'us', are routinely de-authorized, and dismissed as neither credible nor coherent. Some researchers have stressed the possibilities inherent in the 'inversion' of Othering, whereby Others are given legitimacy as informants on Othering (rather than heard – if at all – merely as subjects' descriptions of their own subjugated position). Present-day ethnographers, for example, have recently begun to take seriously the accounts given by eighteenth- and nineteenth-century 'natives' of their western 'discoverers', with the intention of 'decentring' or 'disprivileging' the early ethnographers' reports (Abeyesekere, 1992; Todorov, 1984; both cited in Vidich and Lyman, 1994). Cultural theorists have explored the contemporary representations of 'us' by people from Other cultures. A recent study of Otherness in advertising analysed depictions of westerners in Japanese advertisements, aiming to 'demonstrate to an American audience what the process of "othering" is all about by looking at a situation in which white Westerners are the object of that process' (O'Barr, 1994: 15). Writing about the domination enacted by elite white women in the USA on the women of colour who work for them as domestics, sociologist Judith Rollins (1985) delivers her analysis from the vantage point of the women employed as domestics: 'reversing who would typically be relied upon to tell the "real" story and who would be portrayed as Other, Rollins allows readers to hear how much subjugated women know about them-Selves and about Others' (Fine, 1994: 77). Other recent examples of Others 'writing back' include lesbians writing about heterosexuality (Kitzinger and Wilkinson, 1994; Wilkinson and Kitzinger, 1994); black feminists and people of colour writing about whiteness (e.g. [charles][7], 1992, 1993; Wong, 1994); and, of course, women writing about men (Griffin and Wetherell, 1992). These approaches interrupt the conventional processes of representation, whereby 'we' look at the Others and describe what 'we' see. To look instead at the Others looking at 'us' is to relativize and problematize 'our' own perspective: it can be uncomfortable, unsettling or painful, but it is an essential beginning if the process of Othering is to be interrupted.

Thirdly, the study of dominant group members can yield information about the ways in which Self is constructed through and against the construction of the Other. Just as accounts written by early ethnographers reveal more about their authors' own social and cultural preoccupations than they do about the 'primitive tribes' which were the object of their study, so more generally the words of people with power speaking or writing about Others can reveal the processes involved in Othering. For example, researchers have usually read the traditional psychological and psychiatric literatures on lesbianism *in order to find out about lesbians*, so colluding in the process of Othering. An alternative approach, embodied in the first two chapters of Celia Kitzinger's (1987) book, *The Social Construction of Lesbianism*, is to ask instead: 'What can we learn from the literature about the construction of social scientific accounts?' and 'What can we learn from the literature about attempts to manage and control homosexuality?' In other words, what is said by psychologists and psychiatrists about lesbians is understood as revealing information about their preoccupations as members of a (predominantly heterosexual) academic elite, charged with the special responsibility of constructing authorized accounts of Others. In a parallel study, Harlan Hahn (1983, cited in Fine, 1994) has reviewed the work of non-disabled researchers on disability:

> only to conclude that by reading their work we learn more about these researchers' terror of disability than we do about the persons with disabilities about whom they presumably have written. Hahn theorizes that nondisabled researchers carry existential and aesthetic anxieties about bodily dis-integrity that they project onto the bodies of persons with disabilities. Their narratives are laced with anxieties as if they were simply in the bodies of 'them' rather than (un)settled within the (un)consciousness of the researchers. (Fine, 1994: 78)

As Michelle Fine (1994) points out, listening to the voices of privilege to understand how Othering works involves processes which differ depending on the social location of the listener. To listen, as a lesbian, to the voices of researchers on lesbianism is different from listening, as a non-disabled woman, to the voices of researchers on disability: our own contradictory 'partialities and pluralities' (Fine, 1994: 79) have to be part of the interrogation.

Finally, there are repeated suggestions that 'dialogue' with Others can be more illuminating than the monologue of the single researcher presenting 'data' about Others (Fowler, 1994): our work should be not so much about the *Other* as about the *interplay between* the researcher and the Other. In the introduction to *Writing Culture*, Clifford (1986) argues that ethnographers should attempt to create a text within a context of collaborative story-making which celebrates dialogue over monologue, polyphony over monophonic authority. Given that the object of knowledge (in this case, the Other) cannot be separated from the knower, and given the commonplace construction of the Other as the mirror-image of the dominant group, a 'dialogic' account (which privileges neither the powerful nor the Others) seems to Edward Sampson (1993) to offer the most hopeful approach to 'a genuinely democratic society'. Currently (and Sampson acknowledges this), it is hard to see how Others can be equal partners in this 'dialogue', but he holds fast to his vision in which (in the closing sentences of his book):

> dialogic partners . . . take us on yet another voyage of mutual adventure and discovery . . . We learn how many possibilities there are, how open we must be to this diverse range, and how no one voice can be quieted without losing the greatest opportunity of

all: to converse with otherness and to learn about our own otherness in and through those conversations. (Sampson, 1993: 187)

Having (somewhat selectively) reviewed the existing literature on Othering, we now move on to introduce the arguments and experiences of the authors in this book, and to highlight the contributions they make in advancing our theories and understandings of 'representing the Other'.

Moving Forward: Current Contributions

Contributors to this book are in agreement that traditional social science is still 'usually about someone else or something out there' (Brown) and that traditional *psychological* research, in particular, is 'predicated on the assumption that the subject of the research is "Other" to the researcher' (Adrian Coyle). They point out, however, that feminists, along with other critical social scientists, have challenged positivist notions of science, so that now, in some circles at least, 'an ethic of involvement has replaced an ethic of objectivity': 'if you see an article by a colleague on breast cancer, you write to see how she is, wonder when she was diagnosed. If you see an article on Alzheimer's, you assume someone's got a parent or in-law to help' (Barbara Katz Rothman). It may now be the case that *not* to belong to the group you represent is to raise 'the problem of credentials' (Deborah Marks). Joan C. Chrisler, a thin woman working with fat women, describes how: 'During the first group meeting someone would invariably ask me if I'd ever had a "weight problem" myself. When I answered "no", a veil seemed to descend between us, and it took weeks of work on my part to shift it.' Manjit Bola cogently summarizes the problem when she says:

> Many feminists have suggested that drawing on one's own personal experience is the key to doing feminist research. Similarity between the researcher and the researched is assumed, and the use of shared experience as data is presented as good feminist theory and practice . . . By contrast with the celebration of shared experience, there has been very little written by feminists about the impact of *differences* between the researcher and researched . . . Would women be comfortable with someone whose only similarity with them was gender-based?

While the overwhelming majority of contributors challenge 'the assumption that shared gender is commonality enough' (Marian Titley and Becky Chasey), most nonetheless insist upon the necessity of representing people different from oneself. A note of caution is sounded by Erica Burman who points out that:

> the costs of representation within the dominant order that defines [the Other] may out-weigh the benefits . . . the process of bringing into focus, of knowledging, can consti-tute an act of epistemic violence or alienation that disempowers or distorts, so that commenting on the absences within the dominant representations may be a more respectful and a more enabling political intervention.

But most of the contributors join Anna Livia in criticizing what she calls the 'silence-equals-respect' position: citing her own (fictionalized) account of an Australia without any Aboriginal women, Anna Livia argues that we are accountable not just for what we say, but also for what we leave out. 'Feminist analysis would be very partial if we could only speak of that which we had personally experienced' (Sheila Jeffreys), and 'it is the responsibility of feminists who have status and authority in the public world to question their exclusionary practices' (Anita Harris). Rosalind Edwards, in particular, criticizes the 'universalist pretensions contained in much white western feminist research and writing', arguing that, whatever the 'problems and contradictions' invoked by her whiteness, to fail to include black women in her research would be 'even more indefensible'. We cannot defend 'leaving out' Others, because the 'act of making the other invisible' (Langton, cited in Marion Martin and Beth Humphries) is itself a common form of Othering. '[P]art of our task is actively and publicly to question their continued absence and silence', say Marian Titley and Becky Chasey, from their position as young women who work with old women. They continue:

> To avoid openly discussing old women protects us from the charge of 'wrongful representation', while seeming to credit us with acknowledging the limits of our professional and personal experience. However, by avoiding this risk we are complicit in the continued devaluing of old women's experiences. Both we and they are then silenced.

The feminist project of 'representing the Other' – which is endorsed as necessary (even essential) by most of the book's contributors – involves researchers in a number of dilemmas, two of which will be highlighted here. The first is the dilemma of conflicting commitments: that is, many feminists want *both* to enable the voices of Others to be heard, *and* to create social and political change for or on behalf of those Others. As we shall see, these two commitments are not always compatible, and several contributors discuss the ethical and practical difficulties which arise when they come into conflict. The second dilemma relates to the negotiation of Otherness and difference, such that *both* 'refusing' difference *and* 'insisting' on difference can be used as much to maintain existing structures of power and powerless as to subvert them.

Commitments in Conflict?

Two commitments run through many of the contributions: (a) the commitment to enabling Others to be heard; and (b) the commitment to creating changes in the world.

In relation to this first commitment, some writers present themselves merely as conduits through which the words of Others can be made audible and visible. For Ann McNulty, the task is to 'support women in finding their own words' and 'not continuing to speak on someone else's behalf after it's ceased to be useful'. For Barbara Katz Rothman, 'it was a project in bearing witness ... I did think that I could pass through me the grief, anguish, fears, worries, strength and courage that these women showed me, and make that clear and visible to others.' For many writers, speaking on behalf of Others became necessary because Others were not able to speak, or were not allowed to speak, on their own behalves: 'I have had access to institutional contexts in which I was able to represent (as in "speak for") young people as individuals or as a group where no young women (or men) would ever have been allowed to speak, still less been heard' (Christine Griffin).

Just as Mary Crawford (1993: 44) uses the credibility bestowed upon her as a heterosexual woman to 'subvert heterosexism' in the classroom, so Joan C. Chrisler uses the credibility bestowed upon her as a thin psychologist to 'support fat liberation'. However, as Gabriele Griffin points out, 'we may resent someone whom we see as more powerful than ourselves representing us, purely because this act is an expression of their power relative to our powerlessness.' The problem of the costs of representation (in terms of reinscribing the patterns of privilege which created the Othering in the first place) become particularly acute under these circumstances and have continually to be juggled against the costs of silence.

The second commitment which threads throughout these chapters is the commitment to creating social change. Diane Bell's writing about the rape of Aboriginal women by Aboriginal men derives from her perception of the need to 'make a defiant feminist statement on rape'. For Marian Titley and Becky Chasey, the commitment is to ensure adequate delivery of service provision within the British National Health Service to old women who, as a group, 'are recipients of a significant proportion of health and social care, yet are largely excluded from policy-making and service development'. For Diana E.H. Russell: 'My goal in "representing the Other" [women in the South African liberation movement] was to provide them with the opportunity to publicize their cause in the USA and to move Americans to support the armed struggle against apartheid.'

These two commitments – to 'giving voice' and to effecting social change – do not always sit easily together. There is, of course, the practical problem that policy-makers are generally more easily persuaded by large-scale survey research, concise quantitative data and experimental evidence, than they are by collections of personal subjective accounts from a relatively small number of people (see Adrian Coyle's contribution for a discussion of this). More fundamentally, however, these two commitments may appear incompatible because the Others to whom researchers are committed to 'giving voice' very often do not share the researchers' commitment to social change. The voices of Others rarely speak in a direct and straightforward way of the need for a feminist revolution, or for the overthrow of systems of power and domination.

As the contributors say, part of the problem is that no one group of Others speaks in a single voice: they are never a homogenous group with just one point of view which can faithfully be represented. Anita Harris reflects that 'one of the biggest problems I have faced as a researcher is in dealing with the many contradictory stories and interpretations offered by young women of their experiences.' We cannot abdicate our political responsibility by claiming simply to 'discover' and faithfully report the 'right-on' politics of the Others of whom we write. The Jewish friends of (gentile) writer Anna Livia, disagreed *with each other* when she consulted them as to the appropriateness of her description of Hassidic Jews in North London. Similarly, Sheila Jeffreys points out that:

> the voices of prostitutes even within the literature of the prostitutes' rights movement of the 1970s and 1980s do not agree. The main voices in this literature proclaimed that prostitution was a job just like any other or even a form of sexual self-determination for women. But others described prostitution as seriously and inevitably abusive . . .

Feminists cannot hide from using their political intelligence behind the argument that only prostitutes can speak about their experience when such very diametrically opposite views are all posing as the truth of prostitution.

When some (or even most) of the self-representations offered by Others are at variance with the researcher's own politicized representations, the conflict between acting merely as a 'conduit' for Others' views, and acting specifically to promote social change, becomes particularly acute. We have written of this problem elsewhere:

> Many women in our interviews (on sexual harassment) and focus groups (on breast cancer) say things not easily incorporated into our own radical feminist theories. While I (CK) think sexual harassment is a pervasive and outrageous abuse of male power, many women I interview tell me that 'it's not that much of a problem', that it's comparatively 'rare', and that it is 'all part of normal relationships between men and women'. While I (SW) admire lesbian and feminist writing on breast cancer which stresses the political issues involved, deplores women's dependence on male approval, and challenges the idea that mastectomy is something to be concealed, women in my focus groups persistently ascribe individualistic victim-blaming 'causes' to their cancer, worry about their attractiveness to men, and express shame about their 'deformity'. (Kitzinger and Wilkinson, 1995)

The contributors to the present volume raise similar concerns: the self-representations of young women, for example, are often, says Anita Harris, 'celebrations of achieving images damaging to their health and autonomy'. Such observations lead several of the contributors to a consideration of how to proceed when their own political analysis and commitment to social change conflicts with the self-representations and views of their research participants. Amparo Bonilla Campos says:

> In my research on young people choosing their careers, what the figures show is that this is a social thing, that career choice is clearly structured by social class and by gender. But young people represent themselves as making individual choices. So they dismiss equal opportunity policies as not being important at all . . . I wouldn't expect that my interpretations would be the same as my participants' point of view because mostly my participants aren't feminists. You just have to realize that sometimes the people you are researching are not going to agree with you . . .

Adrian Coyle makes a very similar point:

> researchers and research participants have . . . different frameworks for interpreting the experiences under study . . . For example, women participating in feminist research may not invoke the role of patriarchal social structures when making sense of their experiences because of the invisible organizational function of patriarchy in shaping an oppressive, 'take-for-granted' world. Indeed, if they are aware of the negative aspects of the social representations of feminism, participants may resist the researcher locating their experiences within a feminist analytic framework.

In reflecting on how she deals with 'hostility' from fat women who do not share her commitment to 'fat liberation', Joan C. Chrisler draws a distinction between 're-presenting' and 'representing' – a distinction initially made by Marx (*Darstellung/Vertretung*) and developed by Spivak (1986), who contends that it is not fruitful to undertake projects of representation with the hope that we will be able to let our subjects' voices or experience speak their own truths. As Adrian

Coyle says, 'claims concerning the capacity of any research approach to reflect the voices of research participants in an "uncontaminated" way are simply elements of a discourse of legitimation.' Katie MacMillan similarly advances the argument that 'the practice of giving research subjects a "voice" within academic texts, whether by speaking for them or by letting them speak for themselves, is always and inevitably a textual device that retains and reinforces, rather than weakens, the academic author's authority.' There is always, says Spivak (1986), a tension between simply 're-presenting' our subjects (describing them, painting a portrait of them, speaking 'about' them) and 'representing' them (acting as their proxies or advocates, speaking 'for' them).

> Instead of 're-presenting' fat women in images of how they could change themselves, I would 'represent' them as an advocate for their right to be as they are.
>   Of course, most fat women don't want to be as they are; they want to be thin . . . Whenever I speak about these issues, whether in the classroom, at a professional conference, or at a public lecture, an angry woman will invariably tell me that she has struggled with her weight all her life, has recently made considerable progress, and resents my suggestion that she will not one day meet her goal. (Joan C. Chrisler)

The problem is, as Erica Burman points out, that the stories told us by Others are not transparent accounts of the world: they are 'constructed through both micro- and meta-representational practices'. However we interpret the task of 'representing Others', we have to recognize the complexity of the stories that 'they' as well as 'we' tell, and not imagine that simply 'enabling them to be heard' will unproblematically translate into revolutionary social and political change.

Negotiating Otherness: Refusing Difference, Affirming Difference

A crucial contribution to discussions of Othering arises out of contributors' arguments illustrating the ways in which both the *refusal* of Others' difference (what Amanda Kottler describes as the similarity perspective) and, equally, the *affirmation* of Others' difference, can be used as much to oppress as to liberate. Oppression can operate through *refusal* to acknowledge the differences of those in relation to whom we occupy positions of privilege, whether this refusal is expressed either in the liberal insistence on 'colour-blindness', *or* in the post-modern insistence on the dazzling diversity of experience within and between socially constructed and constantly shifting categories, such that no one 'difference' is afforded any more significance than any other. Equally, however, oppression can operate through the *affirmation* of differences (even if re-valued as 'positive') because this affirmation serves to underwrite and to reinscribe distinctions between people – distinctions which are not 'essentially' real, but which are constructed precisely in order to provide the rationale and justification for oppressive practices. The debate about 'differences' is familiar to feminist psychologists from the 'sex differences' discussions which polarize, on the one hand, those who *refuse* (or, more accurately, in their terms, whose empirical evidence fails to support) the existence of differences between men and women, and, on the other hand, those who *affirm* (and celebrate) women's lives and experiences as different and distinctive from those of men (see Kitzinger, 1994b).

Both the *refusal* and the *affirmation* of sex differences have been lauded as liberationary; equally, both have been deplored as reactionary. This same tension between the *refusal* and the *affirmation* of difference reasserts itself in relation to the question of representing Others.

As with much previous writing on questions of Othering, the contributors here continue to struggle with questions of overlapping categories and shifting identities in their discussions of who 'we' are and who the Other is. '"We" doesn't really get one very far', says Barbara Katz Rothman: 'We who? Can I use "we" only for "women like me"? And what makes a woman "like me"? Is it age, race, sexual orientation(s), reproductive history, familial status, education or job situation?' Diana E.H. Russell documents her difficult decision, as a white researcher on sexual abuse in South Africa, to limit herself to white interviewees only, but she points out that these included white women who, along other dimensions of power and powerlessness, were very much her Others (e.g. middle-class and working-class white women, Afrikaners etc.). In making her decision, Diana E.H. Russell chose, in Magdalene Ang-Lygate's words, 'to privilege the *racialization* of [herself]' (our emphasis) over, for example, her (upper) class position. According to Magdalene Ang-Lygate, the problem of defining 'us' in relation to Others lies in its implied reduction of overlapping and intersecting oppressions to simple binary equations:

> as a Chinese woman researching other Chinese women, it would be methodologically misleading for me to assume that I 'belonged' simply because I am myself Chinese, if I neglected to account for other social differences based on ethnicity, sexuality, class, religion and so on . . . Only in choosing to privilege the racialization of myself and my research participants can I say that we belong to the same group, because the moment we admit the possibility of other concurrent categories of Otherness, group membership becomes repeatedly re-negotiable.

Moreover, researcher and researched may have different ideas about who 'we' are – and the researcher's claim to be included in the 'we' of the research subjects may be rejected by them. Rosalind Edwards found herself 'brought up short' by this discrepancy:

> I had been jolted by the meeting of my own identity – Ros Edwards, approachable woman researcher who had been a mature student and a lone mother, and was 'on their side' – with a racialized categorization as an untrustworthy white institutional figure. This categorization was not resonant with my experiences and conception of self.

First, then, the *refusal* of difference arises from a clear awareness that the idea of 'an incontrovertible difference which determines groups of people and differentiates them clearly from each other', the notion of 'specific categories linked to some essential feature such as sexual orientation or racial identity as the ground on which group identity is founded' (Gabriele Griffin) rests on deeply essentialist ideas. As progressive (white) academics involved in the anti-apartheid struggle argue, 'different races and ethnic groups, unique cultures and traditions, do not exist in any ultimate sense in South Africa, and are real only to the extent that they are the product of a particular world view' (Amanda Kottler). 'Differences' are continually reinscribed by means of structural and institutional power (Marion Martin and Beth Humphries) such that 'imaginary lines' (Magdalene Ang-Lygate) are 'socially constructed' (Diane Bell) between Self and Other: we need to 'resist attempts to categorize us as Other from a perspective not our own' (Magdalene Ang-Lygate).

Several contributors emphasize that, in relation to many forms of Othering, people do not and cannot occupy 'fixed' positions: Anne Woollett describes her own changing self-definition from 'infertile' to 'childless' woman, and Deborah Marks points out that 'most people are likely to experience some form of disability, at some stage in their life. This renders unstable any attempt to make sharp demarcations between being able-bodied and disabled.' In her discussion of representations of people with disabilities, Deborah Marks comments that 'the "Other" is always a construction which relies on the fears and fantasies we have about ourselves as much as the fears and fantasies we have about "Others"'. This is echoed by Marian Titley and Becky Chasey who, in their consideration of young women's representation of old women, suggest that we may 'exaggerate the sense of Otherness' of old women because of 'the fear that our own old age might be similar; that their current reality might be our own future'. But even in relation to categories more stable than those of (dis)ability and age, the boundaries are neither fixed nor 'natural'. Diane Bell asks us to refuse the 'rigidity of the bounded category of race', to 'emphasize relationality' and 'connectedness', and to see the 'permeable membranes' between us. In *refusing* difference, many of the contributors draw on postmodern, social constructionist or discursive perspectives, claiming that 'in viewing such distinctions as linguistically managed it becomes possible to challenge their naturalness and thus the legitimacy of the practices they sustain' (Anna Madill). According to Jean Carabine:

> Adopting the term 'Other' risks restricting our thinking to the boundaries of the Other/Same coupling and to the power relations arising out of that relationship. A focus on Other is problematic because it tends to shift the debate back to a preoccupation with binary oppositions and runs the risk of locking differences . . . up in the oppositional categories of oppressor and oppressed.

Secondly, and by contrast, *affirmation* of difference is central to many contributions. Christine Griffin quotes Audre Lorde's concern about 'the failure of academic feminists to recognise difference as a crucial strength', and Gabriele Griffin asks us to consider 'how differential power among women . . . can be utilized *for* women' arguing that 'it is only through the acknowledgement of difference, and the impetus to use that difference in favour of other women, that representing Others can become a tool for change.' Tracey L. Hurd and Alice McIntyre point to the ways in which tacit and unexplored assumptions of sameness cause problems in allowing researcher and researched to collude in the reproduction of 'lived, *but critically unexamined*, life experiences'. They give the example of 'white talk' in white-on-white participatory research and express 'disquiet' at the similarities between themselves and their participants: 'I increased the level of Othering to counteract my heartfelt similarity to my research participants . . . I sought to remove myself as a participant voice' (Tracey L. Hurd).

Adrian Coyle suggests that pretending commonality with his HIV-positive subjects would be to invoke a 'fictitious sympathy':

> Some fellow HIV/AIDS researchers of indeterminate HIV status with whom I have discussed this issue have sought to create some sort of link with HIV-positive research participants, reasoning 'well, I may not know my HIV status but I do act as if I were HIV positive', by which they usually mean practising safer sex. However, knowing that you are HIV positive involves much more than this: potentially, it involves having to live with a host of uncertainties about health, illness and physical and social functioning. Having listened to HIV-positive gay men recounting what are often incredibly traumatic experiences related to their HIV status, I would find it utterly patronizing to suggest a meaningful commonality of experience between myself and them.

More generally, the problem, as both Amanda Kottler and Jean Carabine point out, albeit from rather different perspectives, lies in finding 'a way of speaking about differences without reinvoking a racializing [or otherwise oppressive] discourse' (Amanda Kottler, our parentheses). The paradox of acknowledging the 'reality' of oppressions based on 'unreal' distinctions is addressed in The Spoken Word, in which Manjit Bola, Amparo Bonilla Campos and Hannah Frith challenge Jean Carabine's statement that it might be 'helpful to stop thinking about all this as though it's something *fixed* – seeing instead that these are imaginary boundaries which can be shifted and that we *are* shifting between them at different times.' As Manjit Bola says, 'many of the positions that we're in are *not* imaginary'; as Amparo Bonilla Campos adds, 'they are socially constructed for *reasons* and they have real effects in the world'; and as Hannah Frith concludes: 'Differences are not all equal. Differences are structured along lines of power and powerlessness. . . .' In sum, while it is undeniably the case that differences between people are socially constructed such that divergence from the norms of privileged groups carry negative and oppressive meanings, it is equally the case that differences so constructed (while not 'real' in any absolute or essential sense) have real and material consequences, and that these consequences are not erased by a simple refusal to 'notice' them.

One way of dealing with this apparent paradox of 'constructed' differences and their 'material' consequences, is to shift the focus away from questions of similarity and difference between Self and Other and to focus instead on the construction of Self and Other in relation. Erica Burman asks that 'we should work to recognize ourselves in Others . . . to understand the dynamics of mutual investment and provisional privilege.' She proposes that:

> if the Others I represent are in some respects also me then *my* representation of *them* should reflect on its process. Rather than the voyeuristic, spec(tac)ular logic of the one-way mirror beloved of psychology, it should present new perspectives on the disciplinary matrix that makes us as well as them.

Where Next?

As Kathy Doherty reminds us: 'certain types of research are encouraged and others are actively undermined in academia – from the gatekeeping process right through to funding, time limits, and all the rest of it.' In a similar vein, Marion

Martin and Beth Humphries caution against an individualist reading of the problems here. Individualist renditions of the research relationship, in which similarities may be emphasized, or in which differences may be given a positive valence, are not sufficient to overcome institutional and structural power. As Yeatman (1993, cited in Marion Martin and Beth Humphries) points out, what is often avoided by these is the 'complexity of dialogue that arises between subjects who understand themselves to be complexly like and different from each other, but are differently *positioned*'. This different positioning (across colonialist and neo-colonialist boundaries) 'tore apart possibilities for collaboration' between Marion Martin, Beth Humphries and their would-be collaborator from the third world: 'The differences which we had come to see positively, and to work with creatively, were placed under extreme stress . . . Our research relationship carried with it the history of our countries. . . .' In focusing on the behaviour of researchers at the level of interpersonal interaction, we run the risk of overlooking the institutional context which shapes this behaviour, and through which it gains meaning. Failure to analyse structural (as opposed to interpersonal) relationships can lead – as in their case – to 'confusion', 'anger', 'alienation' – and ultimately to the destruction of the research collaboration itself.

Overall, and perhaps inevitably, we (the editors) see this book as raising more questions than it answers – but also as raising them in ways which we hope will encourage feminists, particularly feminist *psychologists*, to engage with and to pursue questions of Othering in our research and practice. We would like to see, in feminist psychology, more recognition of Others other than 'women', and more consideration – at the level of both theory and practice – of the ways in which our commitment to 'giving voice' conflicts with our commitment to social and political change. We hope too that (paralleling developments in 'sex differences' research, cf. Kitzinger, 1994b), some of the current emphasis on the extent to which women are the same as, or different from, each other may shift to an exploration of the ways in which those samenesses and differences are *constructed*, the *purposes* they serve, and their *material* effects in the world. Constructing the mindedness and agency of Others is so pervasive and so much a part of communication that it is difficult to imagine proceeding without it. In particular, it is important to engage with these patterns of representation because even if we achieve an Otherless academic discourse, many people and institutions have a great deal at stake in creating and managing Others. Representing Others, whether we do it ourselves as an heuristic device to make sense of what we call our data, or whether we detect it going on elsewhere, is an important topic of study in its own right. At the same time, the work of people attempting to break out of the Otherness we have constructed them into has a vital role to play in achieving a *reflexive* knowledge which is sufficiently fluid to admit of being 'ruptured' with 'uppity voices' (Fine, 1994: 75).

In conclusion, then, Othering is not something which feminists, including feminist psychologists, can afford to ignore. Unless we actively engage with the process of Othering as *topic*, we run the risk of uncritically reproducing it in our own research and writing. Only by making Other*ing* (rather than Other*ness*) the focus of our attention, and by exploring the ways in which it is done and undone, reinforced and undermined, can we open up the possibility, finally, of interrupting its oppressive discourse.

Notes

1 Where ideas or quotations are referenced, as here, using author names only (without a date), they are references to contributions in this volume.

2 The others to date are Wilkinson and Kitzinger (1993) and Bhavnani and Phoenix (1994).

3 The 'Call for Short Contributions' (inspired in part by the earlier submission of Anna Livia's paper, included in this volume) was published by Sue Wilkinson, as Editor of the *Feminism & Psychology* Special Feature on 'Representing the Other'. Because of the overwhelming response, this Special Feature was published in two parts (see *Feminism & Psychology* 6[1] and 6[2]). Additionally, some of the pieces submitted were published separately in the 'Observations and Commentaries' section of the journal, which is edited by Celia Kitzinger (see *Feminism & Psychology* 5[4]); others could appear only in this volume. Because we worked intensively together in selecting and editing these pieces overall, we do not wish, in this book, to claim individual responsibility for editing the different 'sections' under whose headings these pieces originally appeared (and which *are* individually credited in the journal). Indeed, we have combined the Special Feature, the Observations and Commentaries, and the new pieces under the single heading, 'Short Contributions'. Consequently (with the sole exception of Part III: The Spoken Word, which was coordinated and edited by Celia Kitzinger and is so credited both here and in the journal), this book should be read as jointly edited in its entirety.

4 All submissions to the journal were subject to the normal peer review process, and we would particularly like to thank the reviewers (almost a hundred of them!) for their thoughtful and prompt responses to our requests for comments on these pieces. Because of time pressures towards the final stages of this project, a disproportionate burden of the reviewing fell upon members of the journal Editorial Group, so particular thanks to Kum-Kum Bhavnani, Mary Boyle, Erica Burman and Harriette Marshall for their help.

5 We are not being inconsistent in our references to contributors here: 'Brown' is his only name; he wants no other.

6 When in this chapter we use terms such as 'black', 'white', 'Chinese', 'British', 'woman of colour', 'third world' and so on, we have been careful to use the terms employed by the authors to whose work we are referring. We recognize that these terms, and the 'categories' to which they refer, are socially constructed and politically contested, hence the importance of using authors' own words in representing their ideas.

7 This author has said: 'Helen (charles) likes the shape of her name to be respected. The fact that the "family" names of many black people originate in the nomenclature of slave-owners means that naming has not been a matter of free choice for centuries' ([charles], 1993: 272).

References

Adorno T.W., Frenkel-Brunswick, E., Levinson, D.J. and Sanford, R.N. (1950) *The Authoritarian Personality*. New York: Harper and Row.

Afshar, Haleh and Maynard, Mary (1994) 'Introduction: The Dynamics of "Race" and Gender', in Haleh Afshar and Mary Maynard (eds) *The Dynamics of 'Race' and Gender: Some Feminist Interventions*. London: Taylor and Francis.

Alcoff, Linda (1994) 'The Problem of Speaking for Others', in Susan Ostrov Weisser and Jennifer Fleischner (eds) *Feminist Nightmares – Women at Odds: Feminism and the Problem of Sisterhood*. New York: New York University Press.

Allport, G. (1954) *The Nature of Prejudice*. Reading, MA: Addison-Wesley.

Amos, V. and Parmar, P. (1984) 'Challenging Imperial Feminism', *Feminist Review* 17: 3–20.

Andersen, Margaret, L. (1993) 'Studying across Difference: Race, Class, and Gender in Qualitative

Research', in John H. Stanfield and Rutledge M. Dennis (eds) *Race and Ethnicity in Research Methods*. London: Sage.

Aziz, Razia (1992) 'Feminism and the Challenge of Racism: Deviance or Difference', in Helen Crowley and Susan Himmelweit (eds) *Knowing Women: Feminism and Knowledge*. Cambridge, UK: Polity Press in association with Blackwell Publishers and the Open University.

de Beauvoir, Simone (1949/53) *The Second Sex*. New York: Knopf.

Belenky, Mary, Clinchy, Blythe, Goldberger, Nancy and Tarule, Jill (1986) *Women's Ways of Knowing*. New York: Basic Books.

Bhavnani, Kum-Kum (1993) 'Tracing the Contours: Feminist Research and Feminist Objectivity', *Women's Studies International Forum* 16 (2): 95–104.

Bhavnani, Kum-Kum and Phoenix, Ann (eds) (1994) *Shifting Identities Shifting Racisms: A 'Feminism & Psychology' Reader*. London: Sage.

Borland, Katherine (1991) '"That's Not What I Said": Interpretive Conflict in Oral Narrative Research', in Sherna Berger Gluck and Daphne Patai (eds) *Women's Words: The Feminist Practice of Oral History*. London: Routledge.

Burman, Erica (1994) *Deconstructing Developmental Psychology*. London: Routledge.

Carr, Helen (1988) 'In Other Words: Native American Women's Autobiography', in Bella Brodzki and Celeste Schenck (eds) *Life/Lines: Theorizing Women's Autobiography*. Ithaca: Cornell University Press.

(charles), Helen (1992) 'Whiteness – The Relevance of Politically Colouring the "Non"', in Hilary Hinds, Anne Phoenix and Jackie Stacey (eds) *Working Out: New Directions for Women's Studies*. London: Falmer.

(charles), Helen (1993) 'A Homogeneous Habit? Heterosexual Display in the English Holiday Camp', in Sue Wilkinson and Celia Kitzinger (eds) *Heterosexuality: A 'Feminism & Psychology' Reader*. London: Sage.

Cixous, Helene (1983/92) 'The Laugh of the Medusa', in E. Abel and E.K. Abel (eds) *The Signs Reader: Women, Gender and Scholarship*. Chicago: University of Chicago Press.

Cixous, Helene and Clement, C. (1975/86) *The Newly Born Woman*. Minneapolis: University of Minnesota Press.

Clifford, James (1986) 'Introduction', in James Clifford and George E. Marcus (eds) *Writing Culture*. Berkeley: University of California Press.

Clifford, James and Marcus, George E. (eds) (1986) *Writing Culture*. Berkeley: University of California Press.

Crawford, Mary (1993) 'Identity, "Passing" and Subversion', in Sue Wilkinson and Celia Kitzinger (eds) *Heterosexuality: A Feminism & Psychology Reader*. London: Sage.

Crenshaw, Kimberle (1992) 'Whose Story Is It, Anyway? Feminist and Antiracist Appropriations of Anita Hill', in Toni Morrison (ed.) *Race-ing Justice, En-gendering Power*. New York: Pantheon Books.

Croghan, Rose (1993) 'Sleeping with the Enemy: Mothers in Heterosexual Relationships', in Sue Wilkinson and Celia Kitzinger (eds) *Heterosexuality: A 'Feminism & Psychology' Reader*. London: Sage.

Daly, Mary (1978) *Gyn/Ecology: The Metaethics of Radical Feminism*. Boston: Beacon Press.

Evans, Mary (1983) 'Simone de Beauvoir: Dilemmas of a Feminist Radical', in Dale Spender (ed.) *Feminist Theorists: Three Centuries of Women's Intellectual Traditions*. London: The Women's Press.

Felstiner, Mary Lowenthal (1980) 'Seeing *The Second Sex* through the Second Wave', *Feminist Studies* 6 (2): 247–77.

Fine, Michelle (1994) 'Working the Hyphens: Reinventing Self and Other in Qualitative Research', in Norman K. Denzin and Yvonna S. Lincoln (eds) *Handbook of Qualitative Research*. London: Sage.

Fowler, Catherine S. (1994) 'Beginning to Understand: Twenty-Eight Years of Fieldwork in the Great Basin of Western North America', in Don D. Fowler and Donald L. Hardesty (eds) *Others Knowing Others: Perspectives on Ethnographic Careers*. Washington: Smithsonian Institution Press.

Fowler, Don D. and Hardesty, Donald L. (eds) (1994) *Others Knowing Others: Perspectives on Ethnographic Careers*. Washington: Smithsonian Institution Press.

Ganguly, Keya (1992) 'Accounting for Others: Feminism and Representation', in Lana F. Rakow (ed.) *Women Making Meaning: New Feminist Directions in Communication*. New York: Routledge.

Gilligan, Carol (1982) *In a Different Voice*. Cambridge, MA: Harvard University Press.

Gluck, Sherna Berger and Patai, Daphne (1991) 'Introduction', in Sherna Berger Gluck and Daphne Patai (eds) *Women's Words: The Feminist Practice of Oral History*. London: Routledge.

Griffin, Christine and Wetherell, Margaret (eds) (1992) 'Open Forum: Feminist Psychology and the Study of Men and Masculinity', *Feminism & Psychology: An International Journal* 2 (2): 133–68.

Guillaumin, Colette (1972/95) *Racism, Sexism, Power and Ideology*. London: Routledge.

Hill Collins, Patricia (1990) *Black Feminist Thought: Knowledge, Consciousness, and the Politics of Empowerment*. New York: Routledge.

Hollway, Wendy (1995) 'Feminist Discourses and Women's Heterosexual Desire', in Sue Wilkinson and Celia Kitzinger (eds) *Feminism and Discourse: Psychological Perspectives*. London: Sage.

hooks, bell (1990) *Yearning: Race, Gender and Cultural Politics*. Boston: South End Press.

Irigaray, Luce (1981) 'This Sex which Is Not One', in E. Marks and I. de Courtivron (eds) *New French Feminisms*. London: Harvester.

Jackson, Stevi, Prince, Jane and Young, Pauline (1993) 'Science, Medicine and Reproductive Technology: Introduction', in Stevi Jackson (ed.) *Women's Studies: A Reader*. London: Harvester Wheatsheaf.

Jordan, June (1989) 'Report from the Bahamas', in *Moving Towards Home*. London: Virago Press.

Kitzinger, Celia (1987) *The Social Construction of Lesbianism*. London: Sage.

Kitzinger, Celia (1994a) 'Experiential Authority and Heterosexuality', in Gabriele Griffin (ed.), *Changing our Lives: Women in/to Women's Studies*. London: Pluto.

Kitzinger, Celia (ed.) (1994b) 'Special Feature: Should Psychologists Study Sex Differences?', *Feminism & Psychology: An International Journal* 4 (4): 506–46.

Kitzinger, Celia and Perkins, Rachel (1993) *Changing our Minds: Lesbian Feminism and Psychology*. London: Onlywomen Press; New York: New York University Press.

Kitzinger, Celia and Wilkinson, Sue (1993) 'Theorizing Heterosexuality', in Sue Wilkinson and Celia Kitzinger (eds) *Heterosexuality: A 'Feminism & Psychology' Reader*. London: Sage.

Kitzinger, Celia and Wilkinson, Sue (1994) 'Virgins and Queers: Rehabilitating Heterosexuality?', *Gender & Society (Special Issue on Sexual Identities/ Sexual Communities)* 8 (3): 444–63.

Kitzinger, Celia and Wilkinson, Sue (1995) 'The Challenge of "Experience" for Feminist Psychology: False Consciousness, Invalidation and Denial', paper presented at the British Psychological Society's Psychology of Women Section Annual Conference, University of Leeds, July (currently under submission).

Kristeva, Julia (1980) *Desire in Language: A Semiotic Approach to Literature and Art*. Oxford: Blackwell.

Lacan, Jacques (1977) *Ecrits: A Selection*. London: Tavistock.

Lennon, Kathleen and Margaret Whitford (1994) 'Introduction', in Kathleen Lennon and Margaret Whitford (eds) *Knowing the Difference: Feminist Perspectives in Epistemology*. London: Routledge.

Liddle, Joanna and Rai, Shirin M. (1993) 'Between Feminism and Orientalism', in Mary Kennedy, Cathy Lubelska and Val Walsh (eds) *Making Connections: Women's Studies, Women's Movements, Women's Lives*. London: Taylor and Francis.

Lorde, Audre (1984) *Sister Outsider*. Trumansburg, NY: The Crossing Press.

McGrane, B. (1989) *Beyond Anthropology: Society and the Other*. New York: Columbia University Press.

Mama, Amina (1995) *Beyond the Masks: Race, Gender and Subjectivity*. London: Routledge.

Mani, Lata (1990) 'Multiple Mediations: Feminist Scholarship in the Age of Multinational Reception', *Feminist Review* 35: 24–41.

Miller, Alice (1984) *For Your Own Good: Hidden Cruelty in Child-Rearing and the Roots of Violence*. Trans. Hildegarde Hannum and Hunter Hannum. New York: Farrar, Straus and Giroux.

Mohanty, Chandra (1988) 'Under Western Eyes: Feminist Scholarship and Colonial Discourse', *Feminist Review* 30: 61–88.

Morrison, Toni (1992) *Playing in the Dark: Whiteness and the Literary Imagination*. Cambridge MA: Harvard University Press.

O'Barr, William, M. (1994) *Culture and the Ad: Exploring Otherness in the World of Advertising.* Boulder, CO: Westview Press.

Olson, Karen and Linda Shopes (1991) 'Crossing Boundaries, Building Bridges: Doing Oral History among Working-class Women and Men', in Sherna Berger Gluck and Daphne Patai (eds) *Women's Words: The Feminist Practice of Oral History.* London: Routledge.

Patai, Daphne (1991) 'US Academics and Third World Women: Is Ethical Research Possible?', in Sherna Berger Gluck and Daphne Patai (eds) *Women's Words: The Feminist Practice of Oral History.* London: Routledge.

Personal Narratives Group (1989) 'Truths', in The Personal Narratives Group (ed.) *Interpreting Women's Lives: Feminist Theory and Personal Narratives.* Bloomington, IN: Indiana University Press.

Radway, Janice (1986) 'Identifying Ideological Seams: Mass Culture, Analytic Method and Political Practice', *Communication* 9: 92–123.

Riley, Denise (1988) *'Am I That Name?' Feminism and the Category of 'Women' in History.* London: Macmillan.

Rollins, Judith (1985) *Between Women: Domestics and their Employers.* Philadelphia: Temple University Press.

Said, Edward (1978) *Orientalism.* New York: Pantheon.

Said, Edward W. (1989) 'Representing the Colonized: Anthropology's Interlocutors', *Critical Inquiry* 14: 205–25.

Salazar, Claudia (1991) 'A Third World Woman's Text: Between the Politics of Criticism and Cultural Politics', in Sherna Berger Gluck and Daphne Patai (eds) *Women's Words: The Feminist Practice of Oral History.* London: Routledge.

Sampson, Edward E. (1993) *Celebrating the Other: A Dialogic Account of Human Nature.* London: Harvester Wheatsheaf.

Scheman, Naomi (1993) 'Though This be Method, Yet There is Madness in It: Paranoia and Liberal Epistemology', in Louise M. Antony and Charlotte Will (eds) *A Mind of One's Own: Feminist Essays on Reason and Objectivity.* Boulder, CO: Westview Press.

Segal, Lynne (1994) *Straight Sex: The Politics of Pleasure.* London: Virago.

Seifer, Nancy (1976) *Nobody Speaks for Me! Self Portraits of American Working Class Women.* New York: Simon and Schuster.

Sinister Wisdom Collective (1990) 'Editorial', *Sinister Wisdom* 42 (4): 1–6.

Smith, Anna Marie (1995) 'The Regulation of Lesbian Sexuality through Erasure: The Case of Jennifer Saunders', in Karla Jay (ed.) *Lesbian Erotics.* New York: New York University Press.

Spelman, Elizabeth V. (1988) *Inessential Woman: Problems of Exclusion in Feminist Thought.* London: The Women's Press.

Spender, Dale (1982) *Women of Ideas and What Men Have Done to Them.* London: Pandora.

Spivak, Gayatri (1986) *In Other Worlds: Essays in Cultural Politics.* London: Methuen.

Trinh, T. Minh-ha (1989) *Woman, Native, Other: Writing Postcoloniality and Feminism.* Bloomington, IN: Indiana University Press.

Ussher, Jane (1991) *Women's Madness: Misogyny or Mental Illness?* London: Harvester Wheatsheaf.

Van Maanen, John (1995) 'An End to Innocence: The Ethnography of Ethnography', in Van Maanen, John (ed.) *Representation in Ethnography.* London: Sage.

Vidich, Arthur J. and Lyman, Stanford M. (1994) 'Qualitative Methods: Their History in Sociology and Anthropology', in Norman K. Denzin and Yvonna S. Lincoln (eds) *Handbook of Qualitative Research.* London: Sage.

White, Evelyn C. (1990) *The Black Women's Health Book: Speaking for Ourselves.* Seattle: Seal Press.

Wilkinson, Sue and Kitzinger, Celia (eds) (1993) *Heterosexuality: A 'Feminism & Psychology' Reader.* London: Sage.

Wilkinson, Sue and Kitzinger, Celia (1994) 'The Social Construction of Heterosexuality', *Journal of Gender Studies* 3 (3): 305–14.

Williamson, Judith (1986) 'The Problems of Being Popular', *New Socialist* (September): 14–15.

Winzeler, Robert L. (1994) 'Interpreting Skulls: Reflections of Fieldwork in Malaysia', in Don D. Fowler and Donald L. Hardesty (eds) *Others Knowing Others: Perspectives on Ethnographic*

Careers. Washington: Smithsonian Institution Press.

Wong, L. Mun (1994) 'Di(s)-secting and Dis(s)-closing "Whiteness": Two Tales about Psychology', in Kum-Kum Bhavnani and Ann Phoenix (eds) *Shifting Identities Shifting Racisms: A 'Feminism & Psychology' Reader*. London: Sage.

Yuval-Davis, Nira (1993) 'The (Dis)Comfort of Being "Hetero"', in Sue Wilkinson and Celia Kitzinger (eds) *Heterosexuality: A 'Feminism & Psychology' Reader*. London: Sage.

Zita, Jacquelyn N. (1994) 'Jeffner Allen: A Lesbian Portrait', in Claudia Card (ed.) *Adventures in Lesbian Philosophy*. Bloomington, IN: Indiana University Press.

2

Daring to Presume

Anna Livia

Sinister Wisdom, the literary journal 'for the Lesbian Imagination in the Arts and Politics' published this editorial statement:

> we've decided not to consider work written as first person narrative cross-culturally (a white dyke writing in the voice of a black dyke, a Christian writing in the voice of a Jew, for instance) . . . no one should ever 'speak for' or assume another's voice . . . it becomes a form of colonisation. (*Sinister Wisdom* Collective, 1990: 4)

It is now commonplace to find, in lesbian and feminist circles, the idea that it is presumptuous for a writer to create characters who are quite different from herself: for white women to describe the emotions of black women, for example.

Sister Gin (1975), by the white lesbian writer June Arnold, is set in North Carolina and tells the story of a group of old white women who wreak inventive revenge on rapists. The last ten pages are devoted to a conversation between Su, the white heroine, and her alter ego, Sister Gin (presumed white), in which Su offers two possible accounts which Miss May (black, maid to one of the other white women) might have given of her sister's rape. The book ends with Sister Gin's verdict, delivered to Su and, by implication, to the author: 'You just can't speak for Miss May, that's all. Let her go out the door. And she doesn't need you to hold it for her either.' It reads to me as a justification for Miss May's silence, but if the author cannot speak for her character, then who can? Miss May is destined to remain speechless. June Arnold seems to reserve her silence-equals-respect stance for her black characters: she was at least 20 years younger than her oldest character, Mamie Carter, but expresses no qualms about imagining *her* experience because, I assume, they are both white.

Thirteenth Moon's special issue on 'Working-class Experience' (1983) included an article on the writing of *Folly* (1982) by its author, Maureen Brady, and a review of the novel by Bertha Harris. Together they provided the term 'presumption' to name questions I'd been considering in my own fiction.

Maureen Brady, a white lesbian, writes of her feeling that it would be presumptuous to imagine the thoughts of her black characters:

> To tell a story of mill workers in North Carolina and to do this out of a desire for wholeness in myself, I needed to have black as well as white characters, else I would erase blacks in much the same way working-class women (and especially working-class lesbians) were erased in most of the white women's literature, and some of the black women's literature, I read . . . Often as I moved into the areas of my imagination where I expected to find information about black women characters I was creating, I came up

against the charge of the electric fence . . . Most of my tension took the form of fear that it would be presumptuous of me to enter a territory in which I wasn't sure how much I could know. (1983: 148–9)

Around the same time, I expressed my concerns about being presumptuous to Audre Lorde, who responded in her wonderfully clear-headed way, 'But these characters are yours. You've taken them on and so they belong to you. You cannot be presumptuous, you can only be wrong.' (Brady, 1983: 150)

In her review of *Folly* Bertha Harris comments, not on the black characters (maybe she thought that would be presumptuous, as she is white), but on the working-class characters. On behalf of 'my mother (and my cousins and aunts and the girls I left behind)', she proceeds to 'rap' Maureen Brady's 'knuckles':

The Worthy Poor . . . have been written about again: *Folly* is legion. Now clean, fed, sober, politically pro forma, at honest work, should they have further expectations (like being written about well and truly), let them eat cake . . . *Folly* is a melange of presumptuous intimacy, sins of omission and hagiography (as if the poor needed more saints). (1983: 178)

I asked a black Jewish friend what she thought of this issue. She agreed with Audre Lorde: the main problem facing black lesbians in literature (let alone black Jewish lesbians) is almost complete absence. At least if a black lesbian were in there *somewhere*, my friend said, she could quarrel with the portrayal, start a conversation. The black lesbian writer and critic, Jewelle Gomez (1988), writes of 'the value of the ability to live outside of ourselves'. She declares, 'that ability is at the core of any true liberation struggle'. In whose interest is it that white women should feel black experience is so different from ours as to be unimaginable? Or that sighted women should believe the thoughts of blind women to be on such a different pattern that we will not venture to guess them? When gentile women read the work of Jewish women, it must be because we assume we will understand some, I venture to say even most, of what has been written. Probably we will not understand as much as other Jewish women, but enough to feel the book is worth our engagement.

When I read the articles in *Thirteenth Moon* I was writing a scene in my novel *Accommodation Offered* (1985), where a white gentile lesbian returns to London from Paris after thinking, living, in France for two years. She describes everything with an almost dehumanizing distance because, although she recognizes it, it is not really hers again. She looks at the houses, the streets, the little girls skipping, other people out walking, all with the same panoramic lens. This is Stamford Hill, North London, an area where a large community of Hassidic Jews live. She looks at the women's wigs, their navy blue dresses covering knee and elbow; the men's wide-brimmed hats and sideburns; how the children's frocks seem hot and heavy even in the middle of summer. One Jewish woman I know read the description and felt very strongly that the scene should be omitted. It was fine to describe girls skipping as part of the landscape; girls appear frequently in literature in all manner of moods. Hassidic Jews, however, are almost always described by gentiles as if they're not quite human. The wigs and sideburns are often as far as a gentile bothers to look. I asked other friends what they thought. Another Jewish woman felt just as strongly the Stamford Hill Hassidim should stay. To erase them would be like wiping them out all over again, literally, with white-out. The ball was back now in my court to make my decision about my fiction. Only, at the time, I didn't regard it in that way. It was my (Jewish) lover who pointed out the humour of my friends' 'very Jewish' response: the respect for a good, and good-humoured, discussion, seeing many sides of a question and upholding them passionately. I had felt that my two bands of experts were at war with one another and I took the easier way out: I removed the description of the Hassidim, because if they weren't there, no one could quarrel with me. As a writer, the mistake I made was to hand over my decision to someone else, to set up other women as experts with a seal of approval to grant or deny.

Recently a feminist publishing house in the USA was considering a novel by a sighted woman with a blind character in it. Worried about the portrayal of the blind character, they asked a blind women's group if they would like to listen to a tape of the manuscript and comment. This is a perfectly reasonable thing to do, and I believe the publishers in question were simply seeking the opinion of a group of women who might have thought more about the issue than they themselves had yet had reason to. But it does raise the question of the publishers' responsibility. It would be wrong to turn the manuscript over to the group of blind women for a seal of approval, to be produced if other women criticized the book's portrayal of blindness. Our group of 'experts', however formed, should not be a pretext for absolving ourselves of responsibility.

When I started writing I was aware of the feminist tenet that the writer is accountable for what she creates, but it did not occur to me that I might also be accountable for what I left out. Some years after I published *Relatively Norma* (1982), which tells the story of a white lesbian who flies to Australia to come out to her mother, I was asked by a black Australian why I had not included any Aboriginal characters in the novel. I was surprised by the question, had not thought it was my business to write about Aboriginals. I told her I had not met any Aboriginals when I wrote the book and didn't want to create a sentimental fairy tale where all women play happily together and racial segregation does not exist. Australia is an extremely divided country and the fact that I had not met any black Australians during my first six months' stay seemed to me very significant.

It is too late to start rewriting *Relatively Norma* now, but the questions remain. By the time I published *Bulldozer Rising* (1988), I felt strongly that it *was* my business to write about characters very unlike myself. I did not want to be limited to a literature of autobiography or a politics of 'me and my friends'. *Bulldozer Rising* is a fantasy novel about old women, set in a future city where good citizens die at 41. Its cast of characters includes old and young, fat and thin, citizen and foreigner. I found it most difficult to write about fat women. Although I felt it was important to write about women unlike myself, I still felt uneasy about doing research. Aware that as a young, thin, university-educated WASP with a BBC accent it was going to be easier for me to get whatever I wrote published than for my 'subject', I decided to restrict myself to what I read or observed rather than asking individual women for raw material. This must sound somewhat arbitrary, but I felt that whatever was already published was in the

public domain, and so open to my scrutiny, whereas seeking individual statements was more like anthropology.

The author's personal experience is a reasonable criterion on which to judge a
novel. We must take on the whole world; we cannot afford 'no go areas' of the
imagination; we cannot afford to refuse an opinion on any subject. If we insist
that no one may write about anyone's experience save her own, we are con-
demning ourselves to a literature of reporting.

The Heterosexual's Lesbian

This raises the question of how, as a white lesbian novelist, I feel when writers in
a more privileged position create characters from my community.

I picked eight works of fiction by heterosexual women writers – feminist, or
feminist-influenced – published between 1975 and 1985: *Female Friends*,
1974/1981, Fay Weldon; *The Women's Room*, 1977, Marilyn French; 'Dulse'
from *The Moons of Jupiter*, 1977/1991, Alice Munro; *Benefits*, 1979, Zöe
Fairbairns; *Birds of Passage*, 1981, Bernice Reubens; *The Women of Brewster
Place*, 1980/1983, Gloria Naylor; 'Listening' from *Later the Same Day*, 1985/
1986, Grace Paley; *Solstice*, 1985, Joyce Carol Oates. The question of sexual
identity arises immediately: how can you tell these authors are not lesbians?
Some are indeed said to sleep or to have slept with women, but there is no indication of this in their biographies or subsequent interviews, so it seems fair to
assume they are working within a heterosexual framework and, more important,
that their novels are sold and read as heterosexual fiction. The works themselves
cover a range of genres from science fiction (*Benefits*) through situation comedy
(*Female Friends* and *Birds of Passage*) to social realism (*The Women's Room*)
and postmodern stories about story-telling ('Listening'). I hoped their portrayal
of lesbians would be similarly dissimilar. In fact they fall fairly easily into three
major divisions depending on how many lesbians are present in the text: the
absent lesbian; the failed heterosexual; and the plot convenience.

The Absent Lesbian

Those novels most pleasant and tolerant of the lesbian possibility as simply
existing alongside the heterosexual imperative, turned out to be those in which
the lesbian does not appear, but is discussed in her absence.

In 'Dulse' Lydia's affair with Duncan is over and she retreats to an island to
ponder. There she meets old Mr Stanley who comes to the island every year in
search of memories of Willa Cather – an earlier summer visitor – and a crew
laying phone cables. Lydia imagines what each of the crew would be like as a
lover. Following this pattern, she should next imagine sleeping with Mr Stanley
but instead she speaks to him of Willa Cather. She muses about lesbian
sexuality: 'But was she lucky [to be a lesbian] or was she not and was it [sex]
alright with that woman?' (Munro, 1991: 58). A frank and personal curiosity. The
adjective 'alright' is beautifully underplayed: no sense of prurient interest. But
the dead Cather hardly poses a threat.

'Listening' is the last story in Paley's latest collection. It starts with Faith – Paley's ubiquitous story-teller – retelling conversations between men. Husband Jack objects, 'Why don't you tell me stories told by women about women?' 'Those are too private', says Faith (Paley, 1986: 203). After Jack goes off to Arizona for a love affair, Faith is stopped in traffic by a red light. Symbolic, a red stop light: time to reflect on her life. She watches a young man cross the road and comments, 'He's nice, isn't he?' A sexual comment, she's thinking about the hang of his penis. A comment which does not take account of the fact that her friend, Cassie, sitting beside her in the car, is a lesbian. Cassie comments, 'Just a bourgeois on his way home.' 'To everyday life', Faith adds. Whereupon Cassie explodes: 'To whose everyday life? . . . Why don't you tell my story? . . . I don't even mean my whole story, that's my job.' The last sentence seems to presage the later *Sinister Wisdom* statement: 'No one should ever "speak for" or "assume" another's voice.' Cassie continues: 'It's been women and men, women and men, fucking, fucking. Goddamnit, where the hell is my woman and woman, woman-loving life in all this?' and Faith replies with the shock of recognition, 'it must feel like a great absence of yourself' (Paley, 1986: 210). The double irony of this obviously well-intentioned statement is that Cassie has been sitting in the car next to Faith, a fellow traveller, yet Faith has been acting, and is still acting, as though she were not there. The verb is present, not past: 'it must feel', the situation (Cassie's absence) continues despite her presence.

The Failed Heterosexual

In these texts the lesbian does appear as a full participant in the narrative, and is horribly punished for it. Often there will be only one lesbian, emphasizing her symbolic significance: because of this isolation she can only be defined in heterosexual terms and found wanting. Novels in this division are characterized by forced sex: the lesbian is raped, or nearly raped, as an explicit response to her sexuality. This is, sadly, the largest of the three divisions, including *Female Friends*, *Birds of Passage*, *The Women of Brewster Place* and *Solstice*.

Where there are two lesbians, the situation is even worse, and the fact is explicitly commented on. The chapter of *The Women of Brewster Place* devoted to the lesbian couple is titled 'The Two', whereas other chapters bear the name of the characters they present: 'Mattie Michaels', 'Luciella Louise Turner' etc. The lesbians are introduced as a couple: 'At first they seemed like such nice girls.' At the end, 'no one remembered when they moved in . . . It had to be before Ben's death.' Their presence is noted only as it related to Ben.

In each of the texts in this section, evidence of previous heterosexuality – or desire for it – is used to point a moral and all the lesbians, save Lorraine of *The Women of Brewster Place*, used to sleep with men, or would like to. Lorraine's lover, Theresa, used to be straight and consequently has a much easier relationship with the world. 'You've never been with a man' she says, '[it's] as much part of life as eating or breathing or growing old' (Naylor 1983: 138). Lorraine finds heterosex disgusting and is brutally punished for this sentiment. The leader of the gang who rapes her sneers, 'that's what you need . . . after we're through with you, you ain't never gonna want no more pussy' (Naylor 1983: 170).

In *Birds of Passage* two 60-year-old widows go on a cruise together: one is raped every night by a waiter, the other lies awake till dawn waiting for the same waiter to come to her. She thinks of him as her 'lover'. On the same cruise are a third widow and her daughter, Alice, lesbian escapee from an emotionally weary-ing relationship. 'Alice did not love Nellie. She was simply moved by her . . . by her raging, rigid body, stiff still from her father's rape' (Reubens, 1981: 54). Alice whispers to her pillow every night, 'Please God, for God's sake, let me love a man again' (Reubens, 1981: 122). She is nearly raped by the waiter who is raping the widow. His thoughts echo those of the gang leader in *The Women of Brewster Place*: 'he knew from eavesdropping of her man hatred and he knew above all exactly what she bloody well needed' (Reubens, 1981: 167). In Venice Alice throws herself into a canal and is rescued by a would-be pick-pocket who gives her mouth-to-mouth resuscitation: 'without being able to help herself she responded to his kiss' (Reubens, 1981: 125). Then she is cured of her lesbianism, can get rid of her ugly dungarees and pull the beautiful silk dress out from the bottom of her suitcase. What makes a lesbian is rape; paradoxically, what cures her is also rape.

It is important to examine the author's treatment of her lesbian characters in comparison to that of other characters in the same text. Both *Female Friends* and *Birds of Passage* are intended to be humorous and it would be wrong to under-estimate their commitment to farce and incongruity. All the characters are a little pathetic, ineffectual and rather sad, but the lesbians are even more ludicrous, even more unlikeable. Oliver, in *Female Friends*, forces his wife, Chloe, to have sex with the French au pair, Françoise, his mistress, while he watches. Chloe sighs, 'it has been a long and trying day. This is really no more remarkable than any-thing else' (Weldon, 1981: 199). She ends up enjoying herself, laughing at 'her husband and her victory is complete'. But Françoise's breasts are black and blue; Oliver turns her over and fucks her to get his wife's attention back. This amounts to rape since Françoise is frightened and struggles to get away from him. She too is only a lesbian (or in fact bisexual) because 'a relationship with a woman had become a political necessity'. Her lover was a confectioner who used to stick pins through the hearts of sugar bridegrooms, until the day she accused Françoise of lesbianism and eloped with Françoise's fiancé. Again, lesbianism and separation from men are portrayed as ridiculous and inauthentic.

In *Solstice* the relationship between the heroine and another woman is of central importance, though described in reaction to failed heterosexual romance. Here lesbianism seems to offer a third term, a way out of the calamitous male/female dyad. It expresses a form of separatism, but a separatism in reaction. A possibility for specific purposes and for a limited time. Despite the structural differences between this and the other novels, there is the same message of sexual violence and male revenge. Sheila hugs Monica and kisses her on the lips after a dinner party, this in front of Jack, another guest. Jack invites Monica out soon after – and rapes her. In the face of her protests, he defends himself: 'you, a friend of Sheila Trask's'. The last he has seen of Sheila was when she was kiss-ing Monica. Rape follows inevitably from imputed lesbianism.

The Plot Convenience

These novels give some sense of the possibilities of lesbian community, or of women relating principally to each other in more than isolated couples. It is here that I place *The Women's Room* and *Benefits*. In these novels, though lesbianism is accepted as a life choice for some women, the lesbian characters turn out to be some kind of plot convenience, shedding light on other characters or moving the plot forward.

In *The Women's Room* a group of women graduate students revolves around Iso's apartment because Iso, the lesbian – the only real lesbian, even in this women's community there can be only one – has no other ties, no husband, no babies. Iso is there whenever the others need her, massaging foreheads, fixing endless drinks, giving up her sofa, offering her body. When she finally manages to feel put upon, she realizes 'she would have to find a little man in her' (French, 1977: 443). Although she is not raped, she still needs a man inside her. She explains, 'I've spent my life a sort of beggar standing outside the restaurant waiting for table scraps . . . forever is not something I can hope for' (French, 1977: 453). But it could be, if she were not trapped in a heterosexual novel.

Benefits is a sci-fi novel about the British welfare system. Lesbians are present at every level of the text: lesbian mothers must learn to decorate their prison cells tastefully from a catalogue. To complete the cure, they are forced to have sex with a man – the old theme of raping lesbians into heterosexuality: a theme which Fairbairns uses on purpose to point out both its prevalence and its horror. 'Big muscular, denim-clad Posy with the puggish face and mighty strength' (shades of Alice in *Birds of Passage*) is sent to Australia at the end of Part One, ostensibly to foment a women's revolution. She leaves with the erstwhile heterosexual Marsha. It seems odd to get rid of the two strongest female characters so early on, and indeed their trip to Australia turns out to be a plot convenience allowing conservative policies to develop without their intervention. While the London streets are described in such concrete detail you can see, hear and smell them, Australia is just one big beach – clearly a non-place, not London. The lesbian relationship also turns out to be a non-relationship. After 15 years Marsha expresses a wish to return to London. 'You made me into a lesbian and now you're leaving me', Posy complains. Marsha objects in amazement that she thought Posy was the lesbian (Fairbairns, 1979: 64). It stretches one's credulity to accept that the two women have been together for 15 years without ever having a conversation about their first night together or their previous relationships. Although an explicitly feminist text, there is the usual insinuation that women ought to be sleeping with men: 'Some people say it's a cop-out to say you're bisexual, all proper feminists are lesbian. I suspect it's a cop-out to give up men when you've never had one' (Fairbairns, 1979: 22). Added to this is the suggestion that lesbian sexuality is inauthentic, as in Marsha's musings about Posy, 'Had her sex life been a succession of women seeking gentle love and political correctness when what she really wanted was a man to enter her through her self-ruptured hymen?' (Fairbairns, 1979: 67). Posy's demise is as ridiculous as her sexual politics: she is carried on the shoulders of a delighted crowd of Third World peasants, who then drop her, and she dies. Little seems to have changed since D.H. Lawrence's *The Fox* where the lesbian is struck dead by a falling tree.

The heterosexual's lesbian, then, is that way because of a bad sexual experience with a man; she lies in bed yearning for a man; and may be cured by an even worse experience with another man. She is used symbolically in a battle against men; she represents a third term in answer to the male/female dyad; offers a cosy all-nurturing bolt-hole for her straight sisters; she is a plot convenience. The portrayal of the lesbian character forces the reader to ask: if she really is a lesbian what on earth is she doing in this book?

Given the level of violence and trivialization, the insinuations of inauthenticity, should we call for a moratorium on heterosexual lesbians? My answer to this question is still, despite everything, a resounding 'no'. Not because the lesbians in question almost all turn out to be bisexual really and so don't count. That kind of argument always seems to me like linguistic gerrymandering where you move the electoral boundaries to exclude those who are not of your opinion. But because I agree wholeheartedly with Jewelle Gomez, 'the ability to live outside ourselves . . . is at the core of any liberation struggle' (*Trivia*, Spring 1988: 47). To heterosexual women writers I say not 'stop' but 'start'.

But this is fiction, you may object, these are characters. What can they tell us about the usefulness, or otherwise, of the boundaries drawn among real people, organized into particular social and cultural groups either the same, or different from the ones I'm in, with more or less power than my group? Since the condemnation of Salman Rushdie's *Satanic Verses* by certain Islamic leaders, and the author's consequent life in hiding, are we still sure that fact and fiction are so easily separable, or that everyone makes the separation at the same point?

Take three cases. One: Dorothy Allison, the American novelist, and Kate Bornstein, a performance artist who is also a male-to-female transsexual (Bell, 1993b), ask their students to invent a character of the opposite sex from themselves. A very different approach to creativity from that of the current *Sinister Wisdom* Collective quoted above. Two: Diana 'Danny' Torr runs 'Drag-King-For-A-Day' workshops where female students not only create a male persona, but must appear at a 'passing event' Torr has arranged for them (Bell, 1993a). They go to a local art show as the male characters they have created and 'succeed' as long as other people react to them as men. The passing event represents a crossover from pretence to real life. Three: A white woman who was once in a writing group with me would boast of the fact that she was so good at reproducing black American English and creating convincing black characters that she had had stories accepted in black magazines without the editors realizing she was white. Not only are the characters she creates black, but the author herself is assumed to be black although she does not state explicitly what her race is.

Faced with these three examples, one instantly wants to draw a clear, boldface line between writing and acting exercises in which people sharpen their imaginations by pretending to be someone they could never be in real life, and the act of passing oneself off as something one is not. But where, exactly, does sympathetic understanding end and cultural appropriation begin? The exercises are unobjectionable, even the 'passing event' sounds amusing but the white writer who lets her readers think she is black seems deceitful, as though she is taking something which is not hers. The cut-off line is not between the conventions of fiction and the intention to delude: both the drag kings and the white writer intend to delude. Passing oneself off as belonging to a group which has higher status, or simply more power, than one's own may be scorned as social climbing but is at least understandable given prevailing hierarchies. The drag kings are trying out men's power, even the term 'drag' is a tip that they don't quite mean it, will not continue in male guise beyond the evening. Pretending to have less power than one has, however, is a more serious threat and disempowered groups are naturally wary of giving up what little they have to someone who started off with more. When a white writer prompts her readers to believe she is black so she can gain publication in a black magazine, she takes up part of the modest amount of time and space intended for a black author.

Presumption is tricky. One of those pompous latinate terms, it lies somewhere between the equally latinate 'conjecture' and 'appropriation'. Conjecture is good, one is tempted to simplify, appropriation bad. Conjecture is a way of conjuring up new visions, throwing old ideas together in a new way, whereas appropriation is singling something out as yours, taking it away from someone else so they can no longer enjoy it. We need to presume, we also need to tell the truth.

Note

This chapter combines ideas previously discussed in 'You Can Only Be Wrong', *The Women's Review of Books*, Vol. VI: 10–11 (July 1986) and in 'The Heterosexual's Lesbian', a paper presented at The Modern Languages Convention, New York, USA (December 1992).

References

Arnold, June (1975) *Sister Gin*. New York: Daughters.
Bell, Shannon (1993a) 'Finding the Male Within and Taking Him Cruising: Drag-King-For-A-Day', in *The Last Sex: Feminism and Outlaw Bodies*. New York: St Martin's Press: 91–7.
Bell, Shannon (1993b) 'Kate Bornstein: A Transgender Transexual Postmodern Tiresias', in *The Last Sex: Feminism and Outlaw Bodies*. New York: St Martin's Press: 104–20.
Brady, Maureen (1982) *Folly*. New York: The Crossing Press.
Brady, Maureen (1983) 'Article on the Writing of *Folly*', *Thirteenth Moon* (Special Issue on Working-class Experience).
Fairbairns, Zöe (1979) *Benefits*. London: Virago.
French, Marilyn (1977) *The Women's Room*. New York: Summit.
Gomez, Jewelle (1988) 'Imagine a Lesbian, a Black Lesbian', *Trivia*, Spring.
Harris, Bertha (1983) 'Review of *Folly* by Maureen Brady', *Thirteenth Moon* (Special Issue on Working-class Experience).
Livia, Anna (1982) *Relatively Norma*. London: Onlywomen Press.
Livia, Anna (1985) *Accommodation Offered*. London: Onlywomen Press.
Livia, Anna (1988) *Bulldozer Rising*. London: Onlywomen Press.
Munro, Alice (1991) 'Dulse', in *The Moons of Jupiter*. New York: Random House (first published 1977).
Naylor, Gloria (1983) *The Women of Brewster Place*. Harmondsworth, Middlesex: Penguin (first published 1980).
Oates, Joyce Carol (1985) *Solstice*. New York: EP Dutton.

Paley, Grace (1986) 'Listening', in *Later the Same Day*. Harmondsworth, Middlesex: Penguin (first published 1985).

Reubens, Bernice (1981) *Birds of Passage*. London: Hamish Hamilton.

Sinister Wisdom Collective (1990) 'Editorial', *Sinister Wisdom* 42 (4): 1–6.

Weldon, Fay (1981) *Female Friends*. London: Picador (first published 1974).

PART II
SHORT CONTRIBUTIONS

3

The Mother of Invention: Necessity, Writing and Representation

Liz Stanley

Feminism, Research and Representation

There are (at least) four major feminist positions argued regarding the representational issues involved in carrying out feminist research. Many, but by no means all, feminist researchers recognize the existence of critical issues which make the relationship between 'feminism' and 'research' in some sense troublesome and, concomitantly, the representational aspects of research are implicated here. That is, that, among its other characteristics and functions, research is conventionally seen as a presumptively one-to-one depiction and analysis of some aspect of social life, although increasingly there are challenges to such representational claims. The major feminist positions here are:

- Acceptance of the conventional foundationalist view of research, that there is a single reality 'out there' which good research can depict and explain, and, accordingly, that there is a one-to-one relationship between reality and representation in (good) feminist research.
- Recognition of (moral, ethical, political) issues concerning power in the research and writing process, in particular the power of the researcher through (often unacknowledged) knowledge-claims that written research both can and should represent the realities of other people's, here women's, lives.
- Recognition of (intellectual, epistemological) issues regarding both the foundationalist supposition of a single and unseamed reality 'out there', and also of making representational claims: that is, rejection of the assumption that it is possible to represent (using any or all possible forms) in a one-to-one way.
- Insistence that the issues involved (of either the second or the third kind) are so great that the only adequate feminist response is to eschew the representation of other lives altogether.

The fourth feminist position here, the 'shouldn't do it' argument, is strongly articulated by Joyce Treblicot (1988, 1990a,b). Treblicot's view is that: '*I speak only for myself* . . . in the sense that I intend my words to express only my understanding of the world' (1990b: 18, emphasis in original); '*I do not try to get other wimmin to accept my beliefs in place of their own* . . . I should not try to mold wimmin's minds' (1990b: 19–20, emphasis in original); '*There is no "given"* . . . ultimately and in principle, *only* I speak for myself . . . I need to rewrite for myself the entire world as patriarchy has presented it to me' (1990b: 21, emphases in original); 'The methods discussed here are *dyke* methods because dykism . . . is a rejection of/separation from patriarchy . . . I respond to domination with a commitment to discover/create spaces in which domination cannot exist' (1990b: 28, emphasis in original).

The nub of Treblicot's argument is that representation is by definition an epistemological and therefore an ethical exploitation (Treblicot, 1990a: 2–3). My interest stems partly from her clear articulation of the fourth position regarding representation, partly because she references my own work with Sue Wise (Stanley and Wise, 1983) as giving her 'both content and courage' (Treblicot, 1990a: 1) and, relatedly, because I do not understand her grounds for the claimed synonymity between her arguments and my own, and nor do I accept the claimed synonymity anyway.

Stanley and Wise (1983) argue that feminist research derives from the analytic exploration of feminist consciousness as a form of praxis: the combined experience and analysis of what it is to be a woman in sexist society; that is, a set of practices conducted by 'insiders' to women's oppression (1983: 31–2). Relatedly,we propose that the means of accomplishing this is through making the researcher and her consciousness the central focus of research (1983: 49), in particular by exploring her analytic processes of understanding within written accounts of research. We outline 'how to do it' in terms of explicating 'the personal'; that is, coming analytically (not just descriptively) to grips with the everyday experiences of the processes of finding out (1983: 134–49), counterposing an insistence on the epistemological and political ramifications of a feminist social science focused on researcher involvement (1983: 165–8) against conventional notions of 'science' and the 'objective' and 'detached' researcher (1983: 108–13). We look at criticisms of this argument (1983: 49–51) and in particular we reject the view that it proposes research based on 'a sample of one' which is thereby ridiculously limited (1983: 168–73). Instead we insist that 'the researcher's experience' includes indirect as well as direct experience and knowledge gained second – and third – as well as first-hand.

Stanley and Wise (1983) thus actually advance a variant on position two with regard to the power issues at the heart of the representational view of research, arguing that research should proceed from an analytic engagement with the situational specificities of knowledge production. Relatedly, the text also contains an early statement of the third position regarding representation, proposing that research, conventionally claimed as the 'accurate' representation of other lives, is more accurately to be construed as the disguised presentation of the knowledge-production processes researchers engage in. It proposes that researchers should know from the inside whatever they research, in the sense of making clear the specificities of their intellectual engagement. Stanley and Wise (1993: 1–15, 186–233) add to this epistemological engagement, insisting that representational claims must be surrendered in favour of *analytically* accountable feminist research accounts which display their argumentative processes in detailed ways which can be critically engaged with by readers.

Paradoxically, then, in no sense does the Stanley and Wise (1983) text argue for the position assigned to it by Treblicot, that of eschewing representation of other lives. It is instead concerned with outlining a set of intellectual practices which will display in analytic detail how such representations are pieced together and the grounds for the knowledge-claims made from them, a very different approach from Treblicot's.

Representation and Writing

I now look in more detail at these means of displaying, if not dissolving, the issues in representation referred to above. These are discussed in Stanley and Wise (1993) and elsewhere (1993: 189, 193, 209–10; Stanley, 1992, 1995) as 'intellectual autobiography', an approach concerned with explicating the processes by which understanding and conclusions are reached. Such an approach rejects the key foundationalist myth of the detached scientific observer/ researcher; it instead positions an experiencing and comprehending subject at the heart of intellectual and research life, a subject whose ontologically based reasoning processes provide the grounds for knowledge-claims and thus for all epistemological endeavour.

Centring the activities of the feminist researcher within research writing does not mean treating intellectual autobiography as a *narrative* ('the real truth, this time') which claims a new kind of referentiality. Instead it is concerned with *analytic* processes and engagements, thereby displaying the representational and other issues involved in these processes and the conclusions derived from them. This is a supremely epistemological project, in the sense that it is concerned with explicating how knowledge is produced and under what conditions, the grounds of knowledge-claims and the strengths and weaknesses of these. It is also a *radical* epistemological project, concerned with how such explications can thereby provide the grounds for assembling *competing* knowledge-claims. It recognizes both that knowledge is grounded (i.e. has an ontological base) and that its radicalism depends on the very representationality that it criticizes (i.e. the analytic explications that constitute intellectual autobiography themselves trade upon referential claims – that there is a relationship, even if complex, between such an account and the reality it is 'about' if not 'of').

'Research' is at basis an account of events and persons which makes (expert) knowledge-claims about these; how people (claim to) know the social world more generally, as well as in research narrowly conceived, necessarily trades upon representation. 'The representation of other lives' should thus be seen as part of the wider and more fundamental problematic concerning the necessity of representation as the basic means of knowing the social world. Representation is not dissolvable, an optional extra. Given its epistemological necessity, intellectual autobiography constitutes a means by which the issues identified by feminists can be displayed, made apparent, grappled with, and through which readers are empowered to engage with the knowledge-production processes of research and writing and the claims made from these, by enabling readers to perceive these textually, and perhaps also to challenge the grounds of such claims. Certainly this remains a textual engagement: not the research experience itself, but one written (or visual or oral) representation of it. However, this is an open representation, presenting an active text with which readers can engage, and it seems to me decidedly preferable to the closed texts of conventional research with their 'take it or leave it' quality.

Necessity and the Mother of Invention

Earlier I used the idea of necessity in relation to the a priori nature of representation within accounts of the social world. I now use it in another sense, through looking at where ideas and research come from; that is, the resonance between the intellectual or ideational, and the experiential, emotional and political aspects of our lives. Most researchers accept that, in addition to purely utilitarian purposes (i.e. because of job definitions), they also carry out research because: it is socially and/or intellectually meaningful; it engages their intellectual, political and other interests; it challenges their existing skills or knowledge. However, talking to feminist researchers suggests an additional factor here, that of a felt *necessity* to carry out particular research because of the topic and/or the approach and the perceived resonance between these and the personal context of the researcher. Necessity in this sense has motivated much of the research I have carried out: in published works I have often spoken 'in my own voice' about research because of the resonance between the ideational and the personal: between the issues that such research/writing has exemplified and raised, and issues and concerns in my life 'outside research'. I briefly discuss some of the representational issues raised above in relation to three pieces of 'necessary' research which have been concerned, not with 'other lives' in the sense of distanced 'subjects', but rather those very particular others, my own father and mother, who have had as many – if not more – rights as I in the relationships between us. But then again, perhaps this is more a measure of a respect for them and of their lives which was repeatedly negotiated and renegotiated, but which conventional (malestream?) ways of thinking about research subjects typically either abrogates or denies.

The 'Our Mothers' Voices' project was concerned with representations of women's class in academic feminist writing (Stanley, 1985). It was shared with three other feminist sociologists who were also working class by birth, and embarked upon because we felt strongly that there was a serious representational problem around the class/power issues involved in (middle-class) feminist theorizations of (working-class) women's lives. Although issues of power were involved (i.e. position two regarding representation), the more disturbing aspect was the excision of the experience of working-class women: the 'reality' posed in the research was little or nothing like the experience (i.e. position three). We sought to counter this in two closely linked ways, by using our mothers' very varied experiences of 'being working class' as articulated (on tape, in writing, through comments on photographs) by them, and by insisting upon this complexity and difference to deconstruct 'working class' away from the impoverished simplistic monolith of theory.

For me at least, issues here concerning representation lay with the theoretically derived feminist work and not our own; and my own mother was thrilled at the possibility that aspects of her life and those of other working-class women could legitimately be seen as research. However, not all of our mothers felt this way, and the project foundered on one of them using different variants of silence and truncated speech to signal her implicit refusal to participate, and one of us being circumstantially unable, given a family terminal illness, to participate without enormous emotional cost.

The 'Behind the Scenes' project (Stanley, 1990) was carried out in part to look at the representational issues that exist with regard to official and local authority statistics and the ways in which different statistical sets are presumed to relate to each other, but in larger part because of the 'necessity effect' outlined above. The particular statistics involved were my father's committal to a psychogeriatric institution under a section of the (British) Mental Health Act following a series of strokes, then his later death; and the necessity came out of my intellectual anger at the poverty of the statistics to represent the grievous experiential realities involved. My research involved looking at the statistics involved and the simplistic definitional presumptions which underlie them, counterposing against these the enormous complexities involved in different family experiences of 'sectioning' under the Act and 'death'. It centred 'intellectual autobiography', that is, my own processes of changing understanding, and not these experiences themselves.

There both were and were not representational issues involved in writing about these linked events. There was certainly no question of a position four outcome, of *not* researching and writing about them, in large part because the necessity I felt about this research came out of a necessity shared with my mother to talk about what had happened: over a lengthy period we discussed this over and over. The writing was engaged upon because of my perception of linked representational issues concerning power (that of statistical research) and referentiality (the poverty of the statistics in the face of the experiences they are supposedly 'of') – that is, positions two and three concerning representation were both involved; and I explored these issues via intellectual autobiography. However, there were further issues concerning the necessary reference within this to my parents' experiences. My mother knew that I was writing about what these events suggested about the statistics, but she had little comprehension of what this might mean in terms of the public revelation of deeply felt aspects of her and my father's lives; while I tried to minimize such 'revelation' by writing and speaking as though I were dealing with other 'other lives': making my 'subjects' anonymous, removing myself, excising the 'necessity' aspect of the research. As the point of publication arrived, when I needed to discuss with my mother precisely what she would agree to having published and what she would not, she herself experienced a stroke, one more cataclysmic and consequential than any my father had suffered.

The discussion between my mother and I had developed considerably, to become a mutually agreed project which I now call 'My Mother's Voice?' (Stanley, 1995), taped conversations about family history, being working class in Portsmouth between the wars, the relationship (literally so in our family) between Romany and settled working-class people, working-class girls and their lives, the impact of the 1939–45 war on class and gender expectations, the post-war demolition of working-class community and habitas. What started as a collaborative project became entirely one-sided, for my mother's stroke caused so much damage that she became partially paralysed, partially blind and completely unable to understand or articulate speech. Any meaningful giving and receiving of 'consent' became impossible. Although my focus was and remained an intellectual autobiographical one, I was consequently left with unresolved issues concerning my use of the representational element necessarily present within this.

I continue to write about this two-year period of silence and death filled with the clamour of reflection about the nature of 'self' and other, 'identity' and communication, the beginning and ending of 'life', and so on (Stanley, 1993). I do so through the medium of my fieldwork notebooks, kept from before my mother's stroke until after her death; and the focus remains intellectual autobiography in which I try to make the representational issues surrounding referentiality visible and accountable within the conclusions I draw and the claims I make in doing so. However, those other representational issues, concerning power and the exploitation of other lives within research, remain and in this case are truly indissoluble, for, from the outset, the one person who could 'give consent' was unable to.

In so far as I have any 'conclusion', this remains what it was in 1983, and it is incontrovertibly *contra* that reached by Joyce Treblicot. It is that there are no easy or simple or categorical answers to the real and complex ethical and epistemological issues which feminists have identified in relation to research referentiality; that these issues shouldn't be ignored (although those of a foundationalist inclination, the first position on representation outlined, do precisely this); and nor can they be dissolved, as Treblicot appears to think. I continue to believe that 'intellectual autobiography' provides a useful means to handle, by displaying in a clear way, the analytic issues involved; thereby readers can better engage with the resultant knowledge-claims; and, while issues concerning power and representation and epistemology and referentiality uncomfortably remain, within this approach these are at least made visible and engaged with, rather than explained away by wishful thinking in a variant of political correctness. By no means incidentally, Treblicot's use of my and Sue Wise's work displays the political and ethical issues surrounding mis/representation in feminist research/writing; I have the means to protest – our 'subjects' are rarely able to bite back.

References

Stanley, Liz (1985) 'Our Mothers' Voices, paper given at the Third International Congress on Women, Dublin.

Stanley, Liz (1990) 'A Referral Was Made: Behind the Scenes During the Creation of a Social Services Department Elderly Statistic', in Liz Stanley (ed.) *Feminist Praxis*, pp. 113–22. London: Routledge.

Stanley, Liz (1992) *The Auto/Biographical I: Theory and Practice of Feminist Auto/Biography*. Manchester: Manchester University Press.

Stanley, Liz (1993) 'The Knowing Because Experiencing Subject: Narrative, Lives and Auto/Biography', *Women's Studies International Forum* 16: 205–15.

Stanley, Liz (1995) 'My Mother's Voice? On Being "a Native" in Academia', in Val Walsh and Louise Morley (eds) *Feminist Academics: Creative Agents of Change*, pp. 183–93. London: Taylor and Francis.

Stanley, Liz and Wise, Sue (1983) *Breaking Out: Feminist Consciousness and Feminist Research*. London: Routledge.

Stanley, Liz and Wise, Sue (1993) *Breaking Out Again: Feminist Ontology and Epistemology*. London: Routledge.

Treblicot, Joyce (1988) 'Dyke Methods, or, Principles for the Discovery/Creation of the Withstanding', *Hypatia* 3: 1–13.

Treblicot, Joyce (1990a) 'More Dyke Methods', *Hypatia* 5: 140–4.

Treblicot, Joyce (1990b) 'Dyke Methods', in Jefner Allen (ed.) *Lesbian Philosophies and Cultures*, pp. 15–29. New York: SUNY Press.

4

Bearing Witness: Representing Women's Experiences of Prenatal Diagnosis

Barbara Katz Rothman

So what would *you* do, people ask, knowing that I have done a book on women's experiences with amniocentesis for prenatal diagnosis (Rothman, 1986/1993). Would I be tested? Would I abort for Downs Syndrome? For a neural tube defect? For what? How would I decide? And they have the hardest time believing me when I say I have *no* idea what I would do.

I was 26 at my first pregnancy, back in the mid-1970s when almost no one was talking about prenatal diagnosis. And I was 33 in the early 1980s with my second pregnancy, just a bit too young by the standards of that time – if no longer – to have to deal with it. This did not become a topic of concern and interest to me until later on, shortly after the birth of that second child, when I was through with my doctoral work, placed as an assistant professor and looking for a 'next project'. So when I write about prenatal diagnosis and the enormous burdens it places on women, women who choose not to use it no less and no more than women who choose to use it, I am not writing out of a personal experience. Time was, that gave a person credentials. Made you objective, you know. No longer. In the circles I travel in now, if you see an article by a colleague on breast cancer, you write to see how she is, wonder when she was diagnosed. If you see an article on Alzheimer's, you assume someone's got a parent or in-law to help. I can track my colleagues' progression through the life cycle, through crises and passages, by article and book titles. An ethic of involvement has replaced an ethic of objectivity: clarifying and being 'up front' about one's stake replaces the notion that one should have no stake.

So where does that put me, as someone who has not been faced with the decisions and 'choices' that I describe? Not only do I not know what I would do myself, I really am unsure what anyone ought to do, am unsure what moral posture one should take on selective abortion. Because all attempts to find the moral stance on this do seem like just that: posturing. Prenatal diagnosis, with its potential for selective abortion, is about responsibility. Whether one chooses to have the testing and have the abortion if the news be bad, or one chooses not to have the testing and bear the child no matter what its diagnosable condition, one has taken on an unthinkable responsibility, the burden of another person's life.

Of course, motherhood is itself always to take on that burden, when you come right down to it. To choose, to choose not to choose, to have, to have not, to bear, to bear not, is to bear responsibility. In that sense then my motherhood, my mothering of the two children I have borne and the one that I have not, gives me authority, places me, grounds me. But where are we headed here? Can I represent these women only because I am a mother? Is every bit of my ability to understand what these women say grounded in my own motherhood? Or can we say that living itself imposes responsibility, that all morally sentient beings experience responsibility, and at least occasionally experience it as a burden, and so all people can then potentially understand the situation of women who are asked to choose whether and how to make use of prenatal diagnosis. That is certainly the assumption I make in my writing: I do not write *to* mothers, but to all people with moral sensibility.

My goal as I wrote that book (Rothman, 1986/1993) was to get people to understand: it was a project in bearing witness. I did not believe that anything I wrote would change anything in the world, would make burdens any lighter, ease responsibility, free choices. But I did think that I could pass through me the grief, anguish, fears, worries, strength and courage that these women showed me, and make that clear and visible to others. 'Representing' has two meanings, and in my work I move between them constantly. On the one hand, I represent these women as in a portrait: mine is a representational art. I need to find a way of making the highly edited, selected words of a very few people represent, draw a picture of, the situation of many. On the other hand, my representation is also a political representation: through my voice I represent theirs. I am their representative to the world that reads my words, hears me speak.

That these are different projects became clearest to me not in the writing of the book, but in its initial editing. The book has a fairly unimaginative organization. I begin by giving some of the history of prenatal diagnosis, including the history of abortion in America. I then portray the players in prenatal diagnosis: the genetic counsellors who offer the tests, and the women who choose whether or not to use them. In the first draft of the book, there was a chapter on the genetic counsellors, describing them, their backgrounds, their work, their feelings about what they were doing. The book editor read that draft and said that chapter on genetic counsellors did not work, did not belong in the book. It didn't fit in, she said. Well why not? Of course it fits in, I argued. I was logical, rational and (of course) right. It most certainly did fit in, logically and rationally. But when I let the problem sit for a while, and then read through the manuscript, I could see her point. The chapter on genetic counsellors didn't actually fit in. It wasn't a problem in logic: it was a problem in 'tone'. I represented the genetic counsellors accurately, I believe. I showed who they are and what they are doing and something about why they are doing it. It was a perfectly adequate representation, a portrait I stand behind. But it was not a representation in the second sense, the political sense. The genetic counsellors remained, fundamentally for me, Other. I let them speak, but I was (and am) unwilling to speak for them, to let my voice be used so that theirs can be heard.

Editing, or more accurately, being edited, often brings that problem to my attention. Having someone look at my words, circle them, ask if I really mean what I am saying, forces me to confront just exactly what it is that I am saying.

The case of the floating 'we' may be the best example. I use 'we' a lot when I write. Who exactly 'we' are, I couldn't always tell you. Sometimes I am doing it deliberately to refer to women, i.e. to say things like 'When we are portrayed in gynecology textbooks,' rather than to say when 'women' are portrayed. That use of 'we' argues against the desexed, degendered, depersonalized 'author' and grounds the text in my own embodied voice. I've taken to putting in a standard note to the copy editor telling her (almost always a her) that 'we' are women, that I am one too, and that's OK, it can show. But 'we' women are so astonishingly differently embodied, so – even more overwhelmingly – differently placed socially, that 'we' doesn't really get one very far. We who? Can I use 'we' only for 'women like me'? And what makes a woman 'like me'? Is it age, race, sexual orientation(s), reproductive history, familial status, educational or job situation? In another, equally profound sense, there is no we, there is only me.

That explains, I think, why all of my writing ends up so autobiographical. And I hate autobiography. But who I am, my own particulars, keep cropping up. People who read my academic scholarly work end up knowing all kinds of stuff about my 'personal' life. Because each use of 'we' embeds a 'me', a me I feel I need to be 'up front' about, and a me that I draw upon to clarify, to make my point, to help draw the connecting line between the voice I represent and the ear to which I represent it. If I can make *you* see *me* as someone you can relate to, then the resonance I feel with these people I represent might mean something to you. I am a tool, a resource I can draw upon, in presenting and representing the Other to you. Because you, the reader, are the most unknown of Others.

So what would I do about an amnio? I don't know. But isn't the fact that I don't know, that someone reasonably smart, moderately thoughtful, a woman, a mother, terrifically knowledgable about this – if I don't know what I would do, doesn't that tell you something? If people like *me* feel this way, then can you understand how *we* feel? If I can represent me to you, then maybe you can hear me represent them.

Reference

Rothman, Barbara Katz (1986/1993) *The Tentative Pregnancy*. New York: Viking Penguin.

5

Waking from a Dream of Chinese Shadows

Magdalene Ang-Lygate

One morning, a few weeks after the year-of-the-pig Chinese New Year celebrations, I woke up from a dream muttering in my best Cantonese. I was trying very hard to convince the head waiter at the Loon Fung restaurant that he should sell me three Chinese New Year cards. Given my English-educated Malaysian Chinese background, my fluency was impressive but I sensed that the scenario was surreal – not only because the celebrations were already past but because I somehow knew for a fact that waiters did not sell cards in restaurants. Besides, it could not have been me speaking because I usually spoke Nonya-Cantonese[1] and it was only with the greatest effort and concentration that I could normally make conversation in 'proper' Cantonese. The Self I knew could never have launched herself into the passionate torrent that I heard in my dream. Afterwards, I realized that while I appreciated previously that I dreamt in glorious technicolour – complete with smells, sounds, touch and taste – I had never dreamt in Chinese before. How odd that it had taken all this time for my Chineseness to break into my dream-life. Yet, what did it all mean? Using my best amateur dream interpretation techniques, I got thus far: Chinese New Year cards have something to do with paper and surely that represented the paper I wanted to write on 'Chineseness'. The next part was equally easy to interpret. The number three had to correspond to the third month: March, when the paper was due. But where did the restaurant fit in? Surely it was a bit far-fetched to link year-of-the-pig to food and restaurants. After all there was no eating in my dream restaurant otherwise I would have certainly remembered it!

I suspected it had something to do with 'At the Palace', Chung's (1990) study of operational interactions at a Chinese restaurant and take-away in Manchester where she specifically addressed the twin issues of gender and ethnicity in placing herself as a Chinese woman among other Chinese workers.[2] This paper first caught my attention some years ago because I found myself identifying with Chung. At that time, the fact that we were both Chinese women doing 'academic work', researching into roughly the same subject areas was enough to assure me that we belonged to the same side of Otherness. My own research work – based on the narratives of immigration experiences of Chinese and Filipina women – is about the social construction of diasporic identities and multilayered subjectivities. Hence, theories of differences, diversities and Otherness habitually crowd my mind. The scarcity of feminist empirical investigation into the issues raised by the phenomena of diasporic multilayered subjectivities concerned me enough to want to research and write about them. However, in seeking to situate myself in my research work and in engaging with other Chinese women who, with me, were perceived to be Other, questions about belonging and not belonging began to impinge on me in a different way.

'As feminists how are we to represent members of groups to which we do not ourselves belong – and should we even try?' If we accept the logic that is implicit in binary dualism, it would be reasonable to assume that if one could cross the magic imaginary line that separates Self from the Other, then one would be on familiar territory and could represent the Other from the inside out. This form of reasoning is tidy and has been adopted in some research where it was sufficient for women to investigate other women about women's issues. However, as several feminists of colour (e.g. Anthias and Yuval-Davis, 1992; Mohanty et al., 1991; Moraga and Anzaldúa, 1983) assert, what remains unexplained and unproblematized is the fact that women's realities encompass a whole range of different identities and subjectivities – all of which are enmeshed, interconnected and inseparable along shifting imaginary lines. For example, it is possible for a Malaysian Chinese Nonya resident in Scotland to be married, a mother, lesbian, middle class (to name a few categories) and it is impossible for her to experience reality without simultaneously calling into action the social categories of nationality, gender, 'race', class and sexuality – all of which are themselves negotiated through time and space. It is impossible to conceptualize identities that obey the rules of binary dualism because this would necessitate a complicit silencing of many aspects of our identities. The trouble with asking feminists how we are to represent members of groups to which we do not ourselves belong is that it presupposes that complex realities can be reduced to simple binary equations. Binary dualism may provide a useful system of thinking but it has limited currency in attempts to theorize multilayered, hyphenated, hybridized and potentially conflicting subjectivities. Therefore, as a Chinese woman researching other Chinese women, it would be methodologically misleading for me to assume that I 'belonged' simply because I am myself Chinese, if I neglected to account for other social differences based on ethnicity, sexuality, class, religion and so on. The racialized category 'Chinese' is itself problematic. Anderson (1991) claims that it is largely an imagined identity that can be traced to early European imperialism of the 'east'. Only in choosing to privilege the racialization of myself and my research participants can I say that we belong to the same group, because the moment we admit the possibility of other concurrent categories of Otherness, group membership becomes repeatedly re-negotiable.

For example, as part of my research I tried to gain access to a particular group of Hong Kong Chinese women to interview them. I made initial contact with the leader of the group by telephone, but to my initial dismay, she was reluctant to let me attend their meetings. However, when I realized that because she could not see me over the telephone line, she had assumed from my Anglicized first name and my local Scottish accent that I was Caucasian, I specifically declared myself to be Chinese and her subsequent response to me changed dramatically. 'Oh! If you are Chinese, you are most welcome. I look forward to seeing you next Tuesday.' It was clear that while my status as a Chinese woman gave me an immediate right of access to that group, I was actually not allowed to belong until I revealed my 'true' identity and identified as Chinese, colluding with the myth of authentic ethnicity. In the absence of visible and conversational markers – my skin colour and features, my choice of language, accent and name – my perceived identity allowed me, unintentionally, to masquerade as 'white', and allowed her to decide that I did not belong. The other woman's separate construction of a different reality demonstrated afresh that there was a parallel subjectivity and our individual subjectivities were equally dependent on the two 'realities'. Due to our specific positioning in British colonial history, a Hong Kong Chinese woman has a completely different ethnic and social makeup from a Malaysian Nonya, and our Chineseness alone could not be automatically assumed to be a source of commonality. Still, it was upon this premise that I gained access to a group which would otherwise have excluded me. In this case, the imaginary boundary that demarcated Otherness was shifted by her to let me in. Since that time, more imaginary lines based on sexuality, class, religion and politics have indeed been drawn and I have been routinely excluded or included, depending on the circumstances.

In addition, it is important not to lose sight of the dynamics of hierarchical power relationships, about who attempts to demarcate imaginary boundaries and determines how Otherness is represented. Typically, these are the ways that Chinese women are 'Otherized' – we have been sexualized as women, racialized as Chinese and orientalized as exotic. What are the underlying structures that permit this 'Otherizing' process? Who does the 'Otherizing'? As Anzaldúa puts it, an unnamed 'they' is at work to push women to 'the other side of the other side of the other side' to keep them hidden (Anzaldua, 1994: 3). And if the Self is forever found to be 'kept in the shadows of other', how useful is it to hang on to a way of thinking that ultimately isolates and alienates the Self? Can the researcher-self ever reach that imaginary station from which she can represent the Other from the inside out? As only to be expected, once I started negotiating my way around the Chinese-Other landscape, the Chinese-Woman-Other[3] enclosure, which was neatly but falsely packaged as homogenous, could not be sustained in my struggle to situate myself – a Chinese woman researching other Chinese women. Yet the point is not so much about belonging and not belonging on the basis of identity/identities, but about the relationships of power that ultimately decide whose version of reality becomes the dominant representation. Modes of knowledge production that seek to represent the Other – whether self-defined or not – are not apolitical, not ahistorical, and feminist research that treats women as central actors must also be capable of identifying and challenging material structures that perpetuate practices of dominance and oppression. In stepping out of the shadows of dreams and in identifying the nameless 'they' who refuse to see Otherness as simultaneous difference/diversity, those of us who identify as multi-identitied must continue to resist attempts to categorize us as Other from a perspective not our own.

Notes

1 The term Nonya, pronounced (and sometimes spelt) as Nyonya, refers to a Chinese woman born in the Straits Settlements of Penang, Singapore and Malacca who belongs to an ethnic minority Chinese community assimilated into the dominant Malay culture. Nonya-Cantonese is Cantonese spoken with a mix of English and Malay words. For a discussion on language use in Malaysian culture, see Lim (1994).

2 Chung seemed to make the assumption that the racialized category 'Chinese' was unproblematic because, apart from gender, she made no mention of other social differencess such as ethnicity, class, etc. and perpetuated a prevalent view that all Chinese people – especially Chinese women – were alike.

3 A phrase derived from Trinh's (1989) 'Woman, Native, Other'.

References

Anderson, B. (1991) 'Census, Map, Museum', in *Imagined Communities*. London: Verso (first published 1983).

Anthias, F. and Yuval-Davis, N. (1992) *Racialised Boundaries: Race, Nation, Gender, Colour and Class and the Anti-racist Struggle*. London: Routledge.

Anzaldúa, G. (1994) 'Del Otro Lado', in J. Ramos (ed.) *Companeras: Latina Lesbians*. New York: Routledge.

Chung, Y.K. (1990) 'At the Palace: Researching Gender and Ethnicity in a Chinese Restaurant', in L. Stanley (ed.) *Feminist Praxis: Research, Theory and Epistemology in Feminist Sociology*. London: Routledge.

Lim, S.G. (1994) 'Language, Gender, Race and Nation: A Postcolonial Meditation', in *Writing Southeast Asia in English: Against the Grain, Focus on Asian English Language Literature*. London: Skoob Books.

Mohanty, C.T., Russo, A. and Torres, L. (eds) (1991) *Third World Women and the Politics of Feminism*. Bloomington, IN: Indiana University Press.

Moraga, C. and Anzaldúa, G. (eds) (1983) *This Bridge Called My Back: Writings by Women of Color*. New York: Kitchen Table Press.

Trinh, T.M. (1989) *Woman, Native, Other: Writing Postcoloniality and Feminism*. Bloomington, IN: Indiana University Press.

6

Voices in the Winds of Change

Amanda Kottler

This chapter originates from my experiences in the late 1980s while studying in South Africa at the University of Cape Town, where many of my (all white) lecturers were well-known progressive academics involved in the anti-apartheid struggle. These academics challenged a dominant view, that perceived differences in behaviour patterns could be explained in terms of 'racial' or 'cultural' *difference*. Instead, focusing on *similarities* between cultures, they drew attention to the broader socio-political and economic circumstances in South Africa to explain different behaviour patterns. At the tail end of this period, Harriet Ngubane, a black South African doctoral graduate of Cambridge University (in the UK), was appointed to a Chair. Her views were different from those of my lecturers and were extremely unpopular with them. Unlike her colleagues she embraced 'cultural' difference; she spoke with pride about being Zulu and Different. This was riveting and, in 1988, led to my analysis of the *similarities* and *differences* discourses (Kottler, 1990). The progressive academics positioned in the similarities discourse were critical of essentialist ideas that people's behaviour 'naturally' differs along 'racial' or 'cultural' lines; for example:

> On the one end of the continuum many South Africans are industriously seeking to keep abreast of and to contribute to the development and application of science and techno-logy. Yet, at the other end . . . many South Africans, frequently blacks, find it difficult and even bewildering to adapt to and keep pace with the ever changing demands in their work environment. (Raubenheimer, 1993: 171)

In contrast, they argued that: 'different races and ethnic groups, unique cultures and traditions, do not exist in any ultimate sense in South Africa, and are real only to the extent that they are the product of a *particular world view*' (Boonzaier and Sharp, 1988: 1, my emphasis).

Drawing on critical theory, academics positioned in the similarities discourse actively chose not to focus on differences, and therefore 'cultural' preference, to explain data suggesting that, for example, the black population, because of their cultural beliefs, made more use of 'non-western' methods of medical treatment (traditional healers) than whites, who used only western methods of treatment. Instead, these academics argued that other factors needed to be taken into account in order to explain the different behaviour. For example, the fact that western treatment centres were located almost exclusively in urban centres, long distances from the townships where the black population had been forced to live as a result of apartheid, had serious financial implications. The travelling costs and time involved in reaching the clinics would involve a loss of a substantial portion of hourly wages (Westcott and Wilson, 1979). Such progressive academics argued that these facts, and not 'cultural' or 'racial' preference for any one kind of healing system, influenced people's choice of healer (Boonzaier, 1985).

Such arguments provided persuasive support for the conviction that different practices and belief systems did *not* occur along the divide of western/African, as was suggested by the government of the time and in much of the 'non-progressive' academic literature (Boonzaier and Sharp, 1988). The arguments powerfully countered conclusions drawn from and used to 'justify', for example, building western medical clinics in cities and not in townships, on the basis of research which 'showed' that black people did not need these because they apparently did not use western medicine.

Those positioned in the similarities discourse demonstrated, therefore, that research focusing only on differences in behaviour patterns was inadequate, misleading, and dangerously supportive of apartheid ideology. In common with others (e.g. Parker, 1989), these academics began to problematize the discipline of psychology itself. Largely in response to small but vocal groups of politically active youth (white and black, men and women), they began to ask questions about how psychology might be made more relevant for the general population in South Africa (e.g. Berger and Lazarus, 1987; Dawes, 1986). They argued that modernist psychological practice and theory should be remoulded (e.g. Perkel, 1988), or even abandoned (Foster, 1986).

There had never been any question in my mind that these challenges were important. Relative to 'race' and 'culture', I had been comfortably invested in the similarities discourse prior to Ngubane's arrival on campus. Seeing the distinctions only in terms of apartheid, I had always found the differences discourse disagreeable. But Ngubane made me listen to a new voice. Perhaps because of my own journey, from a marginalized position in the male-dominated commercial setting of accountancy to university as a mature student, I was better able vicariously to introspect (Bacal and Newman, 1990) and therefore to 'hear' this other marginal voice.

Drawing parallels with gender, the 1970s feminist literature, which also drew on socio-economic arguments to explain apparent behavioural differences between the genders, had likewise argued that what made us women was socially constructed. Politically, the message was that women should stop talking of differences because these were 'real' only to the extent that they had been socially constructed. They were, in other words, the product of a *particular world view*. As a female accountant I had tried to take up this position by *acting*, but never quite *feeling* the same as, or comfortable as, 'one of the boys'. Clearly no man or woman can rethink themselves as gender-less. Knowing this obviously made it easier for me to take seriously what Ngubane said. No one could rethink themselves as non-racial, ethnic-less or colour-less then or now in South Africa. Socio-political explanations were, and are, important, but a blanket refusal to look at difference had, and continues to have, serious implications for psychological research and practice. It denies individuals an extremely important subjective experience and their absolute right to speak for themselves.

Ngubane was one of those who, positioned within the differences discourse, refused to be silenced. As a black scholar in South Africa prior to 1986, she had to apply for a special permit to attend a 'white' university. With pride and some humorous delight she returned to South Africa as a Professor at a 'white' university. Her talk of difference was hard to reconcile with the idea that such talk felt collusive with apartheid. This apparent contradiction drew my attention to the multiple and contradictory psychological investments involved in what now appeared to be one discourse: the particular world view discourse. While this could be drawn on by those positioned in a similarities discourse to oppose the essentialism of apartheid, it could also be used paradoxically by those positioned in the differences discourse to support the ideology and practice of apartheid. And it was used by a third group who, like Ngubane, were located in the differences discourse but were, like those positioned in the similarities discourse, also opposed to the essentialism of apartheid, but whose text nevertheless demonstrated a powerful psychological investment in being and feeling 'Zulu', 'African', and ethnically different from 'other' South Africans. Those positioned here did not talk of difference in terms of 'backwardness' like those who believed in the essentialist particular world view discourse (e.g. Raubenheimer, 1993). However, at the time Ngubane's investment in difference was heavily criticized by her academic peers and others. She was asked what she was doing 'in the company of these former colonialists whose forebears conquered and oppressed'. And, it was suggested that she was 'contributing to the intellectual support for apartheid by emphasizing indigenous cultural differences and backwardness on the part of the majority population' (Ngubane, 1988: 9–10).

Some of these challenges in effect questioned Ngubane's authority to speak for and about herself and others with whom she identified. Those positioned in the similarities discourse argued that Ngubane's ideas about being different were no longer valid because she and others like her had been schooled and had long lived outside the cultures about and for whom she spoke. Further, she had been exposed to languages and socio-political practices other than those about which she wrote and could not therefore speak as if being Zulu meant that she had been unaffected by other cultures, i.e. separate and different. In a sense, educated people like Ngubane were being regarded by their critics (black and white) as no longer 'purely' black. Clearly, this denied an aspect of Ngubane's sense of herself: regardless of where she was schooled, or what language she chooses to speak, she believes that there remains a central core of 'pure' and 'uncontaminated' identity as a Zulu. She and others like her, e.g. Gabriel Setiloane, a black man, also chose to regard themselves in a not-unproblematic exclusionary manner, as 'insiders', and argued that their experience as Zulu or Sotho-Tswana people could not be known by outsiders (in Lye and Murray, 1980; Ngubane, 1988). Progressive academics (black and white, men and women) held that this was not so: drawing on the similarities discourse they argued that there are many similarities between blacks and whites and that differences should be de-emphasized. The idea about being different through experiencing an exclusive Zulu identity was considered problematic because it was argued that a discretely bounded, static culture, uninfluenced by the rest of the world, did not exist (Boonzaier and Sharp, 1988).

At the height of this debate there were large-scale changes in South Africa. The African National Congress was unbanned, Nelson Mandela was released from prison and a democratic election was planned. The idea of a '*multiracial*' future South Africa was replaced by the more politically correct idea, consistent with the similarities discourse, of a '*non-racial*' future. At around this time I was involved in the training programme for Clinical Psychologists at the University of Cape Town's Child Guidance Clinic. Following an increase in accusations of 'racism' at the university, this issue was discussed at an all-white supervisors' meeting. As progressive psychologists who had until then steadfastly emphasized similarity the question of how now to talk about difference posed a dilemma. However, because of what was happening at the university generally and at the university clinic in particular, difference had to be acknowledged. For example, on one occasion, a black woman referred to the clinic stated explicitly that she would prefer to see a white clinician. On another, when a 'coloured' family failed to arrive, my black supervisee, Nondwe Mange, said with disappointment that she believed this was because she was black; she said they would have known this hearing her voice on the telephone and from her name. Finally, there was the black boy (J), referred by his mother's white employer, who was paying for J to attend a 'white' school. His teacher reported that J was becoming increasingly disruptive in class and in danger of becoming a 'social problem'. J lived with his mother (a single domestic worker) in a 'township' but often spent weekends with his mother's employer. This exposed him to two distinctly different *material* worlds but, more significantly for Mange, to two distinctly different *cultural* worlds. Speaking from the perspective of the differences discourse, Mange said the teacher's complaint that J would not look her in the eye might be an indication of insolence in one culture (mine and the white teacher's), but that it was a sign of respect in another (hers and J's). Momentarily, firmly positioned again in the similarities discourse, I questioned Mange's ideas: surely because J had been exposed to a variety of cultural values, he would know that at school he should look at the teacher when she spoke to him? To suggest that, because he was black, he would remain culturally unchanged was surely to subscribe to the particular world view discourse and the essentialism of apartheid? Also positioned in the similarities discourse, the employer believed that having been at his new school for some time, J would no longer see children in terms of 'colour' or 'race'. He was surprised when J could tell Mange how many white, black and coloured children there were in his class. Mange was not surprised. For her, like Ngubane, these differences do not go away: they have personal meanings which cannot be ignored. Further, as I was later to realize, it did not follow that those who acknowledged difference were supporting apartheid ideology. In retrospect, it seems that none of those involved in these debates at the time, myself included, recognized what Bhavnani and Phoenix (1994), in particular, have since drawn to our attention – that acknowledging difference, as did Ngubane, could have been part of a process of countering inequality and that all subjectivities/identities are constructed in relation to shifting and varied forms of oppression.

Without this understanding, the confusion at the time raised a number of questions: how best could sense be made of these different views for daily psychological practice? Who could talk for whom and whose voice or voices should be heard? Clearly, in this kind of setting it was imperative to acknowledge difference – but how, given the years of silence? And, more importantly, what would the consequences be?

Drawing on Lorde, Henwood (personal communication) argues that failing to recognize difference among equals is a weakening force. She adds that common interests need not be absent, and so we should not be deflected from seeking to understand the way patterns of oppression have been internalized and used to divide. But, the biggest fear in South Africa was (and indeed still is) that 'differences' texts suggest racism. So strong was this fear in 1988 that I was reluctant to submit for publication locally my concern that there would be serious implications for psychologists working in South Africa if we failed to acknowledge the texts of the differences discourse. The intensity of this fear was to draw my attention to a fourth discourse which I later called *white guilt* (Kottler, 1993).

Given the investment in, and evidence of, difference, we need to reflect on how and why this was so effectively silenced for so long in the progressive literature in South Africa. If such silencing was a weakening force, we must avoid repeating such a mistake. But, we also need to consider the possibility that it need not necessarily be weakening. With hindsight it seems that what felt rational and politically reasonable from one position was politically problematic from another perspective. Given the circumstances, decisions had to be made about self-censorship, although most of this was not conscious: entry into the differences discourse by progressive academics was largely untenable in the 1980s in South Africa.

At the time, Foster (1986: 65) noted that there was a range of possible theoretical frameworks to 'carve out the foundations of a practice which contributes towards the real, not imagined, social arrangements in which full human lives may be lived'. At around the same time there were significant methodological and theoretical advances in psychology in Europe (e.g. Burman, 1991; Hollway, 1984; Parker, 1989, 1990a,b, 1992; Wilkinson, 1986) and yet, although some (white) women, in spite of the academic boycott of South Africa, were using these theories to look at gender issues (e.g. Levett, 1988), no one visible in South Africa took them up in research on ethnic or racial texts without fear of criticism. Why not? Clearly there was a fear that this approach might undermine possible political goals (see, for example Burman, 1991).

Reflecting the sort of impossible tension described by Burman (1991) between academic, political and daily psychological practice, it is obvious that the large-scale changes in South Africa in recent years could never have come from pockets of differently positioned groups with different aims and psychological investments, without an overriding shared goal. Just as the arguments put forward in the 1970s feminist literature produced some changes, so too the focus of the similarities discourse, as the dominant *anti-apartheid discourse*, historically served an extremely important political purpose. But complex psychological and psychoanalytic variables were ignored in these arguments. For this reason, the attempt to 'dissolve' (Parker, 1992: 19) the particular world view discourse which led to the similarities discourse did not result in a 'non-racial' future. The recognition in South Africa of 11 official languages and current talk of 'the rainbow people' provide evidence for this. Ironically, the pressing need to oppose the particular world view discourse has in fact served to keep it systematized and unchallenged (Parker, 1992). And, difference talk continues to be associated with the potential for racism or accusations of racism.

For this reason it was impossible for visible senior progressive psychologists to talk of difference at the time. Those who did were, like Ngubane, criticized severely (e.g. Swartz, 1989 – a white male). What were the consequences? Looking back, clearly the visibility of the similarities discourse arguments was a politically effective strategy. However, some heavy criticism would not be entirely misplaced: advocating the goal of a non-racial South Africa could be seen effectively as enforcing 'political correctness'. By presuming to speak for others there was a carelessness about silencing differences. It took the marginal voices of less visible students, women inevitably positioned on the lower ranks of the academic hierarchy and black South Africans who had lived and studied outside the country in the absence of institutionalized apartheid, to break the silence. These (marginalized) groups spoke for themselves, of *their* subjectively experienced sense of *being different* – and as a result have played a significant role in challenging psychological research and practice in South Africa.

Ngubane (1988: 13) suggested at the time that a 'painstaking assessment of the effects on the traditional cultures of the long years of apartheid, and the direction of resulting change' should be carried out by 'indigenous practitioners'. This raised a host of questions, which remain unanswered today. Can only black people research and speak for blacks, white for whites, women for women, men for men? Perhaps in the end, since we cannot ever totally transcend either our historical position or our prejudgements, the best that can be done, when faced with this kind of dilemma, is to interpret in such a way as to give access to our past and continually open up new possibilities for the future. In South Africa, in particular, we need to do this now by finding a way of speaking about difference without reinvoking a racializing discourse.

Note

My thanks to Erica Burman, Karen Henwood, Ann Levett and Sue Wilkinson for useful commentary and editorial assistance. Thanks also, for many fruitful discussions over the years, to Nondwe Mange and Harriet Ngubane.

References

Bacal, Howard A. and Newman, Kenneth M. (1990) *Theories of Object Relations: Bridges to Self Psychology*. New York: Columbia University Press.
Berger, S. and Lazarus, S. (1987) 'The Views of Community Organizers on the Relevance of Psychological Practice in South Africa', *Psychology in Society* 7: 6–23.
Bhavnani, K-K and Phoenix, A. (1994) *Shifting Identities Shifting Racisms: A 'Feminism & Psychology' Reader*. London: Sage.
Boonzaier, E. (1985) 'Choice of Healer: An Important Area of Interest for General Practitioners', *South African Family Practice* 6 (8): 236–40.

Boonzaier, E and Sharp, J. (1988) *South African Keywords*. Cape Town: David Philip.

Burman, Erica (1991) 'What Discourse is Not', *Philosophical Psychology* 4: 325–40.

Dawes, A.R.L. (1986) 'The Notion of Relevant Psychology with Particular Reference to Africanist Pragmatic Initiatives', *Psychology in Society* 5: 28–48.

Foster, D.H. (1986) 'The South African Crisis of 1985', *Psychology in Society* 5: 49–65.

Hollway, Wendy (1984) 'Gender Difference and the Production of Subjectivity', in J. Henriques et al. (eds) *Changing the Subject*. London: Methuen.

Kottler, Amanda (1990) 'South Africa: Psychology's Dilemma of Multiple Discourses', *Psychology in Society* 13: 27–36.

Kottler, Amanda (1993) 'Riddles of Ethnicity: Implications for Psychologists in South Africa', paper presented at British Psychological Society, Women in Psychology and BPS Psychology of Women Section Annual Conference, University of Sussex, Brighton, England.

Levett, Ann (1988) 'Psychological Trauma: Discourses of Childhood Sexual Abuse', unpublished PhD thesis, University of Cape Town.

Lye, W.F. and Murray, C. (1980) *Transformations on the Highveld: The Tswana and Southern Sotho*. Cape Town: David Philip.

Ngubane, H. (1988) 'Reshaping Social Anthropology', paper presented at the University of Durban-Westville, Durban.

Parker, Ian (1989) *The Crisis in Modern Social Psychology, and How to End it*. London: Routledge.

Parker, Ian (1990a) 'Discourse: Definitions and Contradictions', *Philosophical Psychology* 3 (2): 189–204.

Parker, Ian (1990b) 'Real Things: Discourse, Context and Practice', *Philosophical Psychology* 3 (2): 227–33.

Parker, Ian (1992) *Discourse Dynamics*. London: Routledge.

Perkel, A. (1988) 'Towards a Model for a South African Clinical Psychology', *Psychology in Society* 10: 53–75.

Raubenheimer, I. van W. (1993) 'Psychology in South Africa', *The Psychologist*: 169–71.

Swartz, L. (1989) 'Aspects of Culture in South African Psychiatry', unpublished PhD thesis, University of Cape Town.

Westcott, G. and Wilson, F. (eds) (1979) *Perspectives on the Health System*. Johannesburg: Ravan Press.

Wilkinson, Sue (ed.) (1986) *Feminist Social Psychology: Developing Theory and Practice*. Milton Keynes: Open University Press.

7

Able-Bodied Dilemmas in Teaching Disability Studies

Deborah Marks

I am an able-bodied woman, currently organizing a course in disability studies at Sheffield University in the North of England. The course is interdisciplinary, drawing upon critical work in the social sciences and humanities to interrogate practices around the representation and treatment of disability. The course is based around three broad philosophical propositions. First, we aim to question a model of disability which posits the disability solely within the mind or body of an individual. Rather, disability is seen to be socially constituted (see Abberley, 1987). A person is disabled by virtue of a series of practices which divides populations along lines of 'functional ability' and places barriers to full social participation for specific physically or intellectually 'different' groups. One of these barriers is fundamentally about the lack of control over issues of representation. Radical campaigners involved in disability politics have long complained of the way people with disabilities are represented in the media (Gartner and Joe, 1987) and, in particular, in charity advertising, which presents disabled people as being victims, needy and dependent. Disability has long been used in western culture as a metaphor to represent a range of stigmatized characteristics, including sinfulness and impotence (Hevey, 1992). Second, following on from an analysis of the social model of disability, our philosophy is to see disability as a relational concept, which can only have meaning with reference to unacknowledged assumptions about 'normality'. Drawing upon the work of Foucault (1973, 1977) and Derrida (1976), the course aims to deconstruct the binary opposition set up between normality and abnormality. Third, the course is concerned to examine the psychic consequences of disability, both in terms of the social, psychological and physiological experiences associated with different disabilities and in terms of the existential anxieties of able-bodied people, who fear becoming disabled, dependent, vulnerable, powerless and stigmatized. Drawing upon psychoanalysis, the course is also concerned to explore ways in which people project internal anxieties and fears on to different 'Others', who are made into objects of pity or fear.

The course, as with other initiatives into the study of disability, owes its origins to campaigns organized by the Disability Rights Movement. Since the 1970s, there has been growing awareness of disability as a political and social, rather than a purely medical or charitable, concern. The Disability Rights Movement has increasingly begun to demand a voice for disabled people to represent themselves. A number of British fora, including magazines (such as *Dail* and *Disability Now*), academic journals (*Disability and Society*), and radio programmes (*Does He Take Sugar?* and *In Touch*) have begun this task. These initiatives are either staffed by disabled people, or aim to provide a forum for the concerns of disabled people.

The issues raised by an able-bodied woman running a course in disability call forth the spectre of colonization of the 'Other', spoken about so eloquently by many writers on feminism, disability, racism and heterosexism. My fear is that I will be positioned in relation to disability in the way that men have been positioned in relation to feminism. Despite adopting the language of post-structuralism, the course risks slipping into an examination of 'Others'. This is particularly so given that the majority of applicants so far have been able-bodied professionals with backgrounds in health care and education. How will the minority of disabled students experience their position within the course? To what extent, if any, should experiential learning form a part of the course? How will different perspectives on disability gain a voice in the course? How can the course avoid appropriating disabled people's struggles at a time when Disability Studies is experiencing an increasingly high profile in the academy and in political life?

Such questions raise concerns about the role of able-bodied people in the context of the Disability Rights Movement. Perhaps a useful starting point is to examine the positions available to men within feminism. Some have argued that men may take the role of guilty admirer and supporter of women (Smith, 1987). However, admiration and guilt do not offer a stable basis for support. Both emotions are conflicted and often disguise more hostile and envious emotions. Another position open to men is to act as interrogators of feminism, preventing the women's movement from becoming just another exclusionary, disciplinary discourse. Men's interventions, it has been argued (Smith, 1987), can function as a disrupter of essentialist or universalizing tendencies in feminism. Men's presence in the Women's Movement thus functions as a reminder of the material fact of difference. This justification for men's involvement in feminism has been challenged by Jardine (1987), who suggests that such a strategy is reminiscent of men's familiar judging and scolding of women. I share Jardine's suspicion of such abstract theorizations of the role of men in feminism. Men's wishes to be part of feminism can be seen as colonizing, and policing. Men cannot be feminists, because they do not experience (except through some form of masquerade) what it is to be a woman. (For further discussion of difficulties of this claim, see Butler, 1993.) Instead, Jardine suggests that men might offer a more pragmatic contribution to feminism. She suggests that men ask what they, as teachers and writers, can do to transform the subordination and oppression of women (1987).

Such questions of guilt and admiration are particularly pertinent to the treatment of people with disabilities, who are often seen as heroic victims, struggling 'against the odds'. The idea of functioning as a 'material reminder of difference' seems less relevant to the Disability Rights Movement, which seems generally to be acutely sensitive to issues of difference between disabled people. In order to avoid patronizing representations or offensive self-assertion, I wish to support Jardine's pragmatic approach in examining the role of the able-bodied person in disability issues. Such a pragmatic stance has certainly been the one taken by many disabled people in relation to my appointment as course coordinator. The primary concern of those who have contacted me so far has been that I actively become involved with disability rights campaigning. This might involve efforts to make my own institution more accessible. It would certainly involve support for the *Rights Now* campaign to get the Civil Rights (Disabled People's) Bill on to the British statute books. I have had telephone calls and letters from campaigners, letting me know of their existence, and offering their support in setting up the course and in addressing disabling exclusionary practices. Incidently, I have received more letters of support, encouragement and helpful suggestions setting up this Masters Course in Disability Studies than in any task I've worked on before.

I see my role as course coordinator as two-fold. First, I am concerned with instigating resistance to the constitution, exclusion and oppression of disabled people in a number of fora. This involves being concerned with disability in all research and engaging with the work of disabled writers, involving disabled people in teaching and working alongside others to identify and challenge any exclusionary practices which might be operating in my institution. Such a pragmatic set of concerns enables me to circumvent the problem of my credentials for my work. Similarly, I hope that a pragmatic approach avoids the arrogant enterprise of representing the experience of the disabled 'Other'. The point is to provide a forum in which disabled people's voices may be heard, rather than *representing* the needs, or otherwise, of disabled people.

Second, I am also concerned with more philosophical, post-structuralist questions about the boundaries of the Disability Rights Movement, the construction of identity and the psychic experience of normality and difference. This last concern has led me to reflect upon my own position in relation to disability. Most people are likely to experience some form of disability, at some stage in their life. This renders unstable any attempt to make sharp demarcations between being able-bodied and disabled. I follow many in the civil rights movement in being attracted to the term 'temporarily able-bodied' or 'TAB'. Disability is such a wide and complex term, which cannot be fixed, because the nature of barriers against differences is constantly altering.

While I do not wish to engage in narcissistic confession regarding my interest in learning disability, it is certainly worth noting that I have learnt, only gradually, through critical engagement in studies of disability, that I have a number of personal investments in understanding the experience of stupidity and exclusion. This is likely to be true for many academics, who are attracted to a particular subject area in order to work out unresolved personal issues. This recognition that my interest in learning disability did not emerge out of disengaged intellectual investigation, but came from deeply personal and, until recently, unconscious anxieties was largely a product of reading Valerie Sinason's (1992) book *Mental Handicap and the Human Condition*. Sinason disrupts any sharp demarcation between 'the stupid' and 'the intelligent', and also examines the projections and fears experienced in relation to stupidity. Her work helped me, and students I have discussed this with, to understand that the 'Other' is always a construction, which relies on the fears and fantasies we have about ourselves as much as the fears and fantasies we have about 'Others'.

In conclusion, an appreciation of 'real' political debates feeds into a continuing, although often silent, struggle around difference and stigma. I suspect such struggles are shared by many academic women who find themselves in positions of power (at least in relation to students, but also in terms of the way knowledge is produced), and who are concerned about their place within an academic institution and within a range of differences. In part, my paralysing anxiety reflects a complex constellation of gendered anxieties about not feeling comfortable taking power, responsibility or privileges. However, there is also good reason to feel unease about occupying a position which exists, at least in part, as a result of exclusions of disabled people from entering into the educational hierarchy. Such concerns do not, however, overwhelm me, and, as I have argued, have been eased as a result of much support, and by the adoption of a pragmatic approach.

References

Abberley, P. (1987) 'The Concept of Oppression and the Development of a Social Theory of Disability', *Disability, Handicap and Society* 2 (1): 5–19.

Butler, J. (1993) *Bodies that Matter: On the Discursive Limits of 'Sex'*. London: Routledge.

Derrida, J. (1976) *Of Grammatology*, trans. Gayatri Chakravorty Spivak. Baltimore and London: Johns Hopkins University Press.

Foucault, M. (1973) *Madness and Civilization: A History of Insanity in the Age of Reason* (abridged), trans. Richard Howard. New York: Vintage/Random House.

Foucault, M. (1977) *Discipline and Punish: The Birth of the Prison*, trans. Alan Sheridan. London: Allen Lane.

Gartner, A. and Joe, T. (1987) *Images of the Disabled: Disabling Images*. New York: Praeger.

Hevey, D. (1992) *The Creatures Time Forgot: Photography and Disability Imagery*. London: Routledge.

Jardine, Alice (1987) 'Men in Feminism: Oder di Uomo or Compagnons do Route?', in A. Jardine and P. Smith (eds) *Men in Feminism*. London: Routledge.

Sinason, V. (1992) *Mental Handicap and the Human Condition: New Approaches from the Tavistock*. London: Free Association Books.

Smith, P. (1987) 'Men in Feminism: Men and Feminist Theory', in A. Jardine and P. Smith (eds) *Men in Feminism*. London: Routledge.

8

Infertility: From 'Inside/Out' to 'Outside/In'

Anne Woollett

My aim here is to discuss some issues about representing infertile women from my own experiences, initially as an 'insider', but increasingly over time as a childless woman.

My research (conducted with Naomi Pfeffer) was intended to represent infertile women whose voices and experiences we considered were omitted from current accounts of infertility (Pfeffer and Woollett, 1983; Woollett, 1991). Our own position as infertile women was a common link with the women we interviewed: many welcomed the opportunity to talk to other women who shared what we all considered to be a difficult position. As 'insiders', who had experienced some of the feelings and experiences our participants reported, we felt able to write about women's distress and anger at 'not being heard', and about the ways in which women's feelings were ignored or used against them to argue, for example, that distress was the 'cause' of their infertility, rather than a 'normal' and understandable reaction to the indignities associated with infertility investigations. We also felt able to write about women's sense of isolation when the people they usually counted on for support could not deal with the strong feelings generated by infertility.

Our representation of infertile women also drew on our/their perspectives critically to examine the conceptualizations of infertility and infertile women then current. These were based almost entirely on what was written by doctors, either as books for the lay public or in the newsletters of self-help organizations. In these writings, doctors provided medical information about infertility and infertility investigations, often detailing new 'medical advances'. Infertility was conceptualized as a condition for which a medical solution is most appropriate (although self-help organizations also acknowledged adoption as a solution): because such techniques are available, it is assumed that well-adjusted women will pursue them. The accounts in the newsletters of the self-help organizations of couples who have produced the 'longed-for child', exhorting others 'never to give up hope', reinforce this approach. As a result, there was no discussion about how infertile women (and men) may use the information doctors provide to decide *not* to take up treatment. Such resistance to medical treatment was also undermined by the ways in which 'failure' to pursue medical treatment is construed as maladjustment or poor motivation: those who 'give up' are construed as not trying 'hard enough', as not sufficiently 'committed' to becoming parents, or as having poor or unsupportive relationships – a view reinforced by much psychological research (Woollett, 1992). The doctors and self-help groups, therefore, 'speak for' (and speak to) those women who pursue medical treatment, rather than those who do not, or those for whom treatment does not provide a baby.

Another incentive for giving ourselves/infertile women a voice was the lack of feminist analyses of infertility. Those of our participants who, like ourselves, identified as feminists were distressed to find infertility not represented. Controlling fertility, a key struggle for the Women's Movement at that time, was defined only in terms of contraception and abortion. The relevance of infertility to struggles around reproductive 'choice' and the contribution of infertile women to debates about the medical control of women's reproductive health was not recognized (Worcester and Whatley, 1994).

While we were conducting our research, there were significant changes in the 'solutions' available for infertility, as reproductive technologies (such as IVF) became more available. These gave infertility a high profile, but with fewer than 2500 babies born each year as a result of IVF treatment (HFEA, 1994), the impact of reproductive technologies on the experiences of most infertile women has been less than might be expected from the media and other attention given to such technologies. This lack of impact comes about for a number of reasons. First, such treatments are available to only a small proportion of women who are infertile, because they are costly, and available only at a small number of centres; also they are usually only offered to those considered to be 'socially acceptable' (generally women who are married or in long-term heterosexual relationships). And second, IVF still has a low success rate (in 1994, the Human Embryology and Fertilization Authority reported an average success rate for IVF of 12.7 per cent per treatment cycle) (Pfeffer, 1993).

Feminist writers have responded to the development of the new reproductive technologies by identifying their oppressive nature. In doing so, however, they represent infertile women as universally 'desperate', and castigate them for their willingness to submit to medical technology regardless of its effects (Franklin, 1989; Pfeffer, 1987). There is little attempt to understand the diverse ways in which women make sense of and experience infertility, and hence the reasons why they might submit to/persist with medical treatments. In this way, infertile women are marginalized in feminist writing, and given no part in developing an understanding of, for example, the diverse meanings of motherhood in western industrialized and other cultures (Collins, 1994).

In deconstructing infertility, Naomi Pfeffer and I were particularly committed to addressing the ways in which infertile women had been objectified, and their feelings and experiences ignored or trivialized in medical writing and practice, and in much feminist writing. One way in which we sought to do this was through describing and examining the diverse nature of infertility, including the ways in which women come to be infertile, for example, through their own or a partner's reproductive 'failure', when trying to conceive a first child, or a second or subsequent child. Similarly, we represented women's understandings and experiences of infertility as diverse, for example depending on whether a predominant concern is being childless; being infertile; becoming a mother; or creating a 'family'. Women's strategies for coping with infertility also vary depending, for example, on whether they decide to pursue medical treatment and/or other solutions such as adoption; whether or not the 'cause' of their infertility is known; what the source of the problem is (themselves, a partner, or both); the availability of treatment options; women's social and economic positions (and hence their ability to pay for treatment); women's other interests and identities; the comparative social positions of mothers and non-mothers in their families and cultures; and their support networks (whether the energies of family and friends are taken up with children and child care).

Women's understandings and 'choices' around infertility are extremely diverse and cannot be represented as singular or homogenous. As two infertile and childless women, with a necessarily limited range of experiences, we could not hope to 'speak for' all infertile women. We chose to argue some points more strongly than others, often reflecting our analysis of the limitations of current conceptualizations, and the viewpoints which were not represented (or were rendered pathological) in other accounts. Our criticisms of equating 'good adjustment' and persistence with medical treatment drew, for example, on our reading of what was 'absent' (or rendered pathological) in current accounts. For example, we chose not to research anxiety or stress among IVF patients for practical reasons and because such issues are well/over-represented in psychological accounts. My own choice of issues/areas on which to focus was also related, in part at least, to my own strategies for coping with infertility, for example, my decision not to pursue treatment via these new reproductive technologies but to develop non-mothering identities and activities, and also the reactions of other people to that decision.

I have obviously, therefore, represented some infertile women more than others. Women's strategies for coping with infertility do not appear to relate straightforwardly to their social positions, (such as whether or not they have had children), their economic situations, 'race' or ethnicity, age or sexuality. In some respects, therefore, I feel I represent some positions or infertility choices, rather than some groups of infertile women.

During the time I have been engaged in research and writing about infertility, my own position has changed. I started researching as an infertile woman, but over the years, as I have developed non-mothering identities and interests, I have come to think of myself as 'childless' rather than 'infertile'. The passing of time was important not only to my own experience but to those of the women who participated in the research. Over time women's lives and identities change. Traditionally, and 'normally', this means moving from being childless to being mothers, by giving birth or mothering children not born to them (e.g. through adoption or step-mothering). Over time (as I am aware from my research with mothers) mothers' lives and identities also change: as children grow up, mothers are freed from many of the day-to-day demands of child care, and differences between their lives and interests and those of childless women are often reduced. Less traditionally, some women choose to remain childless from an early age, while others adopt this position gradually, through choice or through circumstances (for example because their culture or situation prevents them from bringing up children on their own). And eventually the menopause renders all women infertile.

This shift in my position, from infertile to childless woman, has been gradual, so it is not easy to assess its impact, and to distinguish this from other influences on my approach to infertility and how I represent infertile women. I am aware, for example, of a continuing commitment to resisting common designations of infertile women as 'mad', 'sad' or 'desperate'. But my perspective must necessarily differ (as the memories of the intensity of the feelings fade) from that of younger women who are undergoing infertility treatment, or those who find it difficult to imagine ways of living a fulfilled life without children.

I find myself increasingly drawn to examining the links and disjunctions between the diverse lives of infertile women, mothers and childless women, and the ways these can be used to make sense of women's reproductive decisions about motherhood and/or infertility. Examining the lives and identities of childless women is enabling me to consider the ways in which 'non-mothering' is a fulfilling and valid way of living and relating for women. This reflects on my own life but is also influenced by the recent increase in research and writing in this area (for example, Morrell, 1994).

In sum, then, my perspective on infertility has changed from that of 'insider' to that of 'Other', but coming as I have to this perspective from the position of insider, it is probably more appropriate to position myself as experienced or privileged 'Other', thereby raising questions about the usefulness of the insider/ outsider dualism.

References

Collins, P.H. (1994) 'Shifting the Centre: Race, Class and Feminist Theorising about Motherhood', in E.N. Glenn, G. Chang and L.R. Forcey (eds) *Mothering: Ideology Experience and Agency*. New York: Routledge.

Franklin, S. (1989) 'Deconstructing "Desperateness": The Social Construction of Infertility in Popular Representations of New Reproductive Technologies', in M. McNeil, I. Varcoe and S. Yearsley (eds) *The New Reproductive Technologies*. London: Macmillan.

Human Fertilization and Embryology Authority (1994) *Third Annual Report*. London: HFEA.

Morrell, C.M. (1994) *Unwomanly Conduct: The Challenges of Intentional Childlessness*. London: Routledge.

Pfeffer, N. (1987) 'Artificial Insemination, In-vitro Fertilization and the Stigma of Infertility', in M. Stanworth (ed.) *Reproductive Technologies: Gender, Motherhood and Medicine*. Cambridge: Polity.

Pfeffer, N. (1993) *The Stork and the Syringe: A Political History of Reproductive Medicine*. Cambridge: Polity.

Pfeffer, N. and Woollett, A. (1983) *Women's Experience of Infertility*. London: Virago.

Woollett, A. (1991) 'Having Children: Account of Childless Women and Women with Reproductive Problems', in A. Phoenix, A. Woollett and E. Lloyd (eds) *Motherhood: Meanings, Practice and Ideology*. London: Sage.

Woollett, A. (1992) 'Psychological Aspects of Infertility and Infertility Investigations', in P. Nicolson and J. Ussher (eds) *The Psychology of Women's Health and Health Care*. London: Macmillan.

Worcester, N. and Whatley, M. (1994) *Women's Health: Readings on Social, Economic and Political Issues*. Dubuque, IA: Kendall-Hunt.

9

Representing Gay Men with HIV/AIDS

Adrian Coyle

Traditional psychological research is predicated on the assumption that the subject of the research is 'Other' to the researcher. Drawing on notions of objectivity and scientific detachment, the researcher representing 'the Other' is able to warrant their representation. By contrast, representations of oneself – and others like oneself – risk accusations of bias: objectivity is supposedly contaminated by the researcher's own 'agenda' and 'issues'. The concern for avoiding 'bias' takes precedence over the potential for 'insider' knowledge of a research issue to enrich research work. As Stanley and Wise note, 'How many other professions . . . make such a fetish out of *ignorance*, elevate it into the only possible claim to professional competence?' (1993: 169, emphasis in original).

This traditional 'take' on psychological research was vividly brought home to me at the beginning of my PhD work on the construction of gay identity (Coyle, 1991). My supervisor obliquely raised questions of objectivity with me. Being unsure about whether to risk her personal and professional disapproval by declaring my sexual identity and hence my potential bias, to my eternal shame, I indignantly assured her that just because I was researching a gay issue, this did not mean that I was gay myself. I can clearly recall the cringeworthy parallel that I drew. Knowing that she had conducted research on unemployment, I suggested that a researcher does not need to be unemployed in order to produce high-quality research on the psychological effects of unemployment. Perhaps the memory of this betrayal of my sexuality, this representation of 'us' as 'the Other', hanging albatross-like around my neck, is what leads me to ensure that no one is left in any doubt about my sexual identity these days. But this experience suggests that I was aware of the desirability, in traditional psychological research, of claiming to represent 'the Other'.

Feminist (and other) researchers have explicitly challenged this traditional notion. In their work, many have stated what Burman (1994) has termed their 'speaking positions', i.e. the ideological frameworks which they bring to bear on their research. Many lesbian and gay researchers have also abandoned the mantle of objective detachment and write as members of the lesbian and gay communities which are the topics of their research. Some explicitly describe their speaking positions (for example, see the Boston Lesbian Psychologies Collective, 1987; Davies et al., 1993; Kitzinger, 1987), while others do so implicitly (for example, see Lampon's [1995] reference to lesbian women as 'we'). Far from detracting from the legitimacy of the research, dissolving the distinction between the researcher and 'the Other' is presented as a way of enhancing legitimacy. The researcher is assumed to be intimately acquainted with the context of her/his research topic and brings an 'insider' perspective to her/his analysis, thus avoiding the errors that less knowledgeable researchers might make. Of course, this assumes that the characteristics shared by the researcher and the participants (such as gender or sexual identity) are not overridden by potentially more significant differences (such as class and race) which render the parties largely alien to each other and which prevent them from entering each other's world. Failure to acknowledge this can lead to researchers expressing 'fictitious sympathy' for their research participants (Stanley and Wise, 1993).

These days, much of my own research and writing is concerned with various aspects of HIV/AIDS, including changes in gay men's sexual behaviour since the advent of HIV/AIDS (work that I was involved in during my time with Project SIGMA – see Davies et al., 1993); gay men's experiences of HIV testing (Beardsell and Coyle, forthcoming) and of other HIV/AIDS services (Coyle and Craig, 1993; Coyle and McGrellis, 1995); and gay men's experiences of AIDS-related bereavement (Coyle and Wright, 1994). Yet often in this work, the commonality between myself as a researcher and those whom I am researching seems tenuous, particularly when interviewing gay men who are HIV positive. In this case, I may share a major salient life experience with the participant (i.e. the experience of trying to construct and maintain a satisfying gay identity) but this commonality is swamped by the difference between us concerning HIV status. I often think things would be easier if I knew that I were HIV positive and could share this with those whom I am interviewing. However, the fact remains that I do not know my HIV status and have no real desire to find out.

Some fellow HIV/AIDS researchers of indeterminate HIV status with whom I have discussed this issue have sought to create some sort of link with HIV-positive research participants, reasoning 'well, I may not know my HIV status but I do act as if I were HIV positive', by which they usually mean practising safer sex. However, knowing that you are HIV positive involves much more than this: potentially, it involves having to live with a host of uncertainties about health, illness and physical and social functioning. Having listened to HIV-positive gay men recounting what are often incredibly traumatic experiences related to their HIV status, I would find it utterly patronizing to suggest a meaningful commonality of experience between myself and them. I can react honestly to those HIV-positive gay men whom I interview and can express anger, sympathy, pain or whatever other reaction is engendered in me by listening to them recount their experiences. Yet because of the difference in HIV status, I often think that we remain 'the Other' to each other.

In a research context, this 'Otherness' is problematic because researchers who study the experiences of any group of people may be regarded as spokespeople for this group and, in academic contexts and in the media, may be invited to comment on issues that affect this group. The only way of dealing honestly with this situation is to refuse to be drawn into a spokesperson role, which is not easy. Such a refusal often means that the researcher appears ill-informed about and not attuned to their research population, even if they explain why they cannot go beyond their interpretations of what their research participants have said.

How then can the process of representing 'the Other' be undertaken responsibly in research? Some researchers have recommended that research reports ought to be returned to those who participated in the research so that participants can assess the legitimacy of the researcher's interpretations of the data (for example, Kuzel and Like, 1991; Reason and Rowan, 1981). One of the aims of this procedure is to obtain a more equitable balance of power within the research process: instead of the researcher acting as the sole arbiter of the meaning, significance and implications of participants' experiences, participants are invited to play an active role in the process of representing their experiences. However, it has been pointed out that – because of differences in experience and training – researchers and research participants have differing relationships with the data and have different frameworks for interpreting the experiences under study (Currie, 1988; Opie, 1992). It should therefore be expected that there will be some disagreement over the interpretation of the data. For example, women participating in feminist research may not invoke the role of patriarchal social structures when making sense of their experiences because of the invisible organizational function of patriarchy in shaping an oppressive, 'taken-for-granted' world. Indeed, if they are aware of the negative aspects of the social representation of feminism, participants may resist the researcher locating their experiences within a feminist analytic framework. The question then arises as to how this or any disagreement over interpretation is resolved or otherwise dealt with. It has been contended that the usual courses of action in this case are to excise the contentious material from the research report (a dubious practice as the contentiousness of the material may indicate its significance to the research question) or to privilege the interpretation of the researcher or the participant (Opie, 1992). Too often feminist and other forms of qualitative research use this strategy of participant checking as a 'bumper sticker' to trumpet the 'authenticity' of the research, without any serious discussion of how the power dynamics of the research situation and any disagreements in interpretation were addressed.

In the literature on this issue, a tension can be detected between giving expression to the 'authentic voice' of the research participants on the one hand and the researcher's interpretations of the data on the other. Within feminism, the importance accorded to the former process springs from a desire to avoid perpetuating the distortion and discrediting of women's experiences by social scientists (Stanley and Wise, 1993). In practice, 'giving voice' in an authentic way may involve procedures such as including copious 'verbatim' quotations from participants in the research report and a deliberate avoidance by the researcher of squeezing replies into ill-fitting analytic categories. However, the extent to which this is possible is debatable. For example, in their original presentation of grounded theory, Glaser and Strauss (1967) note that the researcher does not approach the research task as a *tabula rasa*. Yet, elsewhere they seem to suggest that, properly conducted, the categorization of data can be carried out with minimal contamination from the researcher's framework of assumptions and her/his implicit theories about the research topic. Most writers on grounded theory today acknowledge that the researcher's interpretative framework is actively involved in the analytic process. This means that the end product of the research process arises from a 'flip-flop' between the data and the researcher's ideas (Henwood and Pidgeon, 1992).

It is the same with all other research approaches that claim to facilitate 'authentic' representation of 'the Other'. For example, within cooperative inquiry, the aim is to establish 'a dialogue between research workers and the grass-roots people with whom they work' (Reason, 1988: 2) and actively to involve them in the research process at every stage as co-researchers (Heron, 1981). Yet, in my experience of using this approach, despite making diligent efforts to ensure equality of voice, I found that ultimate authority still resided with the researchers, partly because of the demands of the research process and partly because of the expectations of the co-researchers/participants (Daniels and Coyle, 1993).

The idea that including copious amounts of 'verbatim' quotations in a research report helps to represent participants authentically is also contentious. So-called 'verbatim' quotations are seldom that. The transcription of interviews is rarely complete as contextual information such as participants' tone of voice, loudness, hesitations and non-word sounds are rarely included, except in conversation analytic studies and sometimes in discourse analytic research (Sandelowski, 1994). Also, not all data are included in a research report. A researcher may include many quotations from participants but these are located and function within an overall research narrative that the researcher artfully constructs. Once again, the voices of both the participants and the researcher intermingle in any qualitative research report. Claims concerning the capacity of any research approach to reflect the voices of research participants in an 'uncontaminated' way are simply elements of a discourse of legitimation.

There is also a very good practical reason for deliberately not producing a research report overladen with direct quotation. Those who take part in research on issues that are important to them often do so because they wish to have their experiences aired in a public forum in the hope that this will lead to change that will benefit them and/or others like them. This may also be one of the researcher's aims. Indeed, one of the aims of feminist research has been defined as the instigation of social change that is of benefit to women (Stanley, 1990). In much of my HIV/AIDS research, participants expressed the wish that HIV/AIDS services would be improved or expanded as a result of the research. If I had simply presented their accounts in full or in a slightly edited form, I would have ended up with a thick tome of diverse anecdotes which would surely have been ignored by relevant policy makers. For the same reason, there are problems with Opie's (1992) suggestion that one way to deal meaningfully with disagreements between researchers and participants over the interpretation of data is to highlight areas of contention and interpretative tension within the research report. She acknowledges that to do so may create 'a much more broken and fissured text' (1992: 63), which may be acceptable if writing for an academic audience but is more problematic in contexts where research has been funded by organizations which expect concise, traditionally structured research reports. It is, however, possible to acknowledge and explore areas of disagreement within a traditional report framework without creating a postmodernist, polyvocal but inaccessible text. The problem, of course, is that this exploration is conducted from the researcher's perspective, again privileging her/his voice over those of the research participants.

In writing up my various studies on HIV/AIDS, I was acutely aware of my responsibility to my participants to help effect beneficial change and so had to produce reports that would be accessible to and understandable by those who were in a position to initiate change. In practice, this entailed examining the accounts given by different respondents closely, systematically and repeatedly; being aware of and making explicit my own expectations of the data in the analytic and interpretative processes; and then drawing upon my knowledge of the subject matter and the political context of HIV/AIDS services to make practical suggestions for service development, based upon the recurrent themes in my analysis of participants' accounts and feedback on the analysis from key informants in the HIV/AIDS field (including research participants where possible). This has been my imperfect response to the realization that it is not possible to produce an absolutely 'true' or 'authentic' reflection of 'the Other' because any representation is filtered through the lens of the researcher's understanding and is but one of many potential representations. Instead, it is possible, through systematic analysis, to produce a representation of participants' core, common concerns that stands a reasonable chance of effecting change that will be beneficial to them.

References

Beardsell, S. and Coyle, A. (forthcoming) 'A Review of Research on the Nature and Quality of HIV Testing Services: A Proposal for Process-Based Studies', *Social Science & Medicine*.

Boston Lesbian Psychologies Collective (ed.) (1987) *Lesbian Psychologies*. Chicago: University of Illinois Press.

Burman, E. (1994) 'Experience, Identities and Alliances: Jewish Feminism and Feminist Psychology', *Feminism & Psychology* 4: 155–78.

Coyle, A. (1991) 'The Construction of Gay Identity: Vols 1 & 2', unpublished PhD thesis, University of Surrey.

Coyle, A. and Craig, M. (1993) *A Need to Listen: Service Users' Views of HIV/AIDS Services in North East London*. London: Association of London Authorities/North East Thames Regional Health Authority.

Coyle, A. and McGrellis, S. (1995) 'Strategies for Dealing with Problems Associated with Use of Services for HIV Infection and AIDS Out of Region: Views of Providers and Users', *British Medical Journal* 210: 1636–8.

Coyle, A. and Wright, C. (1994) 'AIDS-related Bereavement among Gay Men: Advancing Psychological Theory and Practice', paper presented at AIDS' Impact: 2nd International Conference on Biopsychosocial Aspects of HIV Infection, Brighton, 7–10 July.

Currie, D. (1988) 'Re-thinking What We Do and How We Do It: A Study of Reproductive Decisions', *Canadian Review of Sociology and Anthropology* 25: 231–53.

Daniels, M. and Coyle, A. (1993) '"Health Dividends": The Use of Co-operative Inquiry as a Health Promotion Intervention with a Group of Unemployed Women', in D.R. Trent and C. Reed (eds) *Promotion of Mental Health: Volume 2*. Aldershot: Avebury.

Davies, P.M., Hickson, F.C.I., Weatherburn, P. and Hunt, A.J. (1993) *Sex, Gay Men and AIDS*. London: Falmer.

Glaser, B.G. and Strauss, A.L. (1967) *The Discovery of Grounded Theory: Strategies for Qualitative Research*. New York: Aldine.

Henwood, K.L. and Pidgeon, N.F. (1992) 'Qualitative Research and Psychological Theorizing', *British Journal of Psychology* 83: 97–111.

Heron, J. (1981) 'Philosophical Basis for a New Paradigm', in P. Reason and J. Rowan (eds) *Human Inquiry: A Sourcebook of New Paradigm Research*. Chichester: John Wiley.

Kitzinger, C. (1987) *The Social Construction of Lesbianism*. London: Sage.

Kuzel, A.J. and Like, R.C. (1991) 'Standards of Trustworthiness for Qualitative Studies in Primary Care', in P. Norton, M. Stewart, F. Tudiver, M. Bass and E. Dunn (eds) *Primary Care Research: Traditional and Innovative Approaches*. Newbury Park, CA: Sage.

Lampon, D. (1995) 'Lesbians and Safer Sex Practices', *Feminism & Psychology* 5: 170–6.

Opie, A. (1992) 'Qualitative Research, Appropriation of the "Other" and Empowerment', *Feminist Review* Spring: 52–69.

Reason, P. (1988) 'Introduction', in P. Reason (ed.) *Human Inquiry in Action: Developments in New Paradigm Research*. London: Sage.

Reason, P. and Rowan, J. (1981) 'Issues of Validity in New Paradigm Research', in P. Reason and J. Rowan (eds) *Human Inquiry: A Sourcebook of New Paradigm Research*. Chichester: John Wiley.

Sandelowski, M. (1994) 'Notes on Transcription', *Research in Nursing & Health* 17: 311–14.

Stanley, L. (1990) 'Feminist Praxis and the Academic Mode of Production: An Editorial Introduction', in L. Stanley (ed.) *Feminist Praxis: Research, Theory and Epistemology in Feminist Sociology*. London: Routledge.

Stanley, L. and Wise, S. (1993) *Breaking Out Again: Feminist Ontology and Epistemology*, 2nd edn. London: Routledge.

10

The Seduction of Sameness: Similarity and Representing the Other

Tracey L. Hurd and Alice McIntyre

There has been much discussion in feminist research of the inherent problems of representing the 'Other' in ways that distance the participants from one another, positioning one as subordinate, and therefore one as privileged. This is clearly exemplified in discussions about men studying women or white women studying women of colour. The complexities of sensitively negotiating the boundaries that emerge out of difference have been eloquently explored (see, for example, Fine, 1992, 1994; Franz and Stewart, 1994; Lykes, 1989, 1994; Morawski, 1994). What has been ignored is the problematic dynamics of representing the Other, that are manifested in research in which the participants are marked more by similarity than by difference. We suggest that *sameness* distances the participants (researcher and researched) from a critical reflexive research process and privileges one point of view over another. This often results in the misrepresentation of the research participants' stories. In this chapter we will explore the tacit assumptions of sameness that operate in two distinct areas of research. As feminist researchers, we argue that the stillness of sameness is an illusion that conceals inherent disparities in social science research.

Although we locate ourselves in different research paradigms, we experience moments of unspoken connection with our participants that seem strikingly similar. As two white female researchers, we bring to our work both complementary and contradictory perspectives. We bring differing life histories to similar experiences as white women in academia. We both explore feminist psychology, yet our work is differentially situated. I (Alice) engage in participatory action research, exploring how white female student teachers make meaning of whiteness. I (Tracey) study the social construction of gender in the language and play of young children. At times we feel our work couldn't be more disparate. Yet there is a co-feeling that emerges in discussions of our work. Although our shared curiosity about the relatedness we feel with our participants invites interesting dialogue, it is the shared discomfort with the unexplored experiences of sameness that informs this chapter.

White-on-White Feminist Participatory Research

I (Alice) recently conducted a feminist participatory research project aimed at exploring the meaning of whiteness with 13 white, middle- and upper-middle-class female undergraduate student teachers at a private northeastern university. I share similar points of entry into the study of whiteness with the participants of my/our research. We share characteristics that profoundly shape our life experiences: sex, race, some aspects of class, and choice of profession. We differ most noticeably in age and level of education.

Through the use of qualitative participatory research methods (e.g. interviews and weekly group sessions), we examined the various ways the participants made meaning of whiteness. My research foci were self- and collective-reflection, collaboration with the participants and a critical analysis of how we/they created knowledge and made meaning of whiteness. My role within this project was not defined by the traditional researcher/subject paradigm. I was the primary researcher responsible for fulfilling the requirements of a dissertation, while simultaneously situating myself as an active agent of change within the research process itself. Such a participatory engagement required that I grapple with uncertainties that emerged while 'working the hyphen' (Fine, 1994) as a researcher-participant.

During one of the group sessions, the participants discussed how they experience being white student teachers interacting with black children. The following is a brief exchange that occurred between two of the participants:

> *Faith*: I think little black kids love white girls. Like I don't like to make that little stereotype but like . . . they play with your hair . . . They just love you.
> *Michelle*: I had so many kids, so many black children, like if I wore [my hair] down at camp this summer, if I wore it down, it was inevitable that they would come and touch my hair. It was inevitable. I I never, if I wore it down, there was never a day where they didn't come and touch my hair.

This exchange was accompanied by a number of the other participants nodding in agreement, sharing similar stories of black children playing with their earrings, sitting on their laps and braiding their blonde hair. My own memories of teaching placed me in familiar territory with the speakers. This cogent feeling of similarity distanced me from countering their assumptions and distorted realities. This affective pull of sameness blurred my vision. The participants' stories resonated so closely to mine that I maintained a 'racially privileged naiveté' (Roman, 1993a: 189) and failed to challenge the participants' constructions of whiteness. Although I was clearly frustrated and angered by their interpretation of the relationship between black children and white teachers, I colluded in the macro-narrative by closing the session with a story about my early days of teaching and the experience of having my hair cornrolled by a fourth grade black girl who lived next door to me. It wasn't until a few days later that my advisor, having listened to the taped session, challenged my reasoning for sharing that story and forced me to see the danger of aligning myself with the participants' lived, *but critically unexamined*, life experiences.

The research question was: How do white female student teachers make meaning of whiteness? This question mandated that I provide space for the sharing of lived experiences. At the same time it was my responsibility, as a feminist participatory researcher, to interrupt what I refer to as 'white talk', talk that serves to insulate white people from examining their (our) role in the perpetuation of racism. The dilemma and risk is when white talk resonates so closely with our collective experiences, that we fail to challenge the 'epistemic standpoints of [our] white students . . .' (Roman, 1993b: 81) and of ourselves. This is especially difficult at moments when the seduction of sameness co-opts the research process.

Children, Feminism and Positivist Developmental Research

The tension between the feminist calling to examine and re-examine assumptions underlying all research and the paradoxically apolitical stance of much child development literature has informed much of my (Tracey's) thinking about developmental psychology. As Erica Burman (1991: 151) pondered in the first issue of *Feminism & Psychology*, '[Is] developmental psychology inevitably tied to normative social interests regulating families, gender and sexuality?' I would argue that it is, but the path to that acknowledgement is blocked by the reliance on methods and assumptions that devalue reflexivity.

In my dissertation research I tried to merge some feminist criticisms of developmental research (Burman, 1991; Parlee, 1992; Unger, 1990) into the design of a positivist study of children's same-gender play. I sought to triangulate methodologies to mitigate against the pitfalls of uni-dimensional research (Reinharz, 1992). As part of this research, I videotaped white middle-class children at play in pairs with a 'mini-world', a shallow container with pebbles, driftwood and rocks with an accompanying assortment of small animal and child figures. As a psychologist, former preschool teacher, mother and former white middle-class child myself, I watched the children with multiply informed expectations. Sometimes I felt like I could almost predict what a child was going to say or do – a feeling that should resonate with excitement for the positivist researcher, guided by null hypotheses ready to be disproved! Instead, I often felt disquieted. I felt that what I was experiencing was, most simply, a feeling of similarity. Although no longer a child, I felt like an insider with the children I was studying – that I owned some of the experience that they were now having.

I confronted this issue in the manner that has, I believe, been the traditional path. I retreated to positivism to try to extricate my 'insider knowledge' from creating pictures that may not have reflected the children's experience. I took refuge in a research design that assured at least some breadth to my analysis. In that design, I increased the level of 'Othering' to counteract my heartfelt similarity to my research participants. I analysed both the children's language and social interaction, with methodologies designed to capture complex profiles (Bronson, 1994; Hurd, 1994). Like decades of researchers before me, I sought to remove myself as a participant voice, and make more objective the necessarily relational process of research (Morawski, 1994).

Cognitive developmental theories have legitimized the Othering of children as necessary, because of their less 'mature' reasoning. Assumptions of sameness – of familiarity with children that arises out of our shared legacy of having been children and having lives variously touched by children – go unproblematized. Thus the inherent subjugation that occurs between the researcher and the researched is legitimized in research with children. In my own case, I layered positivist methodologies to produce multiple lenses. I hoped that these lenses would offer some reflexivity to the research. But while there may be promise in such layering, I'm uncertain if it aids or hinders a feminist understanding of children (Morawski, 1994). Perhaps it simply multiplicatively privileges the researcher-participant over the researched-participant. It is clear, however, that exploring methodologies and thinking critically about resulting participant relationships is a first step towards a feminist psychology of children.

Conclusion

Have we been so caught up in critically examining difference, that we have silently privileged our similarity? Our experiences attest to the inherent struggles of contemplating this question. We now suggest that we learn from the many fine models of sensitively representing difference (Comas-Dias and Greene, 1994; Fine, 1994; hooks, 1984; Kitzinger, 1987; Lykes, 1994; Stewart, 1994) and apply them to our understanding of similarity. In this way we can de-privilege the historical legacy of sameness in psychology and work towards acknowledging the complexities inherent in all feminist research.

Note

The authors participated equally in the writing of this chapter and are listed in alphabetical order. They wish to thank M. Brinton Lykes for her comments on a draft of this chapter.

References

Bronson, Martha B. (1994) 'The Usefulness of an Observational Measure of Young Children's Social and Mastery Behaviors in Early Childhood Classrooms', *Early Childhood Research Quarterly* 9: 19–43.

Burman, Erica (1991) 'Power, Gender and Developmental Psychology', *Feminism & Psychology* 1 (1): 141–52.

Comas-Dias, Lillian and Greene, Beverly (eds) (1994) *Women of Color: Integrating Ethnic and Gender Identities in Psychotherapy*. New York: Guilford.

Fine, Michelle (ed.) (1992) *Disruptive Voices: The Possibilities of Feminist Research*. Ann Arbor, MI: University of Michigan.

Fine, Michelle (1994) 'Working the Hyphens: Reinventing Self and Other in Qualitative Research', in Norman Denzin and Yvonna Lincoln (eds) *Handbook of Qualitative Research*. Thousand Oaks, CA: Sage.

Franz, Carol E. and Stewart, Abigail J. (eds) (1994) *Women Creating Lives: Identities, Resilience, and Resistance*. Boulder, CO: Westview.

hooks, bell (1984) *Feminist Theory: From Margin to Center*. Boston: South End.

Hurd, Tracey L. (1994) 'The Construction of Social Competence and Linguistic Style in the Same-Gender Dyadic Play of Preschool Children', unpublished PhD dissertation, Boston College, Chestnut Hill, MA.

Kitzinger, Celia (1987) *The Social Construction of Lesbianism*. London: Sage.

Lykes, M. Brinton (1989) 'Dialogue with Guatemalan Indian Women: Critical Perspectives on Constructing Collaborative Research', in Rhoda K. Unger (ed.) *Representations: Social Constructions of Gender*. Amityville, NY: Baywood.

Lykes, M. Brinton (1994) 'Speaking Against the Silence: One Maya Woman's Exile and Return', in Carol E. Franz and Abigail J. Stewart (eds) *Women Creating Lives: Identities, Resilience, and Resistance*. Boulder, CO: Westview.

Morawski, Jill G. (1994) *Practicing Feminisms, Reconstructing Psychology: Notes on a Liminal Science*. Ann Arbor, MI: University of Michigan.

Parlee, Mary Brown (1992) 'Feminism and Psychology', in Sue R. Zalk and J. Gordon-Keltner (eds) *Revolutions in Knowledge: Feminism in the Social Sciences*. Boulder, CO: Westview.

Reinharz, Shulamit (1992) *Feminist Methods in Social Science Research*. New York: Oxford University.

Roman, Leslie G. (1993a) '"On the Ground" with Antiracist Pedagogy and Raymond Williams's Unfinished Project to Articulate a Socially Transformative Critical Realism', in Dennis L. Dworkin and Leslie G. Roman (eds) *Views Beyond the Border Country: Raymond Williams and Cultural Politics*. New York: Routledge.

Roman, Leslie G. (1993b) 'White is a Color! White Defensiveness, Postmodernism, and Anti-racist Pedagogy', in Cameron McCarthy and Warren Crichlow (eds) *Race, Identity and Representation in Education*. New York: Routledge.

Stewart, Abigail J. (1994) 'Toward a Feminist Strategy for Studying Women's Lives', in Carol E. Franz and Abigail J. Stewart (eds) *Women Creating Lives: Identities, Resilience, and Resistance*. Boulder, CO: Westview.

Unger, Rhoda K. (1990) 'Imperfect Reflections of Reality: Psychology Constructs Gender', in Rachel T. Hare-Mustin and Jeanne Marecek (eds) *Making a Difference: Psychology and the Construction of Gender*. New Haven, CT: Yale.

11

White Woman Researcher – Black Women Subjects

Rosalind Edwards

Can, or should, white middle-class women academics, such as myself, research and represent in writing the voices of black, mainly working-class, women? For me, the question has always been another way around: can I possibly be justified in leaving them out? This is because I have never set out to interview black women per se. Rather, my research so far has been about particular groups of women, of whom black women formed a part. Black women were a substantial proportion of the population I drew upon in my studies of: mature students in British polytechnics (now universities) and the way in which they combine education and family life; lone mothers' use of day care and their uptake of paid work; and homeless mothers' access to child health services and their families' placement in a particular type of temporary accommodation. I want what I have to say on these topics to be based upon the experiences of *all* of those in these situations.

My commitment to include black women in my research does not mean that I hold a simplistic view of black women (or indeed, white women) as an internally homogenous group. Specific individuals cannot represent or speak on behalf of all members of a social group. I am concerned, though, that my work is informed by the differential experiences of women of different positions and backgrounds. Black feminists have – to great effect – challenged the universalist pretensions contained in much white western feminist research and writing. They argue this work is based upon white women's experiences, and that white feminists should acknowledge the ways in which social divisions around race differentially structure women's positions and experiences (for example, Carby, 1982; Phoenix, 1986; Hill Collins, 1990). I want to take account of this in my explorations – however partial – of women's experiences in specific situations.

Positions

Some black feminists would say I cannot do this. They have gone further than critiquing white feminism's universalist pretensions, to say that white women cannot possibly understand and represent black women's subjectivity and social positioning. At two recent conferences this point was strongly put to me by black feminist researchers in discussions following their own papers. They contended that, as a white woman, my own social position and lived experience meant that either I would not have access to, or would not fully understand and/or would stereotypically misrepresent black women's accounts of their lives. In each case, I argued back. I am not only a white middle-class woman; I am also able-bodied, heterosexual, married–divorced–married, a mother, Jewish; I was a teenager in the 1960s, live in a south coast seaside town, etc., etc. Can I only research women in these positions? In fact, I have been in some of the categories I have researched: as a mature student, a lone mother and part of a homeless family. Was I better placed than others, therefore, to represent these experiences?

The concerns of some black feminist researchers, however, deserve more serious consideration. Most of the elements of the identity I have given myself above are to do with specific and diverse positions in relation to which I can claim a shared experience with some Others, including some black women. But, to be a 'child' of the 1960s, twice married, a mature student and so on, is not necessarily to share a subordinated subject position, and to have to live with and challenge the power relations around oppressions of race and class, etc. Aspects of this perspective would be missing if my work were based on the experiences of white women alone. Indeed, it is black women's resistances – specifically those of African-Caribbean women – that have led me to think about whether or not I can research and understand their lives (currently I think I can) and about whether or not I can represent such understanding in academic writing (here I am more ambivalent).

Resistance to Research Participation

The concerns that some black feminists have about white women's (even if feminist) ability to understand and represent black women's accounts of their lives also appear to be held by black women who are potential research participants. I may not feel justified in omitting black women from my research; but they may not wish to take part in the process.

Gaining access to black women as a white researcher has not been an easy process for me. Very few black mature women students responded to my postal written requests (sent out to relevant women of all races/ethnicities) for interviews discussing how they combined their educational and family lives. Moreover, some of them were angry about being asked to take part in the research and went as a group to complain to their course director. What, they demanded, was the institution doing allowing a white middle-class researcher to get in touch with black women asking to talk to them in their homes about private matters? (Their interpretation of my generic request.) I had a similar experience in a later piece of research on lone mothers' use of day care, in which I asked (so persuasively!) for lone mother interviewees in a letter distributed by the co-ordinator (a white woman) of an all-day playgroup in a multi-ethnic area. Here again, in a meeting at the playgroup, many of the mothers, overwhelmingly black, agreed that they did not wish to participate in the research because they trusted neither the motives nor its likely outcome.

In both instances I was brought up short; although not so much the second time. I had been jolted by the meeting of my own identity – Ros Edwards, approachable woman researcher who had been a mature student and a lone mother, and was 'on their side' – with a racialized categorization as an untrustworthy white institutional figure. This categorization was not resonant with my experiences and conception of self. Black women, of course, are likely to live with such enforced racialized 'Otherness' far more often than I do. While in those moments of refusing to take part in research black women exercise some power, it is my social location as white middle class that protects me from many such categorizations as 'Other'.

In the case of the mature students, I defined the black women's responses as resulting from their experience of educational and other public institutions as white middle-class places and as oppressive. The black mature women students' interpretation of my request for interviewees reveals how acutely aware they were of issues of race when white institutions take an interest in them; even supposedly neutral educational institutions. I saw their resistance as coming from their desire to exercise control (where they could) over their lives through not revealing intimate details (Edwards, 1990).

In the case of the lone mothers, I attributed their reaction to the political context whereby the quality of their parenting was questioned and the British government had just introduced the Child Support Act in an attempt to reduce lone parent families' reliance on state benefits (Edwards, 1993). Interviews with black lone mothers for a later piece of research (mentioned below) reveal that they may regard the British government's preoccupation with lone mothers as a covert attack on black family structures (Song and Edwards, 1995). That my research on lone mothers' use of day care was carried out for an independent voluntary organization held no sway with the black lone mothers. Again, I was a white institutional figure.

Of course, yet another explanation of black women's negative responses to my written approaches might be that I am not very good at my job. In my defence, and from my point of view, in both pieces of research white women did respond positively to exactly the same requests; and other white women researchers have made public similar difficulties in contacting and including black women in their research (for example, Cannon et al., 1991; Jewish Women in London Group, 1989; Thorogood, 1987; Walton, 1986). While I still think that my original explanations hold, I have come to wonder if there is more to be gleaned from this situation.

Other white researchers, in addition to myself, note far less difficulty in gaining access to black people if they approach through social networks and/or ask face-to-face for interviewees (Cannon et al., 1991; Foner, 1979; Walton, 1986). I have found this to be so as well in subsequent pieces of research on homeless mothers and on lone mothers' uptake of paid work.

In both the research studies I have outlined above, black women did not only make individual decisions about not taking part in the research, but came together to resist as a group. Their response to my request for interviewees was not merely on an individual basis, but was also the result of a collective dialogue.

I now think this process may throw some light on the nature of the academic knowledge endeavour in which I am involved.

Dialogue

In attempting to understand both black women's resistance and the academic knowledge endeavour, I have been especially influenced by Patricia Hill Collins' work on black feminist thought (1990). Hill Collins explores the alternative ways that African-American women, in particular, have of producing, recognizing and validating knowledge, forged within the interlocking oppressions of sex, race and class. She argues that Eurocentric, masculinist knowledge suppresses and devalues these alternative knowledge processes. Hill Collins makes a distinction between knowledge and wisdom. Within academic knowledge, wisdom is not part of knowing (see also Luttrell, 1992). For African-American women, the connection of experience and knowledge that forms wisdom is necessary: 'Knowledge without wisdom is adequate for the powerful, but wisdom is essential to the survival of the subordinate' (Hill Collins, 1990: 208).

Hill Collins also states that wisdom does not necessarily require you to have experienced a situation for yourself; but you do need to have been part of an empathetic dialogue with those who have. In this dialogue there is no need to 'decentre' anyone in order to centre someone else; rather, power dynamics are fluid, and the centre is constantly and appropriately pivoted. Each participant's experience is partial, but is also valid. This, I extrapolate (in my own interests!) to mean that it is possible for white women to take part in dialogue and to gain the 'wisdom' necessary to research and understand black women's lives. I can both retain my social location and identity (as white, middle-class, Jewish, twice-married, etc.) and shift to see black women's social location and identity in their own terms. My ambivalence, as I have said, is around representing the results of this process (in the form of interview material about black women's lives) in the academic mode.

Hill Collins refers to taking part in an empathetic dialogue as an interactive 'call-and-response mode'. Thus knowledge/wisdom comes not to be individually owned, but becomes part of the social group's way of knowing about the world. She argues that, in order to resist domination and survive the interlocking oppressions of race, sex and, often, class, African-American women are embedded in call-and-response networks. In Britain, black women's collective rejection of my written requests for interviewees and their acceptance of networked face-to-face requests, for me, are a concrete working of this process.

Academics, however, are part of a very different, and more individualized, form of call-and-response: a critical 'objective' pedagogy that is a sort of 'survival of the fittest'. Arguments that can withstand the greatest assault and survive intact become validated. Hill Collins regards this adversarial method of deciding academic knowledge claims as weighted in favour of those who made the rules – those with more social, economic and professional power. How can any empathetic dialogue have a space within a social scientific way of knowing which postulates a theorizing researching elite as against the experiencing researched subjects? In order to meet the academic knowledge criteria and validation process, we have to recast, and thus distort, the dialogue so as to present a knowledge hierarchy. In presenting my research, I must 'decentre' my research subjects and 'centre' my expert academic voice.

Lacking a Firm Conclusion

The knowledge hierarchy both attracts and repels me. On the one hand, I want my arguments about black – and other – women's lives in specific situations to be heard and to be accepted as having a valid academic status. I am prepared to be adversarial with other academics in order to achieve this, and to utilize the status of academic knowledge-making in dissemination to a wider public. Indeed, it is the very power of 'expert' knowledge that I and other academics can seek to use in challenging public agendas on specific topics.

On the other hand, attempts to intervene in public agendas carry dangers as well as possibilities, in terms of the ends to which material about black women's lives may be put. I also wonder what power relations I perpetuate when I take part in the academic 'survival of the fittest' process. These may well be the very dangers, processes and relations that the black women I approached for interviews resisted, by refusing to take part in my research.

Nevertheless, given that I am an academic woman researcher and enjoy the status I worked so hard to achieve from being a mature student, I continue to work towards including black women in the research I carry out and to approaching them in ways they find acceptable. I have no easy answers to the problems and contradictions of my current thoughts. Nevertheless, as many black feminists have made so clear, I feel that to produce representations and theorizations of the experiences of women in particular situations that are based on white women's accounts alone, but which have wider pretensions, is even more indefensible.

Note

Several reviewers made detailed and helpful comments on this chapter. Space does not allow me to do justice to all the issues they raised, but I am sure my work in the future will benefit from their contributions.

References

Carby, H. (1982) 'White Women Listen! Black Feminism and the Boundaries of Sisterhood', in Centre for Contemporary Cultural Studies (ed.) *The Empire Strikes Back*. London: Hutchinson.

Cannon, L.W., Higginbotham, E. and Leung, M.L.A. (1991) 'Race and Class Bias in Qualitative Research on Women', in J. Lober and S.A. Farrell (eds) *The Social Construction of Gender*. New York: Sage.

Edwards, R. (1990) 'Connecting Method and Epistemology: A White Woman Interviewing Black Women', *Women's Studies International Forum* 13 (5): 477–90.

Edwards, R. (1993) 'Evaluation of the Department of Health's New Under Fives Initiative Lone Parents Projects', a report for the National Children's Bureau.

Foner, N. (1979) *Jamaica Farewell: Jamaican Migrants in London*. London: Routledge and Kegan Paul.

Hill Collins, P. (1990) *Black Feminist Thought: Knowledge, Consciousness and the Politics of Empowerment*. New York: Harper Collins.

Jewish Women in London Group (1989) *Generations of Memories: Voices of Jewish Women*. London: The Women's Press.

Luttrell, W. (1992) 'Working-class Women's Ways of Knowing: Effects of Gender, Race and Class', in J. Wrigley (ed.) *Education and Gender Equality*. London: Falmer.

Phoenix, A. (1986) 'Theories of Gender and Black Families', in G. Weiner and M. Arnot (eds) *Gender Under Scrutiny: New Inquiries in Education*. London: Hutchinson/The Open University.

Song, M. and Edwards, R. (1995) '"Babymothers": Raising Questions about Perspectives on Black Lone Motherhood', paper presented at the Social Policy Association annual conference, Sheffield Hallam University, 18–20 July.

Thorogood, N. (1987) 'Race, Class and Gender: The Politics of Housework', in J. Brannen and G. Wilson (eds) *Give and Take in Families: Studies in Resource Distribution*. London: Allen and Unwin.

Walton, H. (1986) 'White Researchers and Racism', Working Paper No. 10, University of Manchester.

12

Between a Rock and a Hard Place: The Politics of White Feminists Conducting Research on Black Women in South Africa

Diana E.H. Russell

I was born in South Africa into a white, upper-class, English-speaking, Anglican family. In 1962, at the age of 22, I joined the African Resistance Movement, an underground revolutionary organization that bombed government property to destabilize the economy and to protest against apartheid. I left South Africa to study in the United States of America before this organization was decimated by the police in 1964. I ended up staying in the USA and making my home base in the San Francisco Bay Area. In my early 30s, I became a feminist, a perspective which has been central to my life and work ever since.

Still deeply troubled by apartheid, I went back to South Africa in 1987 to interview women in the liberation movement, most of whom were black. My goal in 'representing the Other' was to provide them with the opportunity to publicize their cause in the USA and to move Americans to support the armed struggle against apartheid. Most recently, I conducted interviews with incest survivors in South Africa between 1991 and 1993 (Russell, 1995). Each project posed special dilemmas in terms of 'representing the Other,' but here I will focus on the more recent experience and the special problems of conducting research on a taboo subject.

My objective was to provide research material that would support the South African women who were demanding that violence against women be given greater priority. Most anti-apartheid supporters considered the oppression of women to be a trivial and irrelevant problem, distracting progressive people from the struggle against racism. I wanted to publicize some accounts of women's personal experiences of male violence, because such stories have often succeeded in breaking through people's intellectual and ideological defences, making it more difficult for them to dismiss these manifestations of sexism as insignificant.

I decided to focus on incestuous abuse – the most neglected and misunderstood form of violence against females in South Africa. I hoped that this choice would help to bring this particularly taboo and heinous form of sexual exploitation out of the crowded South African closet. Feminists have been quite successful at raising people's awareness about rape in South Africa, starting the first Rape Crisis

Centre in 1976, and the first battered women's shelter several years later (Mayne, 1989). But they have been much slower to confront the problem of incestuous abuse.

Were I to have interviewed incest survivors in proportion to the racial composition of South Africa in 1991, 75 per cent of them would have been African, 14 per cent white, 9 per cent coloured and 3 per cent Indian South African. Thus most of my interviewees would have been of another race than mine. More importantly, they would have been from racial/ethnic groups that have long been – and continue to be – severely oppressed by white South Africans.

Although traditional survey researchers have often denied the relevance of power and status differences between interviewers and interviewees, as feminists we must strive to be aware of the impact these differences typically have on the quality and content of the information obtained. This serious methodological problem would have been compounded by the political problems entailed had I, a white woman, interviewed black incest survivors. In the USA, Britain and Germany, many feminists of colour, as well as white feminists, would consider my conducting such interviews to be politically insensitive and unacceptable. Even were I to disagree with this assessment, the fact that many other feminists subscribe to this view would probably diminish, or even destroy, the positive consequences that might otherwise result from this research.

On the other hand, it could be argued that it would be wrong – perhaps even an example of cultural imperialism – to assume that the political assessment of my conducting this research would be the same in South Africa as in western nations. Indeed, the very definition of racism frequently differs in South Africa and the USA.

For example, an African-American feminist took me to task because she felt I was being critical of a black South African woman's notion of feminism in an article I had written (1989a). I disagreed that I had been critical, but more to the point, I told her that I had asked the two black South African feminists whose views were the subject of this piece, for their corrections or objections, if any, before I submitted it for publication. They both loved it. The African-American woman considered this irrelevant. I wondered if this wasn't an example of cultural imperialism: assuming that she knew what black South Africans *should* feel about the article, assuming that her principles, according to which I was guilty of racism, were superior to theirs, and assuming that she was in a position to judge the situation better than I was, although she had never visited South Africa or been a student of South African politics.

The dominant liberation politics in South Africa, reflected in the policies of the African National Congress (ANC), explicitly rejects evaluating someone on the basis of their race/colour/ethnicity. Not a single black South African anti-apartheid activist whom I requested to interview for my book, *Lives of Courage: Women for a New South Africa* (1989b), expressed disapproval of the fact that I was white and/or suspicion of my motives. To assume that these women were all being Aunt Tomasinas, because this is how such behaviour might be interpreted in the USA, for example, could be viewed as insulting, matronizing and imperialistic.

Given the demographic and political realities described above, additional dilemmas were posed by the research topic itself – incestuous abuse. Women's incest stories typically portray their families in an extremely negative light, often evoking readers' feelings of anger, disgust, outrage, contempt and moral condemnation. Although the research would merely reflect the ratio of blacks to whites in the population at large, the experience of reading seven gruesome portraits of black families for every one such portrait of a white family would inevitably create the impression that black families are uglier and more reprehensible than white families. Statements by me to the contrary would be unlikely to erase this impression. In a country still dominated at the time by whites, whose racism continues to be deeply entrenched, this depiction of the black community would undoubtedly exacerbate white racism.

Many white South Africans smugly believe that incestuous abuse rarely occurs in their communities, yet believe that it is common in black communities. Some feminists and black South Africans, very few of whom are feminist, would argue that research that appears to reinforce rather than dispel this illusion, is irresponsible and racist. They might well denounce me as a racist for bolstering destructive stereotypes of the black community.

The negative impression of black families could also reinforce some black people's already internalized beliefs that blacks are more likely to commit heinous personal crimes of violence than are whites. White South African feminist Ann Mayne notes that although:

> a significantly higher incidence of rape of black women by white men was reported to the [South African] police than vice versa, both white and black audiences are surprised when we report these statistics because they've really bought the myth . . . that whites don't do such nasty things as rape and batter their wives. (1989: 232–3)

For these and other research-related reasons (for example, it was much easier for me to locate volunteer incest survivors who were white), I stopped interviewing black survivors and limited my study to white women. This choice was also fraught with dilemmas, however, including the fact that this radical change in research design got me into considerable trouble with my white-dominated South African funding agency – the Human Sciences Research Council (HSRC). Boycotted for years by progressive South Africans for serving the interests of the white Afrikaner government, the HSRC was supposed to be cleaning up its act in 1993 by becoming more open to the concerns of black people. My decision to limit my study to white survivors was contrary to the new image they wanted to project. Despite the lengthy rationale I provided for the HSRC, and despite their gross under-funding of this research (approximately $8000 for a full-time, one-year research project), they threatened to withdraw some of their funds.

Two of the reviewers of my Final Report on this research questioned my objectivity (as if this were a quality that they possessed). One of them objected to my statement that most white South Africans would be shocked to find out how much incest was happening in their families, given their racist belief that such despicable behaviour is largely confined to black families (personal communication by Evaluator 2, 11 May 1994). The other reviewer commented:

The impression has been created, rightly or wrongly, that this research was done from a feminist frame of reference and the question can be posed whether this has influenced the objectivity of the researcher and consequently the scientific value of the investigation. (personal communication by Evaluator 3, 11 May 1994)

Having abandoned my original research design primarily because of my concerns about the likely racist consequences does not free me from charges of racism. Some people, both within and outside South Africa, will almost certainly consider me racist for limiting my research to whites. Because the findings will be limited to a small group of white women, they may more readily be dismissed as insignificant and unworthy of serious attention, particularly by the new, democratically elected government in South Africa. The problem isn't only in the small size of the white community. If a member of the 'coloured' community (only 9 per cent of the population) were to limit her/his research to 'coloured' women, it would probably not be viewed as racist.

If it is 'a form of colonisation' to 'speak for or assume another's voice' (*Sinister Wisdom* Collective, 1990: 4), should I, an English South African-born woman, also have excluded white Afrikaners from my study? Afrikaners – the white descendants of early Dutch, German and Huguenot settlers – constitute 56 percent of white South Africans. Although no simple power relationship exists between Afrikaners and English South Africans, English ethnocentrism, in the form of a robust assumption of superiority vis-a-vis Afrikaners, has a long history in South Africa.

Since I *have* included Afrikaners in my study, I could be faulted for being inconsistent and/or racist in thinking that it is acceptable to include a white ethnic group of which I am not a member while excluding all black groups. Certainly, many Afrikaners are likely to protest the very negative picture of their families that emerges in my study, and to argue against its validity on one ground or another.

If I believed that feminists should never represent 'the Other', I would have confined my study to English South Africans, who constitute a mere 43 per cent of whites (i.e. 6–7 per cent of the total population). I should also have excluded all Jews and middle- and working-class English South African women. Let us not forget that some incest survivors also feel they cannot be understood by people who were never similarly abused. To avoid accusations of 'colonization', must I be willing to explain where I stand in 'representing the Other', to the interviewees and/or in my publications? This would require describing my sexual preference, my history of sexual assault, my age, for example – admissions that are likely to have a great impact on some women.

If I accepted that feminists should never represent 'the Other', I would have to confine my research to upper-class, white, South African-born ex-Anglican women in their 50s, who now live in America. If we do not continue to 'take on the whole world,' many of us could not do research or publish material that contributes to furthering radical feminist goals.

Note

I would like to thank Kate McKinley for her helpful editing suggestions. I am also indebted to Barbara Smith for my title ('Between a Rock and a Hard Place: Relationships between Black and Jewish Women', in *Yours in Struggle: Three Feminist Perspectives on Anti-Semitism and Racism.* New York: Long Haul Press, 1984).

References

Mayne, A. (1989) 'Feminism and the Anti-rape Movement', in D.E.H. Russell (ed.) *Lives of Courage: Women for a New South Africa*, pp. 227–40. New York: Basic Books/London: Virago 1990.

Russell, D.E.H. (1989a) 'South African Feminism through the Eyes and Life of Tozi Ntuli', *Feminist Issues* 9 (2): 51–80.

Russell, D.E.H. (ed.) (1989b) *Lives of Courage: Women for a New South Africa.* New York: Basic Books/London: Virago, 1990.

Russell, D.E.H. (1995) *Incestuous Abuse: Its Long-term Effects.* Pretoria: Human Sciences Research Council Publishers.

Sinister Wisdom Collective (1990) 'Editorial' *Sinister Wisdom* 42 (4): 1–6.

13

Politics and Women's Weight

Joan C. Chrisler

The personal is political, and nothing is more personal to North American women than their weight. Yet the suggestion that sociocultural, medical and psychological perspectives on weight and body fat are politically motivated continues to meet with resistance, even in the feminist community (Rothblum, 1994). The 'politically correct' who take care to avoid statements that could be construed as racist, sexist, heterosexist, or ageist seem to think nothing of exhibiting fat oppression, commenting critically on women's body size and shape, and 'blaming' fat women for their 'condition'.

For the past 15 years I have been working on appearance anxiety and body image issues with a special emphasis on weight. I began my work from a clinical perspective when I was leading psychoeducational groups that were designed to facilitate weight loss. Since my decision that it is anti-feminist to do weight loss counselling, I have focused on these issues from the perspective of a theoretician and researcher. Most of my publications on this topic (e.g. Chrisler, 1989, 1993, 1994) have been explicitly political and have taken the position that advice to women to lose weight has less to do with health and fitness than with fat phobia and fat oppression.

I was not surprised to find my views attacked by health care practitioners whose economic interests are threatened by the idea that women should cease trying to lose weight. I knew that even the best intentioned would struggle to hold on to the belief that the advice they had given to their patients or clients was 'for their own good' and based on scientific evidence. (See Chrisler, 1994 and Rothblum, 1990 for critiques of the medical literatures on weight and health.)

Nor was I surprised at the negative reaction from thin women. Weight is generally believed to be under voluntary control, despite considerable evidence to the contrary, and most thin women would prefer to think that it is their behaviour rather than their genetics that is responsible for their body shape. If they can be thin, they think, so can anyone. It is a small step from 'can' to 'should', especially in a society that is in the grip of a health craze. Popular culture has insisted that healthy behaviour results in prevention (Brownell, 1991) to the point where cancer patients are often held responsible for their disease. Thin feminists are no different; in fact, it may be easier to be feminist if one is also 'feminine', i.e. attractive (Rodin et al., 1984; Rothblum, 1994).

What did surprise me was the hostility I experienced first from my clients and later from fat women who read my work or heard me speak. In retrospect the suspicion with which my clients greeted my efforts is easy to understand. I was naive, and they taught me much of what I now know about fat oppression, fat phobia, weight stigma, the difficulty of weight loss and the ease of weight gain. During the first group meeting someone would invariably ask me if I'd ever had a 'weight problem' myself. When I answered 'no', a veil seemed to descend between us, and it took weeks of work on my part to shift it. Their resentment was based on the fact that I was suggesting to them that they could lose weight successfully if they followed my directions. They knew that although almost anyone could lose weight, almost everyone would gain it back again. They doubted my ability to understand their frustration, and they were right.

After my clients raised my consciousness and a careful study of the literature on the physiology of weight regulation convinced me that my work was futile, I concluded that it was neither feminist nor therapeutic to do weight loss counselling (Chrisler, 1989). I found the work of the Fat Liberation Movement (e.g. Shoenfielder and Wieser, 1983) and read many first-person accounts of women's struggles against size discrimination and the tragic effects of unsafe weight loss therapies. I decided that I had a responsibility to educate others about fat oppression. Instead of 're-presenting' fat women in images of how they could change themselves, I would 'represent' them as an advocate for their right to be as they are.

Of course, most fat women don't want to be as they are; they want to be thin. Any suggestion that weight loss efforts are doomed to failure must be immediately rejected in order to preserve their hope that someday they can escape the stigma of obesity, that someday they can approach the beauty ideal. Whenever I speak about these issues, whether in the classroom, at a professional conference or at a public lecture, an angry woman will invariably tell me that she has struggled with her weight all her life, has recently made considerable progress, and resents my suggestion that she will not one day meet her goal. The rest of the audience will then applaud her efforts (both literally and figuratively), leaving me with the knowledge that nothing I say can possibly make any difference. As long as one person insists she has successfully 'controlled herself', the rest can comfortably hold on to their belief that only the lazy will refuse to do so and therefore deserve any discrimination they experience.

I don't blame the fat women who argue with me angrily. I know it isn't easy to give up the struggle to 'fit in' and be 'attractive'. I've often wondered if my body weight doubled, could I take my own advice? Feminists have insisted on freedom of choice and the right to control our own bodies. But as long as the media refuse to show the diversity of women's bodies and society insists that thinness is essential to attractiveness, how free is women's choice to diet? As long as there is no successful weight loss strategy and repeated cycles of weight loss and gain leave women heavier than ever, what control do women actually have?

Should I give up? Will I one day agree that my current form of representation is no better than the previous one? I don't think so. Women of all sizes and shapes experience fat phobia and are complicit in fat oppression, and women of all sizes and shapes must fight against it. Just as white women have a responsibility to work against racism, thin women have a responsibility to work against size discrimination. Whenever my students read an anti-dieting article, the first question they want to ask is, 'Is the author fat?' The implication that fat women are anti-dieting because they are too lazy to diet themselves may make it particularly important for women who are perceived as not needing to diet to fight against fat oppression.

I have never personally experienced the stigma of obesity. The writers in the Fat Liberation Movement can describe it more clearly than I will ever be able to do. Their strength is peer education, and they have had considerable success through their publications, their appearances on television talk shows and their organization of groups such as Ample Opportunity and the National Association to Advance Fat Acceptance (NAAFA). Yet this work has had little impact on professionals who see themselves and are seen by the public as the 'real experts' on weight and health. Perhaps people like me who have training in physiological and health psychology can make some progress in educating the experts. I don't know, but I intend to try whenever I get the chance.

References

Brownell, K. (1991) 'Personal Responsibility and Control over Our Bodies: When Expectation Exceeds Reality', *Health Psychology*, 10: 303–10.

Chrisler, J.C. (1989) 'Should Feminist Therapists do Weight Loss Counselling?' *Women & Therapy* 8 (3): 31–7.

Chrisler, J.C. (1993) 'Feminist Perspectives on Weight Loss Therapy', *Journal of Training and Practice in Professional Psychology* 7: 35–48.

Chrisler, J.C. (1994) 'Reframing Women's Weight: Does Thin Equal Healthy?', in A.J. Dan (ed.) *Reframing Women's Health: Multidisciplinary Research and Practice*, pp. 330–8. Thousand Oaks, CA: Sage.

Rodin, J., Silberstein, L. and Striegel-Moore, R. (1984) 'Women and Weight: A Normative Discontent', *Nebraska Symposium on Motivation* 32: 267–307.

Rothblum, E.D. (1990) 'Women and Weight: Fad and Fiction', *Journal of Psychology* 124: 5–24.

Rothblum, E.D. (1994) '"I'll Die for the Revolution but Don't Ask Me Not to Diet": Feminism and the Continuing Stigmatization of Obesity', in P. Fallon, M.A. Katzman and S.C. Wooley (eds) *Feminist Perspectives on Eating Disorders*, pp. 53–76. New York: Guilford Press.

Shoenfielder, L. and Wieser, B. (1983) *Shadows on a Tightrope: Writings by Women on Fat Oppression*. San Francisco, CA: Spinsters/Aunt Lute.

14

'See Whose Face It Wears': Difference, Otherness and Power

Christine Griffin

I used to think that research situations in which feminist researchers 'spoke for' women in more marginal social positions than themselves should be discouraged. This was during the early 1980s in the context of my involvement in youth work and research with young women (Griffin, 1985). At this time (and still today), most studies about the lives of young people focused on young men who are white, working class, heterosexual and able-bodied (Griffin, 1988). Representation of young people outside these groups remains relatively uncommon, especially young black, lesbian and/or disabled women (exceptions include Mirza, 1992; Trenchard and Warren, 1987).

In early 1980s Britain, before 'post-feminism' had been invented, women had only recently begun to work together to make our voices heard – to each other, quite apart from within the academic realm or wider patriarchal society. Representing *ourselves* was the more urgent political priority: our experiences and our 'truths' as we saw them. Of course those voices were and continue to be extremely diverse, and women's experiences do not necessarily reflect the oppressive or marginal nature of our different social positions in a straightforward way (Griffin, 1996). There is no one female voice, any more than there is one feminist voice, and women's accounts of our lives are not all stories of victimization – or of resistance. During the early 1980s, the tensions between a view of women's experiences as relatively unitary and marked by a common oppression, and a view emphasizing the extent of diversity and power differentials between women, were certainly in evidence, but debates within feminism took rather different forms from those of the 1990s.

Fifteen or more years ago, it was a cause of some concern among western feminist communities when a man began researching a book about women's liberation. David Bouchier (1983) required access to documents and information which at that time were out of the public domain and had been generated in women-only contexts. In the 1990s it is more common for men to take an interest in feminist arguments, although this occurs more frequently in the academic domain (Wetherell and Griffin, 1991). Feminism (or at least some forms of it) has entered the academy and gained a form of (partial) respectability, with all the potentials and dangers that implies. In the 1990s it is commonplace for articles by men to fill the *Guardian* Women's Page (the page dedicated to women's issues in a liberal British newspaper), but in the late 1970s there *was* no *Guardian* Women's Page.

In the context of youth research debates during the early 1980s, a number of specific projects inside and outside the academy reinforced my view of the dangers involved when researchers were engaged in 'representing the Other' in more marginal groups across lines of gender, 'race', sexuality and class. I want to illustrate this point with reference to a particular incident, not because it is especially 'typical', but because it demonstrates some of the very specific problems involved in this area, and because some of the written material has recently been republished in a collection of work by the feminist researcher involved (Nava, 1992).

This involves Mica Nava's (1982) *Feminist Review* article 'Everybody's Views Were Just Broadened', subtitled 'A Girls' Project and Some Responses to Lesbianism'. The publication of this piece led to a series of criticisms including detailed objections to the piece from the management group of the project in which the research had been undertaken. These criticisms were published in the following issue of *Feminist Review* (e.g. Birmingham Lesbian Offensive Group, 1983; Camden Girls' Centre Project, 1983; partially reprinted in Nava, 1992). The issues at stake were presented (in part) by Nava and the then *Feminist Review* collective as involving attempts by some lesbians, feminists and trained youth workers with girls to dictate who should write about lesbianism and youth work with girls (Nava, 1992).

Nava's original article was based on interviews with young women who had attended a 10-week girls' group during 1979 run by feminist youth workers at a London youth centre. Nava focused on the girls' responses to a play staged by a feminist theatre group which included a small section about lesbians. Nava argued that the play broke down the usual taboo against (speaking about) lesbianism, and contributed towards the emergence of a more supportive atmosphere for those young women who identified as lesbian (Nava, 1982). The management group of the girls' project objected to the article on several grounds, in a letter that was subsequently published in *Feminist Review* (Camden Girls' Centre Project, 1983). Their objections centred around Nava's assumption that working with young women and girls formed part of a wider feminist strategy of 'recruiting them into the women's movement' (Nava, 1992: 57); and that this relatively minor intervention (the play) could have had the 'extensive repercussions' claimed by Nava. The management group also objected to Nava's representation of the relationship between lesbianism and feminism, and her apparent condoning of anti-lesbian statements made by some of the girls. They were also concerned at the possibility that individual girls and youth workers might be identifiable from Nava's article. Although all the names used were pseudonyms, the project itself was relatively unusual at the time, and therefore potentially identifiable.

Nava's ill-informed assumptions about the aims of girls' work stemmed from her distance from the work itself. A more extended period of interviews and observation might have improved her understanding of the aims of feminists involved in the project and in girls' work more generally. Nava's equally ill-informed assumptions about the nature of anti-lesbianism and about the complex relationship between lesbianism and feminism were a product of her social position (and lifelong experience) as a heterosexual woman. The publication of this article occurred at a particularly sensitive time for feminist youth work, girls' groups and issues around lesbianism and sexuality. From my perspective, as a feminist and a lesbian involved in research and in youth work with girls in Birmingham, Nava's article was a potentially dangerous document. Any suggestion in the public arena that lesbianism might be discussed in the context of a girls' group would probably have resulted in the closure of the group – a fate which befell a group for young lesbians in Birmingham during the early 1980s. Nava's article could have done irreparable harm to feminist work with girls, but fortunately few mainstream youth workers read *Feminist Review*. The argument that heterosexual women should not write about lesbians does not reflect the full complexity of the various objections to Nava's article, but these issues remain relevant to feminist researchers in the 1990s.

The response of the *Feminist Review* editorial collective to the objections described above was (in part) to point out that 'we do allow heterosexual women to write about lesbians and vice versa' (1983; Nava, 1992: 63). My view now (and then) is that there is seldom an equivalence between heterosexuals writing about lesbians and lesbians writing about heterosexuals, nor between whites writing about black people and black people writing about whites. These are not simply uncontextualized academic or journalistic projects, but texts produced in specific political situations, and the responses of Mica Nava and the *Feminist Review* collective reflected a misunderstanding of the points made by those who objected to Nava's article.

In the early 1980s, I would probably have understood the above incident primarily in terms of who should (or should not) write about whom. Today, I would not object to Mica Nava's piece solely because she was writing as an (undisclosed) heterosexual about the experiences of young lesbians – although I do wonder what her political motives were for doing this. If, as her 1992 book implies, Nava's focus on lesbianism 'just happened', then *why* did she have so little awareness of the central importance of this issue for girls' work at this time? My objections to the piece today also concern the lack of awareness (or even acknowledgement in some instances) on the part of Nava or the *Feminist Review* collective of the issues of accountability and power raised by this incident, and the very real differences (which continue today) between feminists who work as academic researchers and those outside the academy, including in this instance feminist youth workers and the young women involved (Hill Collins, 1991). 'Differences' between researchers and respondents in terms of social positions are closely connected with issues of accountability, and it is important to pay attention to the complex implications of these connections in specific research/ political contexts.

The very process of doing research involves the construction of the focus of study as 'the Other' to some extent (Stanley and Wise, 1983). All researchers, feminist or not, irrespective of 'race', class, gender, age, sexuality, nationality or dis/ability, are involved in 'representing the Other', regardless of the status of those with whom they/we work – even if the focus of our research is ourselves. In order to try to understand what is happening in particular situations, researchers need to take a psychological step back from the focus of study, to develop a form of what ethnomethodologists term 'philosophical detachment' (Billig, 1978). The dilemma for feminists involved in research is to understand and to live with the complexities of this situation. If the research process inevitably involves the construction of an 'object' of study to some extent, then how do we, as feminists, avoid the possibility of appropriating the experiences of Others?

Most of my own research has involved working as an adult interviewing young people, and sometimes as a white woman writing about the lives of young men and young black women, or as a lesbian working with young heterosexual women, so I am no stranger to representing the experiences of members of groups to which I do not belong (Griffin, 1985, 1986). The questions I want to focus on here concern not only the (multiple) social positions of a given researcher and her/his respondents, although these issues *do* make a crucial difference to the politics and outcome of the research process. It is equally important to consider the accountability of researchers to specific constituencies and the political context in which particular research studies take place. In other words, *why* are we (as researchers from particular ethnic, class, age, etc. groups) engaged in the *specific* projects on which we are working?

The key question to be asked about *all* research projects is 'why am I doing this?' The answer may partly involve money, a job and academic kudos, but I am interested in (other) political reasons. More specifically, the question becomes: 'How does (or might) this project contribute to radical social change?' It might appear that this question is less relevant to feminists researching the lives of women with similar experiences to themselves, but the sheer diversity of women's positions means that feminist researchers are seldom considering the lives of those in identical social positions. As feminists involved in research we not only recognize differences between women (and men), but we should also be aware *in detail* of the form those differences can take and the political implications of those differences in terms of material, cultural, ideological and psychological power. Researchers are always 'speaking for' Others. This is not something to be denied or avoided: it is a (potential) power and a responsibility. I have had access to institutional contexts in which I was able to represent (as in 'speak for') young people as individuals or as a group where no young women (or men) would ever have been allowed to speak, still less been heard. Researchers in psychology are frequently granted a particularly powerful expert status which as feminists we can use to challenge potentially damaging constructs (such as False Memory Syndrome for example). The power to 'speak for' Others is just that: a power. It is a power that should not be abused, though it frequently *is* abused, and sometimes by feminists. The development of more sophisticated practical strategies for ensuring accountability are important here, and I am increasingly conscious that feminist researchers spend more time talking about the complexities of research methodology and theoretical concerns than they do about issues relevant to political practice (Griffin, 1995).

When, as a feminist and researcher, I 'speak for' other women (and sometimes 'for' men), I cannot avoid telling *my* story about *their* lives. I can use the voices of Others from (my understanding of) their positions, but I can never speak/write *from* their positions. I cannot become them, I can only pass on selected aspects of (what they have shown me about) their lives. Writing ourselves 'in' to the analysis has been one means for feminists involved in research to challenge the construction of the researched as 'Other' and power differences in the relationship between the researcher and the researched, which it is never possible to overcome altogether (Stanley, 1990). It is possible, of course, to conduct research projects which are totally collaborative; in which *all* research participants are researchers and vice versa (Mies, 1991). These are often action research studies and the increasing involvement (incorporation?) of feminists into traditional academic institutions has made this type of work less common. Even in such collective or collaborative feminist projects, however, differences between women do not disappear, and nor should they. We all have to find a way of acknowledging (the political implications of) our differences without representing each other as 'different from' (the norm) or 'Other than' (the norm). My argument here does not revolve solely around who should 'speak for' Others. We are all multiply positioned in terms of age, gender, sexuality, 'race', class, disability, nationality and more, so perfect 'matching' of researched and researcher is seldom possible, although such issues will always be relevant to the research process (see Griffin and Phoenix, 1994 for further discussion). I would prefer to look at questions of 'difference' in a broader context.

Pointing to the lack of 'any consideration of lesbian consciousness or the consciousness of third world women' at the Second Sex conference in the USA during October 1979, Audre Lorde argued that 'the failure of academic feminists to recognize difference as a crucial strength is a failure to reach beyond the first patriarchal lesson. Divide and conquer, in our world, must become define and empower' (Lorde, 1981: 100). She went on to say, 'I urge each one of us here to reach down into that deep place of knowledge inside herself and touch that terror and loathing of any difference that lives there. See whose face it wears' (Lorde, 1981: 101).

Issues of difference, power and accountability may take different forms in these various arenas, but they remain of central importance to feminist practice inside and outside the academy. The present volume is part of a long series of feminist debates about difference, accountability, academic feminism and the power to 'speak for' other people. Let us try not to lose sight of the full range of issues involved in these debates, and especially not to take for granted the privileged place held by feminist researchers and practitioners in psychology to represent other people's lives.

References

Billig, M. (1978) 'The New Social Psychology and "Fascism"', *European Journal of Social Psychology* 7 (4): 393–432.
Birmingham Lesbian Offensive Group (1983) Letter to Editors, *Feminist Review* 13: 136.

Bouchier, D. (1983) *The Feminist Challenge*. London: Macmillan.

Camden Girls' Centre Project (Management Group) (1983) Letter to Editors, *Feminist Review* 13: 137.

Feminist Review Collective (1983) 'Editorial', *Feminist Review* 13: 134–5.

Griffin, C. (1985) *Typical Girls? Young Women from School to the Job Market*. London: Routledge and Kegan Paul.

Griffin, C. (1986) 'Black and White Youth in a Declining Job Market: Unemployment amongst Asian, Afro-Caribbean and White Young People in Leicester', CMCR Research Series. Centre for Mass Communication Research, Leicester University.

Griffin, C. (1988) 'Youth Research: Young Women and the "Gang of Lads" Model', in J. Hazekamp, W. Meeus and Y. te Poel (eds) *European Contributions to Youth Research*. Amsterdam: Free University Press.

Griffin, C. (1995) 'Feminism, Social Psychology and Qualitative Research', *The Psychologist* 8 (3): 119–21.

Griffin, C. (1996) 'Experiencing Power: Dimensions of Gender, "Race" and Class', in N. Charles and F. Hughes-Freeland (eds) *Practising Feminism*. London: Routledge.

Griffin, C. and Phoenix, A. (1994) 'The Relationship between Qualitative and Quantitative Research: Lessons from Feminist Psychology', *Journal of Community and Applied Social Psychology* 4: 287–98.

Hill Collins, P. (1991) *Black Feminist Thought: Knowledge, Consciousness and the Politics of Empowerment*. Boston: Unwin Hyman.

Lorde, A. (1981) 'The Master's Tools Will Never Dismantle the Master's House', in C. Moraga and G. Anzaldúa (eds) *This Bridge Called My Back: Writings by Radical Women of Color*. Massachusetts: Persephone Press.

Mies, M. (1991) 'Women's Research or Feminist Research? The Debate Surrounding Feminist Science and Methodology', in M.M. Fonow and J.A. Cook (eds) *Beyond Methodology: Feminist Scholarship as Lived Research*. Indianapolis, IN: Indiana University Press.

Mirza, H.S. (1992) *Young, Female and Black*. London: Routledge.

Nava, M. (1982) '"Everybody's Views Were Just Broadened": A Girls' Project and Some Responses to Lesbianism', *Feminist Review*, 10.

Nava, M. (1992) 'A Girls' Project and Some Responses to Lesbianism', in M. Nava (ed.) *Changing Cultures: Feminism, Youth and Consumerism*. London: Sage.

Stanley, L. (1990) *Feminist Praxis*. London: Routledge.

Stanley, L. and Wise, S. (1983) *Breaking Out: Feminism Consciousness and Feminist Research*. London: Routledge and Kegan Paul.

Trenchard, L. and Warren, H. (1987) 'Talking about School: The Experiences of Young Lesbians and Gay Men', in G. Weiner and M. Arnot (eds) *Gender Under Scrutiny: New Inquiries in Education*. Milton Keynes: Open University Press.

Wetherell, M. and Griffin, C. (1991) 'Feminist Psychology and the Study of Men and Masculinity: Part 1: Assumptions and Perspectives', *Feminism & Psychology* 1 (3): 361–92.

15

Representing Other Feminists

Diane Richardson

The term 'feminism' has many different meanings, and perhaps never more so than today. Typically the three classic feminist positions are characterized as radical feminism, Marxist/socialist feminism and liberal feminism. 'Other' feminisms that may or may not be represented in discussions of similarities and differences between feminists include, for example, black feminist perspectives, lesbian feminism, postmodern feminism and eco-feminism. While I would accept Jackie Stacey's (1993) point that too rigid a categorization may lead to an over-simplification of feminist thinking at both the individual and collective level, I am interested in how the use of these categories can lead to strands of feminist thought being (mis)represented in particular ways. I therefore want to consider how feminists represent other feminists and the possible consequences this may have for the development of feminist theory and practice. The example I shall use is the representation of radical feminism.

One of the most common representations of radical feminist thought is that it is essentialist, locating the source of women's oppression in women's biological capacity for motherhood and/or in male biology in terms of sexuality and aggression (see, for example, Abbot and Wallace, 1990). This portrayal of radical feminist analyses as biologically determinist has always struck me as extremely odd, given that within most radical feminist writing it is clear that sexuality and gender difference are understood to be socially constructed and the emphasis is on challenging and changing essentialist notions of male and female sexuality as fixed (see, for example, Dworkin, 1987; Jackson, 1996; Kitzinger, 1987; Richardson, 1993).

Essentialism and social constructionism are relative terms, of course (see Fuss, 1990), and in some cases it is a form of social rather than biological essentialism with which radical feminists are identified. Here the assumption is that radical feminist theories conceptualize women's oppression as universal and unchanging, failing to acknowledge historical and cultural difference. Despite the fact that, as Walby (1990) and others have pointed out, such criticisms are misplaced, such stereotyping may in part explain the perception of radical feminism as overly simplistic and lacking in theoretical analysis, especially of differences between women.

This alleged 'denial of difference' – particularly in terms of class and race – is usually seen as resulting from the claim that women are universally oppressed through patriarchy (see, for example, Denny, 1994). However this is to confuse two issues: the universalism of women's oppression and the theorization of difference between women. While for radical (and certain other) feminists the concept of patriarchy is central to understanding women's oppression, this does not mean that radical feminists believe in the notion of 'woman' as a unitary, absolute category, nor does this mean that they have no interest in theorizing differing and contradictory interests between women. Radical feminists are just as much aware as other feminists of the need to examine the interrelationships between patriarchy and other unequal power relations, such as class inequality and racism (Delphy, 1984; Douglas, 1990).

There is also a tendency within feminist texts to illustrate the 'radical feminist position' through citing a rather narrow range of writers, including, classically, the work of people like Shulamith Firestone (1970), Kate Millet (1970), Susan Brownmiller (1976), Mary Daly (1978), Adrienne Rich (1977, 1980), Susan Griffin (1981) and Andrea Dworkin (1981). Without wanting to deny the importance of such contributions to feminism, this limited representation of radical feminist theories, of which there is a wide variety (see Douglas, 1990), can lead to radical feminism being perceived as monolithic and dated.

Another important theme in representations of radical feminism is the claim that, far from aiding women's liberation, radical feminism is actually oppressive to women. This takes a number of forms. In some cases it is linked with the construction of radical feminism as narrow and judgemental. The flavour of this is captured in the following quote from Jane Ussher:

> Much of the radical feminist theorizing is potentially very anti-woman in its implications and very divisive, setting up criteria for how 'good' women, 'good' feminists should behave, and dismissing those who do not comply . . . This arrogant dictating of appropriate 'feminist' behaviour is no different from the élitism and oppression practised by the patriarchs [*sic*] for centuries. Such feminists may have rejected the phallocentric discourse, but they have in its stead created new discursive practices which are as oppressive and misogynistic as those of the men. (Ussher, 1991: 224–6)

In addition to being seen by certain writers as 'anti-woman', radical feminism has also been labelled by some as 'anti-sex' and moralistic, a social purity movement by any other name (Hunt, 1990). For example, radical feminists have been described as 'sex-negative', silencing some women and making others feel guilty about their sexual feelings and desires. This has been particularly evident in debates about S/M and butch/femme, as well as in recent work on theorizing heterosexuality (see, for example, Segal, 1994).

In Britain, such criticisms have been voiced in the main by socialist feminists, sexual libertarians and by some writers associated with queer and postmodern theory. Implicit in such discussions seems to be the assumption that radical feminist discourse has had more disciplinary power to influence women's lives than have other perspectives, feminist or not. Others, myself included, would seriously question whether radical feminism has the power to constrain women's voices in this way (see, for example, Ramazanoglu, 1993).

In any case, to interpret the problematization of (hetero)sexual desire and pleasure as 'anti-sex' is fundamentally flawed. Critiquing certain constructions of sexuality and forms of sexual desire and practice does not necessarily imply one is against either sexual diversity or pleasure. Also, radical feminists are not alone in criticizing certain forms of sexual practice and desire; so have some so-called sex radicals, queers, socialist and lesbian feminists (e.g. Nichols, 1987; Rubin, 1989; Segal, 1994; Smyth, 1992). A good example of this is the derogatory use of terms like 'vanilla' and 'politically correct' sex.

The view of radical feminism as oppressive is also reflected in the view put forward by certain writers that radical feminism constructs women as passive victims without agency (see, for example, Segal, 1987). This is influenced, in part, by the association of radical feminism with essentialism and social/ biological determinism. The consequence of this, it is argued, is that radical feminism has made women feel powerless and vulnerable. Again, as Bryson (1992) and others have pointed out, to argue that society is structured by male domination is not to suggest that such domination may not successfully be challenged. On the contrary, rather than seeing women in the role of 'victims', radical feminism, like other feminisms, sees women as active agents in the processes of social change.

I have highlighted some of the main ways in which radical feminism is represented as 'Other' to other feminisms. A serious consequence of this (mis)representation and oversimplification of radical feminism as a strand of contemporary feminist thought is that it is frequently dismissed as extreme, out-dated, misguided, theoretically naive and 'prescriptive'. It is also often construed as out of touch with what women's lives are really like and, by allegedly failing to legitimize different women's experiences, as oppressive. I chose this case example because, as someone who has written as a radical feminist, I have all too often found it hard, if nigh on impossible, to recognize my own and other radical feminist work in representations of radical feminism. There are, of course, criticisms that can be made of radical feminist accounts and areas that are under-theorized. For example, Stevi Jackson (1996) draws attention to the need to think further about the ways in which sexuality is constructed at the level of our individual subjectivities. At the same time, many of the criticisms that are levelled at radical feminism are inaccurate and without foundation.

It is, however, not only the question of misrepresentation that concerns me, it is the feeling that radical feminism is continuously held up as the 'bad fairy' of feminism upon whose supposedly narrow shoulders all the ills and failures of feminism can be heaped. This raises for me the question of if and how our political identity and chosen theoretical perspective can interact with how we are positioned as 'Other'. Radical feminism has often been perceived within popular culture as the extreme wing of feminism, with the conflation of radical feminism and lesbian feminism serving to strengthen the view of radical feminism as both unacceptable and 'Other'. More worryingly, as I have tried to demonstrate, it seems that radical feminism is increasingly positioned as political 'Other' in terms of its erasure and/or (mis)representation within feminist and queer writing.

References

Abbot, P. and Wallace, C. (1990) *An Introduction to Sociology: Feminist Perspectives.* London: Routledge.
Brownmiller, S. (1976) *Against Our Will.* Harmondsworth: Penguin.
Bryson, V. (1992) *Feminist Political Theory: An Introduction.* London: Macmillan.
Daly, M. (1978) *Gyn/Ecology: The Metaethics of Radical Feminism.* Boston: Beacon Press.
Delphy, C. (1984) *Close to Home: A Materialist Analysis of Women's Oppression.* London: Hutchinson.
Denny, E. (1994) 'Liberation or Oppression? Radical Feminism and In Vitro Fertilisation', *Sociology of Health and Illness: A Journal of Medical Sociology* 16 (1): 62–80.
Douglas, C.A. (1990) *Love and Politics: Radical Feminist and Lesbian Theories.* San Francisco, CA: ism Press.
Dworkin, A. (1981) *Pornography: Men Possessing Women.* London: Women's Press.
Dworkin, A. (1987) *Intercourse.* London: Secker and Warburg.
Firestone, S. (1970) *The Dialectic of Sex: The Case for Feminist Revolution.* London: Jonathan Cape.
Fuss, D. (1990) *Essentially Speaking: Feminism, Nature and Difference.* London: Routledge.
Griffin, S. (1981) *Pornography and Silence: Culture's Revenge Against Nature.* New York: Harper and Row.
Hunt, M. (1990) 'The De-eroticization of Women's Liberation: Social Purity Movements and the Revolutionary Feminism of Sheila Jeffreys', *Feminist Review* 34: 23–46.
Jackson, S. (1996) 'Heterosexuality and Feminist Theory', in D. Richardson (ed.) *Theorizing Heterosexuality.* Milton Keynes: Open University Press.
Kitzinger, C. (1987) *The Social Construction of Lesbianism.* London: Sage.
Millet, K. (1970) *Sexual Politics.* London: Abacus.
Nichols, M. (1987) 'Lesbian Sexuality: Issues and Developing Theory', in Boston Lesbian Psychologies Collective (eds) *Lesbian Psychologies.* Chicago: University of Illinois Press.
Ramazanoglu, C. (1993) 'Theorizing Heterosexuality: A Response to Wendy Hollway', in S. Wilkinson and C. Kitzinger (eds) *Heterosexuality: A Feminism & Psychology Reader.* London: Sage.
Rich, A. (1977) *Of Woman Born: Motherhood as Experience and Institution.* London: Virago.
Rich, A. (1980) 'Compulsory Heterosexuality and Lesbian Existence', *Signs* 5 (4): 631–60.
Richardson, D. (1993) 'Sexuality and Male Dominance', in D. Richardson and V. Robinson (eds) *Introducing Women's Studies: Feminist Theory and Practice.* London: Macmillan.
Rubin, G. (1989) 'Thinking Sex: Notes for a Radical Theory of the Politics of Sexuality', in C. Vance (ed.) *Pleasure and Danger: Exploring Female Sexuality.* London: Pandora.
Segal, L. (1987) *Is the Future Female? Troubled Thoughts on Contemporary Feminism.* London: Virago.
Segal, L. (1994) *Straight Sex: Rethinking the Politics of Pleasure.* London: Virago.
Smyth, C. (1992) *Lesbians Talk Queer Notions.* London: Scarlet Press.
Stacey, J. (1993) 'Untangling Feminist Theory', in Diane Richardson and Victoria Robinson (eds) *Introducing Women's Studies: Feminist Theory and Practice.* London: Macmillan.
Ussher, J. (1991) *Women's Madness: Misogyny or Mental Illness?* London: Harvester Wheatsheaf.
Walby, S. (1990) *Theorising Patriarchy.* Oxford: Blackwell.

16

'White Women Can't Speak?'

Diane Bell

Speaking out, speaking of, speaking with, speaking about, speaking for . . . What did I say to bring the furies down on my feminist head? At the time it was really very simple. In collaboration with Topsy Napurrula Nelson, an Aboriginal woman from Central Australia with whom, over the past 20 years, I have worked, played, published, travelled, strategized, danced, sung and painted (Bell, 1985; Bell and Nelson, 1989), I called attention to three facts: (1) Aboriginal men are raping Aboriginal women at a rate that qualifies as a human rights abuse and on a scale that constitutes a crisis; but (2) those whose voices we would expect to hear raised in outrage (i.e. Aboriginal Legal Aid and feminists) are, albeit for different reasons, silent on the nature and extent of the abuse; and (3) women's refuges and rape crisis centres modelled on Aboriginal women's traditional use of social space have been successful in providing safe places.

For my part, I contextualized these facts within a discussion of anthropological and legal modes of 'representing' Aboriginal women and the transformation of gender relations in colonial and 'post-colonial' Australia (Bell, 1983/93). Two case studies illustrated the complex dimensions and power plays that serve to privilege race over gender in the politics of Aboriginal self-determination (Bell, 1992). On the issue of conceptualizing rape, I cited a range of opinion regarding the awkward relationship of Aboriginal women to the women's movement (Bell, 1988). For her part, Topsy Napurrula Nelson spoke of the traditional modes of protecting women, of kin-based law, of women's sanctions against violent men, of safe spaces for women and girls, and of the increased vulnerability of Aboriginal women in the towns, fringe camps and on large reservations (Nelson, 1990a).

Our attempt at a joint paper that reflected these ideas became an interplay of voices. In 1988, at a colloquium on the 'Rights of Subordinated Peoples' at La Trobe University, Victoria, Australia, we took turns in explaining what was happening in Aboriginal communities in Central Australia (Bell, 1994). At that time we were made aware that raising the issue of intra-racial rape was going to be contentious. However, we both felt that the incidence of violence against Aboriginal women was increasing; that the legal system needed to understand the complexity of violence against women in cross-cultural contexts; and that the voices of Aboriginal women living in the more traditional communities of Central and Northern Australia were not being heard.

The colonial encounter is inscribed differently on the lives of men and women and, in the locus of violence, we have a clear example of how this difference registers: Aboriginal men are dying in police custody and the horror of this social fact has deeply scarred the Australian population (Johnson, 1991). While some Aboriginal women also die in custody, many more are being brutalized in their home communities (Atkinson, 1990a: 6; Balendra, 1990: 2). Not to engage with the questions that intra-racial rape cases raise leaves rape shrouded in myth, the subject of spirited legal defences based on spurious anthropological evidence by lawyers, or the stuff of repressive law and order campaigns. But who may speak and in what voice?

In titling our piece 'Speaking about Rape is Everyone's Business' (Bell and Nelson, 1989), we were evoking the Aboriginal notion that there are matters that concern men only, others that concern women only, and the possibility that there are still others that concern everyone. It was also an indication that we believed we could speak *to* each other and speak *out* to a wider audience. It was a defiant feminist statement that rape is about power and that silence about rape protects the abusers of power. So we were speaking *out*, not *for* other women.

Women's Studies International Forum (*WSIF*) published a written version of the paper (Bell and Nelson, 1989) and all hell broke loose. In February 1990, a letter bearing no signatures to validate the names typed at the bottom of the second page, and no address, was sent to colleagues and *WSIF*, but was not sent directly to me (although my address was on the article). It accused me of creating divisions within the 'Aboriginal community', appropriating Topsy Nelson's voice by citing her as 'co-author' rather than 'informant', of exhibiting white imperialism, of exercising middle-class privilege and it concluded with the claim that 'sexism does not and will never prevail over racial domination in this country' (Huggins et al., 1991: 507). It was authored by 12 well-educated urban Aboriginal women, none of whom, to the best of my knowledge has any in-depth fieldwork experience in the area of which we had written, but all of whom claimed to speak *for* Aboriginal women. Our title had enraged these women. I had no business to speak. Only Aboriginal women could speak for Aboriginal women. There was no need to specify any other basis.

I sought advice from colleagues who said, 'It will pass', but it didn't; it got worse. At conferences, the rights of white women to work in Central Australia were discussed; journal articles appeared; I was called upon to defend myself on the ABC (Australian Broadcasting Corporation) and in letters to various journals.[1] Our unspeakable article was the basis of many a talk but, I quickly learned, it was rarely read. Jumping on the bandwagon of 'beat up a white feminist anthropologist who is now out of the country' (I had just taken up a position in the USA) was a popular pastime in 1990. Highly imaginative stories of conspiracies to silence the authors of the letter added an extra spice to the retellings. In reality, *WSIF* took legal advice, sought signatures to the letter so that it could be published, and offered to publish a more detailed piece should the women wish to submit one (Rowland, 1991–2). They also sought a response from Topsy Nelson and myself. I tried to correspond with Jackie Huggins but she and her co-authors were not inclined to further discussion with a person such as myself, although they reserved the right to discuss the matters wherever, whenever, and with whomever they pleased and they did so at some length.

Meantime, in the real world, Aboriginal women were speaking out and their stories were of unrelenting violence. Far from overstating the case, we had only touched the surface (Bolger, 1990). Judy Atkinson (1990a), an Aboriginal woman from Queensland, noted that 'in one town no Aboriginal girl over the age of ten had not been raped' and 'rape is a daily occurrence but 88% go unreported, only pack rapes are reported' but, as our cases indicated, even they may not be reported (Bell and Nelson, 1989: 411–12). Under-reporting is a problem in all rape cases but there are particular reasons why, in small kin-based communities, crimes go unreported: victims fear retribution, learn to protect themselves from further abuse by keeping quiet, and the power to intimidate is known to boys and men; police are not always interested and may even be part of the abuse pattern; people are reluctant to see offenders go to jails in distant cities (Atkinson, 1990b: 14, 1990c: 20).

Activists, Aboriginal and non-Aboriginal, who had long agitated for research on the issue of violence against women, wrote thanking us for opening the subject to a wider audience. Several began to tell us of the ways in which their projects and analyses were being threatened and deflected and of how they had been warned not to quote our work. It was right and proper to speak of *inter*-racial rape, but not *intra*-racial rape. You can't study 'rape', one highly qualified Aboriginal woman researcher was told by a senior male Aboriginal bureaucrat. When she persisted, another more compliant woman was appointed to take over the work. Jackie Huggins has told me that she does not cite me and that others follow suit. Dialogue is difficult under these circumstances.

My file on the reception of our article is voluminous and it makes depressing reading. In all these exchanges and fora, the substantive issues raised by our piece disappeared. There were postmodern discourses on difference, subjectivities and representivity aplenty, but not a word on the issue of rape and, in the process, Topsy Nelson was also rendered voiceless. Huggins et al. (1991) demote her to the status of 'informant' – a particularly offensive term in my opinion – and claim that because she cannot speak English, she can't have understood what was in the article! Here I would refer the reader to publications in which she speaks perfectly intelligible English (Nelson, 1990a). Anna Yeatman, one of the self-appointed non-Aboriginal academic chroniclers of the debate, refuses to cite our article as jointly authored and insists it is 'Bell, 1989' (Yeatman, 1993). In the rush to reverence difference and to heed the voices of certain Aboriginal women, it seems that Topsy Nelson cannot have a space. Her difference doesn't count. Or is it too difficult to hear, too destabilizing of the race/gender hierarchy? It does after all promise a way out of the 'no-speak' dilemma. Indignant that she was deemed a dupe of my anthropological pen, Topsy Nelson wrote to Jackie Huggins and *WSIF*:

> I had no Aborigine to write this down. Diane is like a sister; best friend. She wrote all this down for me. That's OK – women to women; it doesn't matter black or white. I want these things written down and read again later. I was telling Diane to write this story for me. (Nelson, 1990b: 507)

This was not the first time Topsy Nelson and I had worked together and, in reviewing our several previous (and often memorable) interactions, I saw a way to build a more dynamic, less guilt ridden appreciation of questions of gender and race. In 'Intra-racial Rape Revisited: On Forging a Feminist Future Beyond Factions and Frightening Politics' (Bell, 1991), I proposed that feminists think seriously about the possibilities of actual friendship and personal trust as the context for dialogue. I sketched examples of positive, woman-affirming, cross-cultural collaborations. I argued that if we think of race as a given, all we can do is react. In such situations our modes of interaction are circumscribed by the construct 'race' and the boundaries of the person become fixed. Before we can engage in dialogue, we have to breach these socially constructed boundaries. Whereas, if we emphasize relationality, and ground our analyses in the specificities of place and personal history, we can focus on connectedness and the rigidity of the bounded category of race gives way to permeable membranes. The shift in emphasis opens up the possibility of theorizing issues of gender and race around particular relationships, and declares that our possibilities are not exhausted by our predicates (*white* woman, *Aboriginal* woman, *radical* feminist, *socialist* feminist). This shift from boundary maintenance to relationality is threatening if one has constructed a politics on the basis of predicates. When the issue is rape, it is our vulnerability as women to rape that grounds the relationality and thus I am suggesting we begin with the issue (rape), not with the construct (race).

In my view, a feminism drawing on female friendship bespeaks a more robust feminist future than one cringing before socially constructed categories. If the cross-cultural politic is to be cooperative, the exchanges have to be two-way: we need to learn to be more sensitive to cultural difference, and Aboriginal women need to see there are women who are sensitive. We need not be cowed by being told we are white and Aboriginal women need to acknowledge, as many have, that feminism has changed the environment in which they operate. In this I think white women have the major responsibility to create and foster the conditions under which dialogue might occur, but that does not mean we should suspend all critical faculties. We need to be able to talk and not be constrained by fear of being called 'racist'. Aboriginal women need to be able to speak and not fear being dismissed as 'guilt tripping'. It's not the end of the relationship to have a disagreement. If Aboriginal and white women can't argue and disagree in a constructive way, then there is room to talk about an element of racism in the relationship. In attempting to imagine safe places in which dialogue might occur, I would caution that not all women are feminists and womanist politics are not necessarily part of Aboriginal female identity.

So to return to the three facts with which I began. Frustrated with the defence-oriented nature of existing services, the Aboriginal Women's Legal Group is moving to create separate services for women. In her award winning 'Our Shame: How Aboriginal Women and Children are Bashed in their own Community – Then Ignored', Rosemary O'Neill (1994) retraces the ground we mapped five years earlier. Our heresies have become received wisdom. At the national level there are Women's Initiatives Programs and the like, but the real action is at the local level, where women such as Topsy Nelson have authority. Out in the communities, away from the power struggles of the organizations that purport to speak for Aborigines, women are confronting the violence. In the Mutitjulu community, Uluru (Ayers Rock), Pitjantjatjarra women like Kunbry Peipei, working with anthropologist Jane Lloyd, are achieving remarkable results on the issue of domestic violence (Finnane, 1995). These women are taking their message from one place to another. Aboriginal women are learning from each other. The media have caught up, the lawyers are paying attention, many Aboriginal women's voices are being heard, but too many academics are still writing commentaries on the commentaries and not engaging with the grim realities.

While the Huggins' orthodoxy no longer reigns, the chilly environment engendered by her attack persists. And, although it is now clear that Topsy Nelson and I spoke the truth, and that our analysis of the legal system was appropriate, I am still being abused, misrepresented, and misquoted in print and slandered by persons with little or no knowledge of the issues, or of my background. It is more convenient to accuse feminists who speak out of being divisive than it is to address the conditions that give rise to violence against women.

Notes

A longer version of this chapter appeared in Diane Bell and Renate Klein (eds) (1996) *Radically Speaking: Feminism Reclaimed*, Melbourne: Spinifex Press. Reproduced with kind permission.

1 I invite the reader to follow the twists and turns and to become familiar with the cases that prompted our article (see Bell and Nelson, 1989; Bell, 1990, 1991, 1992, 1994; Huggins et al., 1991; Larbalestier, 1990; Rowland, 1991–2; Yeatman, 1993).

References

Atkinson, Judy (1990a) 'Violence against Aboriginal Women: Reconstitution of Customary Law – The Way forward', *Aboriginal Law Bulletin* 2 (46): 6–9.
Atkinson, Judy (1990b) 'Violence in Aboriginal Australia: Colonisation and Gender: Part 1', *The Aboriginal and Islander Health Worker* 14 (2): 5–21.
Atkinson, Judy (1990c) 'Violence in Aboriginal Australia: Colonisation and Gender: Part 2', *The Aboriginal and Islander Health Worker* 14 (3): 4–27.
Balendra, Jaya (1990) 'Aboriginalities: Black Violence at Home', *The Independent Monthly* August: 2.
Bell, Diane (1983/93) *Daughters of the Dreaming*. Minneapolis: University of Minnesota Press.
Bell, Diane (1985) 'Topsy Napurrula Nelson: Teacher, Philosopher, Friend', in Diane Barwick, Isobel White and Betty Meehan (eds) *Fighters and Singers*, pp. 1–18. Sydney: Allen and Unwin.
Bell, Diane (1988) 'The Politics of Separation', in Marilyn Strathern (ed.) *Dealing with Inequality*, pp. 112–29. New York: Cambridge University Press.
Bell, Diane (1990) 'Letter to the Editor', *Anthropological Forum* 6 (2): 158–65.
Bell, Diane (1991) 'Intra-racial Rape Revisited: On Forging a Feminist Future Beyond Factions and Frightening Politics', *Women's Studies International Forum* 14 (5): 385–412.
Bell, Diane (1992) 'Considering Gender: Are Human Rights for Women Too? An Australian Case Study', in A.A. An-Na'im (ed.) *Human Rights in Cross-cultural Perspectives*, pp. 339–62. Philadelphia: University of Pennsylvania Press.

Bell, Diane (1994) 'Representing Aboriginal Women: Who Speaks for Whom?', in Oliver Mendelsohn and Uprendra Baxi (eds) *The Rights of Subordinated Peoples*, pp. 221–50. Delhi: Oxford University Press.

Bell, Diane and Nelson, Topsy Napurrula (1989) 'Speaking about Rape is Everyone's Business', *Women's Studies International Forum* 12 (4): 403–16.

Bolger, Audrey (1990) *Aboriginal Women and Violence: A Report for the Criminal Research Council and the Northern Territory Commissioner of Police*. Darwin: ANU.

Finnane, Kieran (1995) 'Domestic Violence: Hints for our Finest', *Alice Springs News* 2 (8): 3.

Huggins, Jackie, Willmot, Jo, Tarrago, Isabel, Willetts, Kathy, Bond, Liz, Holt, Lillian, Bourke, Eleanor, Bik-Salik, Maryann, Fowell, Pat, Schmider, Joann, Craigie, Valerie and McBride-Levi, Linda (1991) 'Letter to the Editor', *Women's Studies International Forum* 14 (5): 506–7.

Johnson, Elliot (1991) *Royal Commission into Aboriginal Deaths in Custody*, National Report. Canberra: AGPS.

Larbalestier, Jan (1990) 'The Politics of Representation: Australian Aboriginal Women and Feminism', *Anthropological Forum* 6 (2): 143–57.

Nelson, Topsy Napurrula (1990a) 'My Story', in Shelley Schreiner and Diane Bell (eds) *This is My Story*, pp. 18–27. Geelong: Centre for Australian Studies, Deakin University.

Nelson, Topsy Napurrula (1990b) 'Letter to the Editor', *Women's Studies International Forum* 14 (5): 507.

O'Neill, Rosemary (1994) 'Our Shame: How Aboriginal Women and Children are Bashed in their own Community – Then Ignored', *The Weekend Australian Review* 18–19 June: 1–2.

Rowland, Robyn (1991–2) 'Correspondence', *Anthropological Forum* 6 (3): 429–35.

Yeatman, Anna (1993) 'Voice and Representation in the Politics of Difference', in Sneja Gunew and Anna Yeatman (eds) *The Politics of Difference*, pp. 228–45. Sydney: Allen and Unwin.

17

Putting Pakeha into the Picture: Analysing Lesbian/Bisexual Politics in Aotearoa/New Zealand

Kate Paulin

'Doing difference' has become an essential aspect of feminist theory in the 1990s. This often involves analysing differences (and similarities) between and within women which result from women's locations across power-saturated matrices of race, gender, class and sexuality (Bhavnani and Phoenix, 1994). However, I have experienced tension between my knowledge of the politics of difference and my ability to enact this attention to difference within my research project (see Bhavnani, 1993). This chapter is a story about my attempts to work through what attending to difference means in relation to my PhD research on lesbian/bisexual politics. I look at the complex and largely unresolvable issues of whether I, as Pakeha[1] and lesbian, should interview bisexual women and, more particularly, whether I should interview Maori bisexual women.

Over the course of my research, I have become increasingly aware that the politics of representation are embedded within my thesis topic. I have had to consider who is permitted to speak on behalf of whom (Gunew and Yeatman, 1993); who mobilizes power; who is oppressed and/or enabled by its effects. I am both immersed in lesbian/bisexual politics and at the same time studying them, which means another set of power relations is invoked. I want to be able to 'speak about' the practices and struggles over meaning in which lesbian and bisexual women are involved (Trinh, 1991: 12).

My awareness of the often hostile nature of interactions between lesbians and bisexual women in 'my lesbian community' made me wonder about the appropriateness of myself as a lesbian researching bisexual women. I knew, for example, that some bisexual women felt lesbians discriminated against them by excluding them from community events. Other bisexual women named lesbians as oppressors. However, I felt I was on safe ground if I focused on the interface between lesbians and bisexual women rather than on bisexual women per se.

I intended to interview only a small number of bisexual women about their experiences of being bisexual and of interacting with lesbian women and lesbian communities. One of the stated aims of the research was to understand how bisexual identity varies with respect to the intersections of class and race. Despite these aims, I did not systematically consider how to incorporate race/ethnicity[2] or class into the interview study. When my supervisor raised the issue of whether I would be interviewing Maori women, my response was a simple no. I did not articulate the reasons why that should be the case.

My implementation of the interview-only-Pakeha policy was quite uneven. When talking to participants about other women from their friendship circle who may have been interested in participating in my research, I said I was only interviewing Pakeha. However, when contacting the coordinators of various bisexual groups, I did not specify to whom I would like to talk – nor did my participant information sheet specify the preferred cultural make-up of my participants.

Nonetheless, because I chose the pragmatic strategy of a snowballing technique for contacting participants, beginning with women I knew, most of my participants were Pakeha (and university educated). Enthusiastic about the diversity in their stories, despite the homogeneity in age, education and ethnicity created by my snowballing strategies, I began organizing to gather more narratives from a much more diverse set of participants: working-class, non-university educated and Maori.

I soon realized though that this mid-thesis expansion was more problematic than it initially seemed. I moved into a dilemma phase. As I saw it, I was only interviewing Maori women on the assumption that Maori women offered a position on bisexuality different from that offered by the Pakeha individuals I had already interviewed. That is, Maori women's stories would only be included as a counterpoint to the debates at centre stage: Pakeha sexuality identity politics. Yet at the same time I wanted to bring in other voices beyond those active in bisexual groups; if I were going to broaden my participant range how could I specifically exclude Maori? Surely that would constitute a glaring and unacceptable silence around race? It felt like I had reached an impasse. Both options seemed politically fraught. Only at this point did I read writing by Maori academics about research.

A number of Maori academics have shown how Pakeha research on Maori is implicated in the ongoing process of colonization (Smith, 1992a). They point out how Pakeha researchers have used monocultural western scientific methods and models that position Maori as inferior 'brown Pakeha' (Walker, 1992: 5). As well as critique there have been moves towards Maori-centred research; research beginning from Maori concerns, conducted by Maori according to Maori knowledge protocols (Cram and McCreanor, 1993). There has been considerable debate about what role Pakeha should play in Maori research with a number of conflicting models circulating. One view is Pakeha cannot possess the cultural knowledge safely to conduct research on Maori and that instead Pakeha should study their own culture. In this model only those with Maori whakapapa (genealogy) can research Maori (see Walker, 1992). Others advocate a sponsorship model where Pakeha who have been 'adopted' by Maori communities and who have shown they can act in culturally appropriate ways can research Maori (see Smith 1992b; Stokes, 1992; Te Awekotuku, 1991). More recently partnership models involving both Maori and non-Maori researchers working together or in parallel projects have been developed (e.g. Park, 1992; see also Cram, 1995).

In retrospect, my initial decision not to interview Maori was based on the model of Maori researching their own and Pakeha doing likewise. This resulted from my association with the feminist-based organizations of Rape Crisis and Women's Refuge. In Aotearoa Women's Refuge is run on a model of separate but complementary service provision and support for Maori and non-Maori women and child survivors of physical violence (Alice, 1990; Lambourn, 1990). Within this understanding of Maori/Pakeha relations it was axiomatic for me not to interview Maori. Not interviewing Maori women was also far easier than engaging with questions of cross-cultural research practices. As Pakeha it was all too easy to ignore race/ethnicity. I realized that my concern with bisexual/lesbian politics had led to a focus on a 'singular sense of difference' (Alice, 1993: 34).

Moreover, my initial decision not to interview Maori women meant that I avoided considering in what ways I would need to do research differently, adequately and appropriately to address both the racial and sexual identity positions of my participants. My subsequent decision to include Maori meant I would be fitting Maori women in *after* the research questions and methods had been determined. The problem was trying to address racial difference within a predetermined, monocultural, western scientific framework of one-to-one interviews. I wanted Maori women to provide racial diversity in relation to bisexuality but expected to be able to insert them into a Pakeha frame of understanding. Lynne Alice (1993: 37) describes this approach as 'an information retrieval exercise' in which the researchers maintain control over 'their commodities' (i.e. Maori participants). The commodification of Maori perspectives for Pakeha use reproduces the position of Maori as marginal to Pakeha that I intended to avoid with my initial decision.

Despite deploying deliberate strategies to problematize psychology in my thesis (e.g. use of feminist, post-structural and queer theories; use of qualitative methods) I realized the extent to which I was still located in scientific discourses. I saw as legitimate my desire to have a whole set of narratives about bisexuality (see Smith, 1992a) – but of course the idea of obtaining a complete range of narratives on bisexuality is a positivist myth. I need to resist the notion of completeness and closure implicit in my desire to gather more narratives. Instead I need to make explicit how the existing narratives (and my reading of them) are particular accounts. I need to show they are partial stories located in historically specific, meaning-making systems (Haraway, 1988). Specifying the partiality of women's accounts about bisexuality involves locating my participants and myself as Pakeha.

Given my existing research structure, it appears that I can most effectively address race by foregrounding Pakeha identity rather than interviewing Maori bisexual women. Therefore I should return to my initial decision only to interview Pakeha. This may sound simple enough but propels me straight into dilemmas about who is Maori, Pakeha or Tauiwi and my role in policing those boundaries[3] around the highly contested signifiers of race and ethnicity. Are the participants Pakeha if they look white? What about Maori women who belong to bisexual networks into which I have already tapped who have expressed interest in participating in my research? My current working solution is to interview

Maori women who come up through snowball sampling, but not *seek out* particular individuals to provide 'the racial difference'. I am ambivalent about this solution, for it offers no clear guidance about what I should do with the transcripts of these interviews. How should I analyse the resulting narratives? One starting point for my analysis must be to theorize difference not as oppositional but as multiple and contradictory (Alice, 1993).

Part of my dilemma about interviewing Maori women arose from my assumption that if I wanted to look at race then I needed to go and find the women who supposedly embodied race: Maori women. This assumption simultaneously constructs Pakeha women as unmarked by race (Jones, 1992). However, Pakeha is a (privileged) 'racial' identity too. Rather than import racial difference into my thesis, it is important that I interrogate the intersections of 'race', gender and sexuality that are 'always already' there in my work. In other words I need to foreground Pakeha identity in my analysis of the interviews by making visible and particular that which is unmarked and universal (Jones, 1992; Walker 1992). Without addressing Pakeha identity my initial position of not interviewing Maori women can easily slip into a position of repeating Maori invisibility and reasserting Pakeha as universal (Brookes and Tennant, 1992).

The starting point for this analysis is the acknowledgement that bisexual/lesbian politics takes place in a context of ongoing colonization and institutional racism rather than in some pure space outside of Maori–Pakeha relations. Considering Pakeha identity rather than interviewing Maori women prompts a series of questions. For example, why is bisexual activism in Aotearoa (almost always) the province of Pakeha women? Do narratives about bisexual community creation draw on Pakeha stories of the settlement of Aotearoa as a new nation created from 'nothing'? How much are models of gay, lesbian and bisexual liberation imported wholesale from Britain and North America rather than being drawn from Maori struggles for self-determination? Does bisexual activism rely on (subvert? reinforce?) 'western' notions of subjectivity, identity and sexuality? What role does Pakeha feminism play in bisexual/lesbian politics?

My initial decision not to interview Maori was an attempt to *simplify* my analysis by concentrating on lesbian/bisexual politics. Asking the questions above is the beginning of my attempt now to deal with the *complexity* of the intersections of 'race' and sexuality (Martin, 1993).

Notes

1 An explanatory note about race relations in Aotearoa (New Zealand): Maori are the tangata whenua (first people) of New Zealand/Aotearoa. The term/identity Pakeha is most often used to refer to descendants of the colonizing (predominantly white British) settlers. The relationship between Maori and Pakeha dominates race relations as Maori have sought to redress the effects of 150 years of colonization. Often this has centred around the status and meaning of the Treaty of Waitangi signed between representatives of the British Crown and representatives of Maori people (see Orange, 1987; Walker, 1990). More recently the term Tauiwi (non-Maori) has been employed to signal that significant numbers of people of colour, from Pacific Islands, Asia and the Indian Subcontinent as well as other 'ethnic' groups live in New Zealand. I focus on Maori–Pakeha relations and acknowledge the exclusion of women of colour (see Gunew and Yeatman, 1993; Jagose, 1988).

2 The meaning of the terms race and ethnicity are highly contested (see Pearson, 1989; Spoonley et al., 1991).

3 I am also heavily involved in policing boundaries around sexuality in my research. What are the implications of my notion of two stable distinct interview groups of lesbian and bisexual women? The idea of stable identities was contested by participants. For example, I interviewed one woman who I thought identified as bisexual, but at the interview she identified as lesbian.

References

Alice, L. (1990) 'A Place to Stand: Feminist Praxis, Racism and Ethnicity', in L. Hill (ed.) *Women's Studies Conference Papers 1990*. Auckland: Women's Studies Association (NZ).

Alice, L. (1993) '"Unlearning Our Privilege as Our Loss": Postcolonial Writing and Textual Production', *Women's Studies Journal* (NZ) 9 (1): 26–46.

Bhavnani, K-K. (1993) 'Tracing the Contours: Feminist Research and Feminist Objectivity', *Women's Studies International Forum* 16 (2): 95–104.

Bhavnani, K-K. and Phoenix, A. (1994) 'Shifting Identities Shifting Racisms: An Introduction', *Feminism & Psychology* 4 (1): 5–18.

Brookes, B. and Tennant, M. (1992) 'Maori and Pakeha Women: Many Histories, Divergent Pasts?', in B. Brookes and M. Tennant (eds) *Women in History 2*. Wellington: Bridget Williams Books.

Cram, F. (1995) 'Ethics and Maori Research', unpublished paper, Psychology Department, University of Auckland.

Cram, F. and McCreanor, T. (1993) 'Towards a Psychology for Aotearoa', *New Zealand Psychological Society Bulletin* 76: 34–7.

Gunew, S. and Yeatman, A. (1993) 'Introduction', in S. Gunew and A. Yeatman (eds) *The Politics of Difference*. Sydney: Allen and Unwin.

Haraway, D. (1988) 'Situated Knowledges: The Science Question in Feminism and the Privilege of Partial Perspective', *Feminist Studies* 14 (3): 575–99.

Jagose, A. (1988) 'The (W)hole Story: Lesbians of Colour in Aotearoa', *Broadsheet (NZ)* September: 30–2.

Jones, D. (1992) 'Looking in My Own Back Yard: The Search for White Feminist Theories of Racism for Aotearoa', in R. Du Plessis (ed.) *Feminist Voices: Women's Studies Text for Aotearoa/New Zealand*. Auckland: Oxford University Press.

Lambourn, B. (1990) 'Parallel Development in Women's Refuge: The Non-Maori Women's Perspective', in L. Hill (ed.) *Women's Studies Conference Papers 1990*. Auckland: Women's Studies Association (NZ).

Martin, B. (1993) 'Lesbian Identity and Autobiographical Difference[s]', in H. Abelove, M. Barale and D.M. Halperin (eds) *The Lesbian and Gay Studies Reader*. New York: Routledge.

Orange, C. (1987) *The Treaty of Waitangi*. Wellington: Allen and Unwin.

Park, J. (1992) 'Research Partnerships: A Discussion Paper Based on Case Studies from "The Place of Alcohol in the Lives of New Zealand Women" Project', *Women's Studies International Forum* 15 (5/6): 581–91.

Pearson, D. (1989) 'Pakeha Ethnicity: Concept or Conundrum' *Sites* 18: 61–72.

Smith, L.T. (1992a) 'Te Raapunga I Te Ao Maarama. The Search for the World of Light', in Research Unit for Maori Education (eds) *Te Tari Rangahau O Te Matuaranga Maori, Monograph 9*. Auckland: University of Auckland.

Smith, L.T. (1992b) 'On Being Culturally Sensitive: The Art of Gathering and Eating Kina Without Pricking Yourself on the Finger', in Research Unit for Maori Education (eds) *Te Tari Rangahau O Te Matuaranga Maori, Monograph 9*. Auckland: University of Auckland.

Spoonley, P., Pearson, D. and MacPherson, P. (eds) (1991) *NgaTake: Ethnic Relations and Racism in Aotearoa/New Zealand*. Palmerston North: Dunmore Press.

Stokes, E. (1992) 'Maori Research and Development', in Research Unit for Maori Education (eds) *Te Tari Rangahau O Te Matuaranga Maori, Monograph 9*. Auckland: University of Auckland.

Te Awekotuku, N. (1991) *He Tikanga Whakaaro: Research Ethics in the Maori Community: A Discussion Paper*. Wellington: Ministry of Maori Affairs.

Trinh, T. Minh-ha (1991) *When the Moon Waxes Red: Representation, Gender and Cultural Politics.* New York: Routledge.

Walker, R. (1990) *Ka Whawhai Tonu: Struggle Without End.* Auckland: Penguin.

Walker, R. (1992) 'A Consumer View of Research', in Research Unit for Maori Education (eds) *Te Tari Rangahau O Te Matuaranga Maori, Monograph 9.* Auckland: University of Auckland.

18

Representation and Difference in Cross-Cultural Research: The Impact of Institutional Structures

Marion Martin and Beth Humphries

This chapter describes the experience of setting up a research study in a third-world[1] country while working across the national boundaries of that country and the UK. From this practice base we raise some issues around the notion of *representation* and *'difference'* in research, that is, ways in which *institutional structures* have an impact on the differences which exist among women, differences which, while having the potential to be creative and constructive, can be exploited in destructive ways. We are concerned that discussions about representation in feminist research tend to be framed in highly individualistic ways, focusing on the behaviour of researchers at an interactional level. One of the criticisms of some versions of feminist postmodernist discourses is their resistance to the analysis of structural relationships (see Hennessy, 1993). While we agree that this acknowledgement of personal differences, and the need to build connections across these differences, is essential, there is a need for further discussion of these within the institutional context in which cross-cultural research may be conducted. We offer this case study towards exploring further this often neglected area of analysis in contemporary feminist research. In so doing, we are concerned that in discussing some of the complexities there is a danger of focusing too much on the negative aspects of our experience. We do not mean to imply that such research should not be pursued. However, it is important to unpack the contradictions, untidiness and contextual constraints on collaborative processes. In examining these issues we may learn strategies to understand and challenge institutional structures.

The Context of Collaboration

The example we give concerns not so much the relationship between researcher and research subjects, but what on the face of it appears to be a more equal relationship, that between the researchers themselves. The focus is a 'collaborative' research study embarked upon with a colleague from a third-world country, which drew together our common interests in women's health. In this study, we were concerned to explore qualitative methods of inquiry informed by principles of equity and participation (Maguire, 1996; Martin, 1994). The opportunity to work together grew out of a link between our universities. While we shared an interest in the research itself, we were separated by differences which included our biographies, professional experiences and international boundaries. Ideological differences were also significant. For example, when we first met, we had very different ways of understanding the world, particularly as this related to our interest in health care. From a background of traditional medical training and hospital-based practice, our colleague understood the causes of ill health largely in medicalized terms, while our understanding arose from a social critique of the political economy of health (Doyal, 1995). Such differences at times brought conflict, as well as depth, to our relationship. Through discussion and the sharing of professional and personal experiences we came to a greater understanding of one another's perspectives and made connections across some of these. However, when we embarked upon collaborative work, we discovered obstacles we had not envisaged in working across cultures in an international research context. These created responses ranging from frustration to confusion to anger and alienation. On reflection it is clear that structured racism and colonialist attitudes underpinned many of the problems we met and made it difficult to put our shared principles into practice in the research itself, ultimately destroying any possibility of collaboration. Some of these problems are discussed below.

The Process of Collaboration

The research proposal was completed relatively quickly, though it was some years before an international funding organization showed an interest in resourcing it. During that time we continued to develop the project, and maintained close contact. When we commenced negotiations with the prospective funder, the multiple layers of structural relations began to have their impact. These involved both the UK university and the funding organization.

The UK University

The political context in which our attempts at collaboration took place was a climate of intensified competition for research resources among universities nationally, in the run-up to the government-determined Research Assessment Exercise, which results in financial rewards to those universities with the 'best' profiles in terms of staff publications and research projects. There was thus pressure to pursue the funding, and to have it credited to the university. Moreover, the substantive area of interest for the research, reproductive health, was attractive to the university because, as an aspect of health of international concern, it was potentially economically productive. This may have been a factor in the university's granting time to pursue the research, albeit within an inflexible timescale. This rigidity was not negotiable, and no consideration was given to the complexities of reorganizing a workload. When the funding organization signalled interest in supporting the research, and liaison systems were being set up between it and the university for securing the money, these were characterized by our being dependent on these systems, yet meeting difficulties both in accessing information and in receiving only partial information about progress.

The Funding Organization

A number of complications arose with the prospective funder. Our plan had been for the study to take place in a region of the third-world country where our colleague had developed contacts, where local people had identified a need and willingness to take part in the research, and where we had made preliminary visits. The funding body wanted the study moved to a different region where they were already supporting projects. They could not be persuaded of the importance of need identified locally (a key principle of our research approach), and were driven by the demands of a project already under way.

It also emerged that the funder's policy (which had previously been for management of the funds within the country where the research would take place) had been changed, and now required that research funds were held by the UK institution rather than the local institution. It was this issue about control of the purse which was the pivotal event leading directly to our relationship fostered over the years being placed under great strain, since the policy was recognized both by us, and by our colleague's institution, as racist. This view was confirmed in a number of ways. An inquiry to the UK headquarters about the reasons for the change in policy brought the (informal) response that in-country institutions were likely to be disorganized, leading to money mismanagement. Further, a feasibility study visit was arranged for one of the UK researchers to visit the overseas country, which included a meeting with the representative of the funding organization. A meeting was set up with the local director of fieldwork for the funding organization (a white European woman). At this meeting our colleague, a figure of international reputation, experienced exclusion, marginalization and invisibility in discussions about the research. Overall, the focus of liaison about the project was with the UK researcher. The differences which we had come to see positively, and to work with creatively, were placed under extreme stress. The issue of racism was taken up with the funding organization, but without satisfactory response. Nor did the UK university show interest in pursuing the issue.

Some Issues

Reinharz (1992), commenting on the paucity of cross-cultural research studies, suggests various reasons for this, such as the time it takes to communicate across international boundaries, or problems associated with working in cumbersome institutions like universities. Add to this the bureaucratic nightmare of extracting agreed funds from the 'aid' organization, and the situation becomes nearly intolerable in terms of the time and energy needed to achieve even simple steps. These institutional layers of structured power are overlaid by the historical, political and economic relationship of the two countries represented by the researchers, and the racism that continues to work through funding bodies as an integral part of neo-colonialism. Our research relationship carried with it the history of our countries, an inextricable part of any plans towards collaboration. This history includes economic dependency through colonialism, continued through neo-colonialism (Mies and Shiva, 1993). Research and development aid is manipulated for political purposes and market interests. The purse strings invariably lie with organizations operating from the first world, who have interests of their own. In this case, the financial interests of the UK university were apparent, and these were linked to the ideological interests of government, non-government and global organizations, in viewing over-population as the central problem of third-world countries.

The representation of our colleague and her university in negotiations with the aid agency was one of invisibility. Discussing the politics of representation in Aboriginal art and film, Langton (1994: 94) says that the most natural form of racism in representation is the 'act of making the other invisible'. In this situation, although our colleague's university was required as a collaborator of the project, it had little influence in the management of resources. The funding organization related primarily to the UK university, and even in a meeting among all the parties, the third-world partner was largely excluded from discussion. Another dimension of this situation concerns internal contradictions resulting from the UK researcher's location within this material structure. The reality reflected an advantage over our colleague, yet both were vulnerable to the decision-making power exercised by a third party. In other words, the first-world feminist researcher must be concerned not only with her representations of the subjects of research, but with the contradictions resulting from her *positioning* and perceived *identification* with those in power. Yeatman (1993) makes the point that what is often avoided is the complexity of dialogue that arises between subjects who understand themselves to be complexly like and different from each other, but are differently *positioned*. Such positioning is, of course, not fixed and we have described attempts to position ourselves differently by challenging the racism we met. Spivak (1990) places responsibility on all those engaged in debates about issues of equality and domination, to enter them from a position of being informed about respective histories, and to take the risks involved in a genuine dialogue. In locating ourselves in that dialogue, we must consider carefully strategies to prevent fragmentation and trivialization, and take account of the problems which arise out of cultural relativism and institutional imperialism. In our situation described here, the rules for the negotiation had been set by the institutions with which we were working. We tried to speak in their languages, to understand their cultures, to play their games, but with a view to using the funding to work according to a different philosophy. When we complained about the behaviour of representatives of the institution, we used a language which was not recognized as legitimate and found minimal response. We are left with the question: is it possible to subvert institutional structures, and so challenge the colonialist enterprise? It *must* be, not in isolated, individualized ways, as in our case study, but rather in community with others who have chosen to enter the same struggle.

Conclusion

When Mohanty (1991) writes of the need for researchers to ground research in their particular historical, political, economic and cultural contexts, it is precisely to the situation we have described that she alludes. While none of these problems will be resolved easily, they need to be acknowledged and discussed at the start of the working relationship, so that institutional contradictions are recognized. Our colleague and ourselves were not without an understanding of these factors, but perhaps were more naive than we might have been about multilayered power in international, inter-institutional and interpersonal terms. In the event our colleague withdrew from collaboration, largely as a result of the racism experienced. The institutional forces had such an impact on our relationship nurtured over several years that they tore apart possibilities for collaboration. Our colleague is unaware of the complaints made to the funding body about the racism experienced, and is likely to view such efforts as futile. Her professional interests and ideological position are such that she is unlikely to want to linger on the process as described here.

One thing is clear to us. Contemporary feminist understandings, rather than retreating into individualistic models of women working across difference, need to articulate the

> systematic operation of social totalities like patriarchy and racism across a range of interrelated material practices. These totalities traverse and define many areas of the social formation – divisions of labor, dimensions of state intervention and civil rights . . . the reimagination of colonial conquest. (Hennessy 1993: xvii)

This case study highlights some of the complex institutional factors at play in situations that sometimes are depicted solely at interactional levels. This over-simplifies and reduces the reality of what are in fact complex, often contradictory, issues surrounding notions of difference and representation. There is a need for reflection on these processes if strategies to challenge them are to be found.

Notes

1. We recognize that the terms 'third world', 'developing world', 'countries of the south', are contested terms. We have chosen the term 'third world' as used by Doyal (1995) to describe countries of Asia, Africa and Latin America, whose political and economic structures have been, and continue to be, distorted through the processes of colonialism and neo-colonialism.

References

Doyal, Lesley (1995) *What Makes Women Sick? Gender and the Political Economy of Health.* London: Macmillan.

Hennessy, Rosemary (1993) *Materialist Feminism and the Politics of Discourse.* London and New York: Routledge.

Langton, Marcia (1994) 'Aboriginal Art and Film: The Politics of Representation', *Race and Class* 35 (4): 89–106.

Maguire, Patricia (1996) 'Proposing a More Feminist Participatory Research: Knowing and Being

Openly Embraced', in Korrie de Koning and Marion Martin (eds) *Participatory Research in Health: Issues and Experiences*, pp. 33–48. London: Zed Books.

Martin, Marion (1994) 'Developing a Feminist Participative Research Framework: Evaluating the Process', in Beth Humphries and Carole Truman (eds) *Re-thinking Social Research: Anti-discriminatory Approaches in Research Methodology*, pp. 123–45. Aldershot: Avebury.

Mies, M. and Shiva, V. (1993) *Ecofeminism*. London: Zed Books.

Mohanty, Chandra T. (1991) 'Under Western Eyes: Feminist Scholarship and Colonial Discourses', in Chandra Talpade Mohanty, Ann Russo and Lourdes Torres (eds) *Third World Women and the Politics of Feminism*, pp. 51–80. Bloomington and Indianapolis, IN: Indiana University Press.

Reinharz, Shulamit (1992) *Feminist Methods in Social Research*. New York: Oxford University Press.

Spivak, Gayatri Chakravorty (1990) *The Post-colonial Critic*. New York: Routledge.

Yeatman, Anna (1993) 'Voice and Representation in the Politics of Difference', in Sneja Gunew and Anna Yeatman (eds) *Feminism and the Politics of Difference*, pp. 228–45. St Leonards, NSW: Allen and Unwin.

19

Questions of Legitimacy? The Fit Between Researcher and Researched

Manjit Bola

Many feminists have suggested that drawing on one's own personal experience is the key to doing feminist research. Similarity between the researcher and the researched is assumed, and the use of shared experience as data is presented as good feminist theory and practice. As Stanley and Wise (1993: 169) say: 'at least a few researchers are not male, white, heterosexual or middle class in origin. Those who aren't should make good use of this by examining, as research, our experiences as female, black, lesbian, working class and so on.' By contrast with the celebration of shared experience, there has been very little written by feminists about the impact of *differences* between the researcher and researched.

My own research, on women's experience of pregnancy, was shaped by three key dimensions of difference, which permeated relations between myself, the researched and the research topic: namely (1) race: I am black (of Asian origin) and the participants were white; (2) appearance: I have vitiligo (white patches of skin); (3) experience: I have no personal experience of pregnancy. Although the difficulties involved in negotiating access to research participants have been discussed elsewhere (e.g. Burgess, 1984; Shaffir et al., 1980), what is rarely explored is the effect of the perceived (in)compatibility between the researcher, the researched and the research topic in limiting and constraining the interview process. My attempts to gain access to women in the early stages of pregnancy illustrate the problems that can arise when the researcher is seen as incompatible with her research topic.

In my research project the gatekeepers to access were medical practitioners of various kinds (consultants, GPs, midwives and nurses). The process of gaining access was lengthy (one year). After gaining permission from the hospital, I received a telephone call from one of the doctors informing me that an obstetrician with whom I had not spoken objected to the study as she had not been consulted and that the women who would potentially take part in the study would be her patients. I went to meet this obstetrician to explain my oversight and to apologize for not having consulted her directly. At the meeting she was quick to point out (by using an example) that Asians did not know how to follow procedures. She remarked that she was on a committee looking into complaints about GPs and did I know that all the complaints and the wrongdoings were related solely to Asian GPs? A racist element was inherent in this encounter and I felt unable to reply. However, having made her point she was quick to take up an active role in helping to recruit women for the study. As I wanted to follow women from the early stages of pregnancy, she pointed out that recruitment would best be achieved via GP practices. She phoned a number of GPs on my behalf and asked them to cooperate.

In trying to gain access, I was wholly unprepared for the subsequent questioning I received concerning my own suitability to conduct this piece of research and the development of my own doubts with regards to this matter. The gatekeepers wanted to know why I (an Asian woman) wanted to carry out research on white middle-class women rather than women from an ethnic minority background. For some, the 'race' of the researcher was not the primary question of legitimacy but rather the mismatch between what I was interested in as a topic of research (pregnancy) and what they *thought* I should be interested in based on my appearance.

Difference in Appearance, Race and Experience

Vitiligo is a condition in which for often unknown reasons colour is lost in certain parts of the skin. In my case I have visible white patches of skin on the face and hands. The vitiligo was of major concern for one gatekeeper in particular. While I was explaining the proposed research project, I was interrupted by the gatekeeper, a doctor, with the following remark: 'It must be awful for you.' As this remark was out of the blue and did not relate in any way to what I was saying, I replied by saying: 'I'm sorry but I don't know what you mean.' He replied by saying: 'Well everybody must look at you twice and wonder what it is. I mean it must be difficult for people to listen and talk to you.' I became aware (as he had pointed out) that I had not been listened to by him, but did not know how to respond. In fact I did not acknowledge his comments verbally and continued to describe the proposed study and asked if he would distribute the leaflets I had produced to any patients who came to him in their early stages of pregnancy. After I left his office, I began to question my suitability to interview women in the light of what I had just experienced. Would the participants be able to listen and talk to me about their pregnancy if, at the forefront of their minds, was this curiosity with what I looked like? Could I make a suitable interviewer given that I do look different? These feelings were carried into each of the interviews I undertook with the participants.

One week after this encounter, a midwife (who was Asian) asked me why I was not investigating the experiences of ethnic minorities. She had come along with some fairly detailed information and offered to provide me with a subject pool. However, I pointed out to her that, although her ideas were extremely interesting and research in the area was needed, I had already invested much time and effort in setting up my research and would therefore like to pursue this before taking on another different project. The midwife then went on to ask me how long I had had the vitiligo. I informed her that it had been over four years and she then went on to ask me why I was not doing research in this area of personal experience and interest, rather than a project on women's experiences of pregnancy.

'Lack of Fit between Researcher and Researched': The Black Researcher's Dilemma

The comments described earlier placed me in a dilemma. Given that research is lacking in areas such as the experiences of ethnic minorities in a variety of situations, and given the perceived lack of congruity between myself, the researched and research topic, was I justified in carrying on? There is, on the one hand, a need for the experiences of ethnic minorities to be explored by black researchers but, on the other hand, it could also become an exercise in marginalization, where black researchers are deemed only to be able to research black participants. This can be a 'no-win' situation: if one examines non-race matters then one is being treacherous, but if one *does*, then this might be seen as typical and the research be considered lower status. These statements are intensely political and served to make me feel uneasy when undertaking my research.

Interviews with Participants

Having spent so much time and effort gaining access, it was a relief to be making contact with potential participants. However, my encounters with the gatekeepers had left me feeling self-conscious about my suitability as an interviewer based on people's perception of my difference. What perceptions would the participants have of me? Would women be comfortable with someone whose only similarity with them was gender-based? This anxiety was further compounded when I read Oakley's (1981) account of her experience, as a white feminist with children of her own, interviewing pregnant women, in which she highlights the value and importance of the similarity between herself and her research participants. Oakley's similarity between self and respondents was based not only on gender but also on past experience. Her participants were able to engage in conversations in which the personal experience of the researcher could be called upon to elicit personal opinions. In terms of how far my personal differences from the women I was interviewing were concerned, the thoughts remained with me and were not raised either by myself or the women (see Phoenix [1994] for a detailed account of the effects of 'difference' on the interview situation). The women seemed to accept my reasons for carrying out the research and, as one woman remarked, the project was my 'baby'. In line with Oakley's suggestion, interviewing women was 'a strategy for documenting women's own accounts of their lives' (1981: 48). However, the possible lines of perceptual difference between the interviewer and interviewees and the relative power in the interview situation is more complex and thought-provoking than Oakley suggests. The notion that power lies with the researcher rather than the researched in interviews did not tie in with how I felt. This may have been due to the disempowerment I had already experienced from the gatekeepers to access. The sense of powerlessness experienced in the interviews could be seen to be one of the major impacts of 'difference'.

Conclusion

The fit between the researcher and the researched, in terms of the perceived similarities and differences, is an important element which may affect the research in complex ways. Details about similarities are often provided by researchers who make the case for shared experience on the grounds of, for example, gender and past experience. These are often used and discussed in research articles as a source of empathy for and a means of building rapport with participants. In my case perceptual difference was paramount in the early stages of the research process (gaining access). Ready acceptance of legitimacy is often related to the similarities one has with the researched. The lack of similarity led to questions of suitability and self-doubts for which I was unprepared. To use the traditional language of psychology, the 'experimenter effects' on the pre-interview stage of the research process is important for consideration in feminist research methodology. Identification with the researched can be, and was in my case, shaped by the opinions of the gatekeepers to access. They had an influential role in placing doubts about my suitability to conduct the research and could have led to the abandonment of this particular piece of research. I would like to argue that perceived researcher characteristics are vital in the shaping of many research projects and should thus be paid more serious attention. Outlining the differences one has from the subject matter and participants can be as informative as the similarities that are seen to exist. We need more exploration, from a feminist perspective, of the impact of difference between researcher and researched, and discussion of how these differences can be theorized from a position of feminist reflexivity.

Note

The author wishes to thank her supervisor, Karen Henwood, for her support and Celia Kitzinger for her editorial assistance with this article.

References

Burgess, R.G. (1984) *In the Field: An Introduction to Field Research*, London: Allen and Unwin.
Oakley, A. (1981) 'Interviewing Women: A Contradiction in Terms', in H. Roberts (ed.) *Doing Feminist Research*. London: Routledge and Kegan Paul.
Phoenix, A. (1994) 'Practising Feminist Research: The Intersection of Gender and "Race" in the Research Process', in J. Purvis and M. Maynard (eds) *Researching Women's Lives from a Feminist Perspective*. London: Falmer.
Shaffir, W.B., Stebbins, R.A. and Turowetz, A. (eds) (1980) *Fieldwork Experience: Qualitative Approaches to Social Research*. New York: St Martin's Press.
Stanley, L. and Wise, S. (1993) *Breaking Out Again: Feminist Ontology and Epistemology*. London: Routledge.

20

The Reproduction of Othering

Brown

Social science is usually about someone else or something out there. A good deal of the work we do, both in the traditional 'hard' methodologies which predominate in psychology and in the 'softer' more innovative fields like discourse analysis and ethnography is about anchoring what we say to the object of our enquiry. Science has a considerable stake in constructing 'out thereness'. Certainly, there have been attempts to substitute a more participative model of enquiry (see *inter alia* Currie and Kazi, 1987; Oakley, 1979) or to style the people in whom one is interested as 'co-researchers' (Moustakas, 1994). However, there are usually limits to this apparently democratic process: the 'co-researchers' being researched do not suddenly appear on the university payroll, for example. The creation of Others in the social sciences, as Fine (1994) reminds us, disproportionately involves the privileged researching and representing 'ethnic minorities', the poor, the 'mentally ill' or even ordinary women. Moreover, according to Fine (1994: 79) an 'even more terrifying' prospect emerges if the research is intended to 'help' the Others thus created. Even ethnographically documenting strategies of liberation and resistance is accomplished in and through the structure of academic privilege. So even when we take Others seriously there will be 'residues of domination' (1994: 81) haunting the warp and weft of our descriptive fabrics.

Given the ethical and political concerns about doing this kind of thing to Others, is there any justification for producing descriptions of people who differ from ourselves in terms of their experience of gender, disability, sexuality, madness or any other distinction which confers privilege on us as describers?

Perhaps we *should* represent Others. On an ethical level, it's probably more justifiable than ignoring them. On an academic level, it is because the Others are difficult to ignore. Whoever the Others might be, they are not solely located in their bodies. The discourse and activity of Others spreads out over a variety of surfaces. Others are writing, talking, painting, photographing, acting, filming, singing as well as participating in everyday life. Others are industriously raising scholarly imaginations on their own situation and how it has been represented in mainstream social science. The intense interest in critically re-reading the classic texts of psychology and identifying the racism, heterosexism and masculine basis of the discipline has been propelled by the efforts of scholars who are black, lesbian and/or feminist. While we can't afford to be complacent about the technologies of oppression embedded in the social sciences, it does suggest that

Others are not just people out there somewhere else. Othering, and being an Other, is an intensely public activity. Moreover, it is activity which in our academic and private lives we struggle to make intelligible. It becomes so through an ongoing choreography of argument whereby the Otherness itself is created and transformed.

Conjectures and Refutations: Intelligible Orgasms?

As an example of this, consider the recent altercations between myself and Wendy Hollway (Brown, 1994; Gilfoyle et al., 1992; Hollway, 1993; 1995). This debate, while it involves a number of contributors, has increasingly developed along lines that are concerned with the agency of Others. My recent suggestions (Brown, 1994) that heterosexual practice, pleasure and desire for women and men are informed by politics and processes of domination are taken by Hollway (1995) to mean that I am denying her 'sexual agency', though this was not what I wrote. Moreover, Hollway takes issue with our earlier article (Gilfoyle et al., 1992) where we described a set of interviews with men and women about sex and relationships. Here we identified the 'pseudo-reciprocal gift discourse', where women were described as somehow giving themselves to men and men were somehow giving them orgasms. Hollway infers that by identifying inequalities in this form of talk we have ridden roughshod over the participants. True, the participants did not launch into diatribes about how unequal it was. However, they didn't say it was equitable either. The lens of feminism, with its especial concern with gender inequality, assists us in understanding how such conversation links in with grander systems and structures. Presuming that fragments of sexuality are equal is just as tendentious.

The whole process gets even more controversial when it is read as 'denying agency'. I have no personal doubt of Hollway's strong subjective sense of herself as an agent, both in her role as an author and as a participant in heterosexuality. However, I am not in the privileged position of knowing Hollway's mind. What interests me is how that agency becomes part of an intelligible public performance. Agency, to my mind, is as much a topic to be explained as it is a resource for substantiating claims to self-determination. The Other, in the form of this mysterious agency of heterosexual desire apparently resident in heterosexual women, doesn't just stay inside. It leaks out over other ideologically contoured surfaces, such as the literary surface of *Feminism & Psychology*. Hollway's expressions of pleasure and desire are immediately intelligible in terms of the public ways in which desire and pleasure are 'accountable' in Shotter's (1993) terms. Hollway's (1993) references to being wrapped in strong tanned arms, to be adored and to being given something, which are foregrounded in her account, are understandable by anyone who has grown up watching movies or television, reading novels, magazines or comics in Europe and North America. Consider also how the terms used connote and consolidate agency. What different imaginations do we raise on the situation of women in heterosexuality if different terminology is used – like being imprisoned or restrained, being despised, having their honour or their maidenheads 'taken'? What if, instead of wrapping her in his arms, a woman were to describe her lover wrapping her in his tentacles or in cling film? Trivial, perhaps, but that's why we understand Hollway as describing something fundamentally accountable as part of her experience, rather than writing science fiction for example. The creation of desiring, heterosexual selves, and consequently desiring, heterosexual Others does not rely on internal personal psychological processes, but is accomplished through language.

Relations in Public: Authorizing Heterosexual Pleasures

A further reason why we need to take the process of people describing Others very seriously is that it goes on in everyday life. Getting to grips with this is not entirely coterminous with turning an imperializing ethnographic gaze on people, but looking at how public expressions of activity make sense in their social context. Going back to the example of heterosexual desire, it is immediately apparent that this is a highly contested field where the contributions in *Feminism & Psychology* are but a drop in a very large and unruly ocean. The literate heterosexual is hailed on every side by a huge number of regulatory discourses, such as popular magazines and books on how to have a better relationship, all of which are actively channelling desire. Heterosexual pleasure doesn't get left to chance. In many ways it is authored. That is, pleasure is a kind of argument which enfolds emotions, bodily sensations and orientations to social relationships. It makes possible particular experiences. In order to do this it has to be scrupulously organized.

As people talk about their relationships they participate in much larger, complex systems of meaning where creating and representing Others goes on. Everyday talk and popular literature are replete with accounts of the mindedness of Other people or their readers. If the people who write for *Feminism & Psychology* don't represent Others, we are avoiding a social process which already describes, fixes and enlists them: a process which creates Others, their desires and pleasures as entities to be worked on, transformed and managed.

Perhaps we should carry on representing Others. Constructing the mindedness and 'agency' of Others is so pervasive and so much a part of communication that it is difficult to imagine proceeding without it. In particular, it is important to engage with these patterns of representation because even if we achieve an 'Otherless' academic discourse, many people and institutions have a great deal at stake in creating and managing Others. Representing Others, whether we do it ourselves as an heuristic device to make sense of what we call our data, or whether we detect it going on elsewhere, is an important topic of study in its own right. At the same time, the work of people attempting to break out of the Otherness we have constructed them into has a vital role to play in achieving a *reflexive* knowledge which is sufficiently fluid to admit of being 'ruptured' with 'uppity voices' (Fine, 1994: 75).

References

Brown (1994) 'Pleasures Untold: Heterosexuality, Power and Radicalism', *Feminism & Psychology* 4 (2): 322–5.

Currie, D. and Kazi, H. (1987) 'Academic Feminism and the Process of Deradicalisation', *Feminist Review* 25: 77–98.

Fine, M. (1994) 'Working the Hyphens: Reinventing Self and Other in Qualitative Research', in N. Denzin and Y.S. Lincoln (eds) *Handbook of Qualitative Research*. Thousand Oaks, CA: Sage.

Gilfoyle, J., Wilson, J. and Brown (1992) 'Sex, Organs and Audiotape: A Discourse Analytic Approach to Talking about Sex and Relationships', *Feminism & Psychology* 2 (2) 209–30.

Hollway, W. (1993) 'Theorizing Heterosexuality: A Response', *Feminism & Psychology* 3 (3): 412–17.

Hollway, W. (1995) 'A Second Bite at the Heterosexual Cherry', *Feminism & Psychology* 5 (1): 126–30.

Moustakas, C. (1994) *Phenomenological Research Methods*. Thousand Oaks, CA: Sage.

Oakley, A. (1979) *From Here to Maternity: Becoming a Mother*. Harmondsworth: Penguin.

Shotter, J. (1993) *Conversational Realities*. Thousand Oaks, CA: Sage.

21

Representing the Prostitute

Sheila Jeffreys

Can feminists theorize prostitution if they have never worked as prostitutes? Feminist analysis would be very partial if we could only speak of that which we had personally experienced. In the absence of personal experience, feminist theorists can rely upon other women's accounts and upon the exercise of their own critical political intelligence. In the area of prostitution the exercise of political intelligence is particularly necessary since the voices of prostitutes even within the literature of the prostitutes' rights movement of the 1970s and 1980s do not agree. The main voices in this literature proclaimed that prostitution was a job just like any other or even a form of sexual self-determination for women. But others described prostitution as seriously and inevitably abusive.

Before the prostitutes' rights movement began, Kate Millett (1975) analysed prostitution in *The Prostitution Papers* as 'paradigmatic, somehow the very core of the female's condition'. It declared her 'subjection right out in the open' more clearly than marriage which hid the cash nexus behind a contract. It turned the woman into a thing to be bought, it effected her 'reification'. It showed that a woman is no more than 'cunt'. The prostitute was selling not really 'sex' but 'degradation' and the john bought 'power over another human being, the dizzy ambition of being lord of another's will for a stated period of time' (Millett, 1975: 56). But Millett considered that authentic action around prostitution had to come from prostitutes themselves 'if anything, ultimately, is to be done or said or decided about prostitution, prostitutes are the only legitimate persons to do it ...' (Millett, 1975: 15). Millett's analysis had become very unfashionable for feminists by the 1980s. Shannon Bell, in her 1994 book *Reading, Writing and Rewriting the Prostitute Body*, offers a postmodern feminist position in which her 'overarching strategy' is to show that there is 'no inherent meaning' in prostitution (Bell, 1994: 1). She does not hesitate to 'represent the Other' with her own meaning which is that the prostitute should be seen as 'worker, healer, sexual surrogate, teacher, therapist, educator, sexual minority, and political activist' (Bell, 1994: 103). Initially the writings of women in prostitution that emerged in the 1970s under the influence of feminism were not celebratory. The collection *Prostitutes: Our Life* contains the oral histories of six of the French women involved in the 1975 prostitutes' strike (Jaget, 1980). The argument of the strike was that prostitution was work which should be respected and decriminalized, but no attempt was made to sanitize it. The three books that emerged from the much more developed prostitutes' rights movement in the late 1980s show a rather different approach. In these texts many of the accounts still show prostitution to be a damaging experience but the main ideological message is much more positive. Feminists who emphasize the injury of prostitution are accused of making prostitutes into victims. These collections are: *Good Girls, Bad Girls: Sex Trade Workers and Feminists Face to Face* (Bell, 1987); *Sex Work: Writings by Women in the Sex Industry* (Delacoste and Alexander, 1988); and *A Vindication of the Rights of Whores* (Pheterson, 1989).

These books were all published by feminist presses and they all directly challenge what is seen as a hostile feminist analysis of prostitution. Prostitutes' rights activists argue that prostitution is not just a job like any other but a form of work with positive advantages. It allows women to be in control, particularly of their sexuality. An example of this positive argument comes from Terry van der Zijden from the Netherlands who says prostitution allows women to enjoy sex without complications and is a way to become 'sexually autonomous' and that sexual self-determination can lead to self-determination 'in all other areas of our existence as women' (cited in Pheterson, 1989: 161). But other prostitutes' voices in this literature adamantly reject the notion that prostitution has anything to do with women's liberation. A French woman in the collection from the 1975 prostitutes' strike asserts, 'Prostitution and sexual liberation have got nothing to do with each other, they're exactly the opposite.' She says it is 'quite absurd' to think that 'there'd be girls who'd do this for pleasure'. She explains that she does not feel 'free' with her body. In fact she feels 'bad about it' and 'self-conscious' and comments: 'I don't really feel like my body's alive, I think of it more as bruised, as a weight' (cited in Jaget, 1980: 112).

At a Canadian conference on pornography and prostitution, Peggy Miller, a member of Toronto's CORP, was positive about the sex in prostitution: 'What is so terrible about fucking for a living? I like it, I can live out my fantasies' (cited in Bell, 1987: 48). But another participant challenges her directly, saying that she was a prostitute for 8 years from the age of 15 and does not believe that she can 'like every sexual act' or work out fantasies with a trick that she's 'putting on an act for'. She asks 'Isn't it about having money to survive?' and says 'If I had had to fuck one more of them – boy, I would have killed him' (cited in Bell, 1987: 50). A woman at the Second Whores Congress pointed out that while some women purported to enjoy their work when they were speaking publicly more negative stories were being told in private (see Pheterson, 1989: 178). Another sceptical participant argued that if Priscilla Alexander's estimate in her theoretical piece, 'Prostitution: a Difficult Issue for Feminists' (in Delacoste and Alexander, 1988), that street prostitutes serviced an average of 1500 men a year, were true, then it was very hard to imagine that in every case they were revelling in sexual freedom. Other prostitutes in this literature argue that prostitution is not suitable for the young. Margo St James at the Canadian conference said prostitution was unsuitable for women under 25 because 'a young person should find their own sexual self before they are subjected to a lot of commercial leering and lusting' (cited in Bell, 1987: 129). The desire to protect young women does give the lie to the very positive accounts of prostitution's advantages.

The positive view of prostitution in the literature is belied by the common experience of very serious violence that many women describe. One French woman describes a 'respectable' client pulling a gun on her and another trying to strangle her. She says that assaults happen 'very often' (cited in Jaget, 1980: 124). All of the French women described the threat and experience of violence as a very negative part of the work. One says she was attacked several times when she began in prostitution, so 'I've reached the point now where I get really scared of all of them, even the regular clients. They could easily come ten times, twenty times, and then one fine day get some crazy idea in their head' (cited in Jaget, 1980: 85).

In one of the 1980s volumes, *Sex Work* (Delacoste and Alexander, 1988), dedicated to refashioning the image of prostitution, many of the women speak of experiencing severe violence or having to take precautions to avoid it. A street prostitute speaks of the precautions she takes such as searching the glovebox, keeping a hand on the door handle at all times. She tells of having had a knife to her throat and having a gun pulled on her and says she has to have a 'sixth sense' (cited in Delacoste and Alexander, 1988: 94). The threat of death is very real, as suggested by the figure in the same volume for the murder of prostitutes in the Seattle area: 81 from 1983 to 1986. An Australian study found that a third of the women had experienced some kind of non-sexual violence, 11 per cent experiencing it on more than seven occasions. A fifth of these women had been raped at work (Perkins and Prestage, 1994: 172). A contemporary female brothel owner in Sydney with lengthy experience does not see the situation in respect of violence against prostitutes as improving: 'The modern client is more demanding, wanting to pay less, looking for kinkier sex and, I believe, more likely to turn to violence' (Barlow, 1994: 139). Women in prostitution who would assert in surveys that they had not been raped would attest to having clients who go 'over-time', a situation that the prostitute is powerless to redress. It is likely that there is an under-reporting problem in surveying prostitutes on experiences of violence (Perkins and Bennett, 1985: 75). Going overtime can be a sign of more serious violence. One brothel prostitute tells of an incident: 'She went overtime so I looked in and there she was, dead, with a leg of a chair shoved through her eye and into her brain' (Perkins and Bennett, 1985: 240).

Toby Summer is the pseudonym of an ex-prostitute who wrote an angry rebuttal of the positive arguments of the Delacoste and Alexander (1988) *Sex Work* anthology. She offers a useful explanation from her own experience of why there is presently such a denial of the damage and celebration of prostitution in pro-prostitution literature. She seeks to explain how prostitution can be said to have 'something to do with *women* owning our own bodies . . .' while at the same time these bodies are being sold 'to men who hate women, whores and lesbians . . .'. She says that though not always a feminist she had always wanted to be 'free'. She felt 'closer to freedom' when espousing what she calls the 'Man's lie' about her independence in prostitution, when she told herself she chose 'even the rapes' and that the 'nausea–alienation–bruises–humiliation–STDs . . . poverty–abortion all were somehow fixable with what amounts to an EST positive attitude'. She lied to herself, she says, because this made her feel better and that she maintained this lie after leaving prostitution even though it allowed no explanation of why she chose to work in a 'hot commercial laundry for $1.00 per hour [rather] than fuck another man' (Summer, 1993: 233). She found that 'confronting how I've been hurt is the hardest thing that I've had to do in my life' (Summer, 1993: 234). It is hard because 'it is humiliating to acknowledge victimization'.

Why are there so few critical theoretical accounts of prostitution from feminists? There has been little attempt to fit prostitution into an analysis of women's oppression apart from Kathleen Barry's *Female Sexual Slavery* (1979), republished as *The Prostitution of Sexuality* (1995). This is so considerably revised as to constitute a quite new book. Barry exercises a critical political intelligence to make the argument that prostitution is a violation of women's human rights. If feminist squeamishness about challenging men's use of women in prostitution is really the result of not wanting to 'represent the Other', or not wanting to choose between Others, then this needs to be got over in the interests of integrating prostitution into a feminist analysis of sexuality and sexual violence.

The desire not to choose constitutes an abandonment of the prostitutes and ex-prostitutes who are critical, such as Toby Summer and the brave feminists who founded groups in the USA such as WHISPER (Women Hurt in Systems of Prostitution Engaged in Revolt) and the Council for Prostitution Alternatives. I suggest that when feminists are deciding what they think about prostitution that they must weigh up women's accounts against what they already know about sexuality and male violence under male supremacy. Rather than backing away from 'judgementalism' or depending on the rhetoric of 'choice', they need to see prostitution in its context, to see how it fits into and shapes the construction of women as objects for men's sexual use, which affects the status of all women. They need to consider how the sexual harassment and unwanted sexual intercourse that prostitutes are paid to endure relate to their own reasonable feminist aims of eliminating male violence for all. Feminists cannot hide from using their political intelligence behind the argument that only prostitutes can speak about their experience when such very diametrically opposite views are all posing as the truth of prostitution.

References

Barlow, Caroline (1994) 'A Brothel Owner's View', in R. Perkins and G. Prestage (eds) *Sex Work and Sex Workers in Australia*. Sydney: UNSW Press.
Barry, K. (1979) *Female Sexual Slavery*. New York: New York University Press.
Barry, K. (1995) *The Prostitution of Sexuality*. New York: New York University Press.
Bell, L. (ed.) (1987) *Good Girls, Bad Girls: Sex Trade Workers and Feminists Face to Face*. Toronto: The Women's Press.
Bell, S. (1994) *Reading, Writing and Rewriting the Prostitute Body*. Bloomington, IN: Indiana University Press.
Delacoste, F. and Alexander, P. (eds) (1988) *Sex Work: Writings by Women in the Sex Industry*. London: Virago.
Jaget, C. (ed.) (1980) *Prostitutes: Our Life*. St Albans, Herts: Falling Wall Press.
Millett, K. (1975) *The Prostitution Papers*. St Albans, Herts: Paladin Books.(First published 1971).
Perkins, R. and Bennett, G. (1985) *Being a Prostitute*. Sydney: George Allen and Unwin.
Perkins, R. and Prestage, G. (1994) *Sex Work and Sex Workers in Australia*. Sydney: UNSW Press.

Pheterson, G. (ed.) (1989) *A Vindication of the Rights of Whores*. Seattle: The Seal Press.

Summer, T. (1993) 'Women, Lesbians and Prostitution: A Workingclass Dyke Speaks Out against Buying Women for Sex', in J. Penelope and S. Wolfe (eds) *Lesbian Culture*. Freedom, CA: The Crossing Press.

22

The Spec(tac)ular Economy of Difference

Erica Burman

I want to reflect on political and psychic investments involved in acts of representing Others as this applies to feminist psychology. Irrespective of my intentions, those actions that I may consider interventions can reproduce the very power relations I am committed to dismantling and constitute me as the power-wielding subject, rather than as excluded object. Thus, although I may claim a position as a feminist in and around psychology, and this is a feminist book, writing this, here, inevitably positions me as an academic accumulating cultural capital. The question is: what else does it do? The phrase 'representing the Other' alludes to feminist and post-colonial studies' appropriation of a (specifically Lacanian) psychoanalytic account of the construction of subjectivity: the sentient Self emerges through differentiation from (an) Other(s). The Self is defined in relation to this/these Other(s), which carry the burden of difference, the excess, the surplus that will not fit. So, the condition of entering the symbolic order is that we are split, and the strivings to regain those features that lie outside its structure of representation institute a fantasy of an earlier time of unity and completeness (a time that never actually existed).

Now how does all this fit in with what I am doing here? I think this framework can be applied at an institutional level (not least since the realm of 'the personal' is constituted by this too). Just because some kind of distinction between Self and Other may be (logically, psychologically) necessary, this significantly *under*-determines *which* differences are taken as primary. A better question is: who defines which differences matter? So, Lacanian theory, after Freud, treats sexual difference and its symbolic associations as the primary axis around which power is owned, exercised and lacked. But this is increasingly challenged by feminists, not only in terms of repudiating the relegation of women to the margins of representability, or celebrating those exclusions as subversive and transformatory, but also in terms of questioning the absolute polarity of the distribution between male/female, inside/outside and Self/Other (Benjamin, 1995).

It seems to me that these are very relevant issues for feminist psychologists. When we speak/write/act as feminist psychologists we are adopting the equivalent of what Juliet Mitchell described in relation to the woman novelist as 'the discourse of the hysteric'.

> Hysteria is the woman's simultaneous acceptance and refusal of the organisation of sexuality under patriarchal capitalism … the hysteric's voice … is *the woman's masculine language* (one has to speak 'masculinely' in a phallocentric world) talking about feminine experience. (Mitchell, 1984: 289–90, emphasis in original)

Psychology, as a particular masculine-invested discipline, wedded to a mythical model of science as the repudiation of all things (supposedly) feminine (emotions, subjectivity, connectedness, contextuality), can only recognize us insofar as we speak in, or in strategic relation to, its terms (Grosz, 1992). Necessary, even perhaps laudable for our feminist interventions, the conditions for our speaking are (apart from the tokenistic gesture) as *psychologists* rather than feminists. We are not made Other through our own processes of representation. But we are positioned as psychological subjects, and subjects of psychology by virtue of separating ourselves from other positions and identifications.

All this poses dilemmas for the project of feminist psychology. Either as feminists we are outside psychology, and therefore disallowed a position from which to intervene, or we are positioned as psychologists and therefore, at least structurally or institutionally, distanced from feminist theory and activity. But look what has happened: in the process of demarcating the polarity, feminism as the excluded Other of representation has been constituted as undifferentiated homogeneity. This recalls the debates in feminist research about the theoretical and political difficulties of according authenticity to those accounts being represented and introduced into the discipline. In claiming to 'speak for' or 'give voice to', not only do we run the risks of being patronizing and colonizing Others' accounts, thereby reproducing the institutional authority of psychology in the act of making claims on behalf of others, we also essentialize (and sometimes individualize or romanticize) those accounts by failing to treat them as constructed through both micro- and meta-representational practices (Kelly et al., 1994).

I am not proposing that we refuse the speaking positions to which we can claim access. This is not possible, desirable or responsible. But what we do need to remind ourselves of is that the act of assuming such positions places us within familiar and well-policed definitions of sameness and differences which, in privileging the first, constitute the second. But what this analysis does is to invite some political strategies for subverting these (doubly) exclusive categorizations. First, we should work to recognize ourselves in Others. I am not here advocating a mere liberal extension of our own qualities and attributes to Others, but rather to understand the dynamics of mutual investment and provisional privilege. So, to enjoy the transgressive position of the feminist psychologist, we rely upon some claim to represent a feminist constituency. This is a fiction, in the sense that there is no such unitary entity and, if there ever were, it was structured by exclusionary practices from which we would want to distance ourselves. But our rights to speak, both as and for feminists, arise from such a fiction – like my right to 'speak for' or invoke 'feminist psychologists'. We need to use this fiction as a productive collective fantasy, with an awareness of its strategic basis.

Second, without being coy about the power of psychology's definitions and the audience its voice commands, we should not presume that the Other will necessarily want (or be able) to be represented by us as feminist psychologists. That is, the costs of representation within the dominant order that defines it may outweigh the benefits. As Kum-Kum Bhavnani (1990) suggests, silence may be a more potent critique than words. This is not to romanticize a domain outside language or other representational practices, but to recognize that the process of bringing into focus, of knowledging, can constitute an act of epistemic violence or alienation that disempowers or distorts, so that commenting on the absences within the dominant representations may be more respectful and a more enabling political intervention.

Third, all this highlights how representation is not neutral and transparent in process as well as outcome. Our practices of representation all too often construct precisely what they claim to reflect or describe. Feminist psychological research is no less vulnerable to this than other research practices. We can make some connections here with matters of political representation. In invoking alternative structures of feminist accountability that lie outside the academy, we may be lamenting a loss and striving to repair a retrospectively constituted community. Such communities may have never actually existed as such, but the process nevertheless may be useful rhetorically if not inspirationally.

Fourth, redrawing the landscape of affiliations and identifications that acknowledge as well as transgress the institutional divides of professional and structural social inequalities allows for the elaboration of ways of working across those differences. These are alliances, coalitions that are built through negotiation and shared work, not identities that can be presumed. The category 'feminist psychologist' may be a partial, tense identity I assume for particular purposes, but how it functions – to interpellate others who might also claim this identity, or to identify those who would disallow it, or to set me up as a psychologist claiming a feminist expertise over other feminists/women – resides more in what I *do* than what I call myself.

In other words, if the Others I represent are in some respects also me then *my* representation of *them* should reflect on its process. Rather than the voyeuristic, spec(tac)ular logic of the one-way mirror beloved of psychology, it should present new perspectives on the disciplinary matrix that makes us as well as them.

References

Benjamin, J. (1995) 'Sameness and Difference: Toward an "Over-inclusive" Theory of Gender Development', in A. Elliot and S. Frosh (eds) *Psychoanalysis in Contexts: Paths between Theory and Modern Culture*. London: Routledge.

Bhavnani, K.-K. (1990) '"What's Power Got to Do with It?" Empowerment and Social Research', in I. Parker and J. Shotter (eds) *Deconstructing Social Psychology*. London: Routledge.

Grosz, E. (1992) 'What is Feminist Theory?', in H. Crowley and S. Himmelweit (eds) *Knowing Women: Feminism and Knowledge*. Cambridge: Polity Press.

Kelly, L., Burton, S. and Regan, L. (1994) 'Researching Women's Lives or Studying Women's Oppression? Reflections on What Constitutes Feminist Research', in M. Maynard and J. Purvis (eds) *Researching Women's Lives from a Feminist Perspective*. London: Taylor and Francis.

Mitchell, J. (1984) 'Psychoanalysis and Child Development', in J. Mitchell (ed.) *Women: The Longest Revolution*. London: Virago.

23

Giving Voice: The Participant Takes Issue

Katie MacMillan

The theme of the following discussion is that the practice of giving research subjects a 'voice' within academic texts, whether by speaking for them or by letting them speak for themselves, is always and inevitably a textual device that retains and reinforces, rather than weakens, the academic author's authority. For example, despite its overt co-authoring by 'Karl, Cynthia, Andrew and Vanessa' (1992), Karl Tomm's article with three of his therapy clients remains his, via his identification as 'primary author', and in statements such as how they (Cynthia, Andrew and Vanessa), 'found this theoretical part of the chapter rather "heavy reading" but realized it was intended for a professional audience' (1992: 134). Furthermore, while Cynthia, Andrew and Vanessa remain anonymous (by their own choice), Karl Tomm is the one included in the front of the book in the list of contributors, and it is his name that is given as copyright holder. The voices of the 'subjects' (Cynthia, Andrew and Vanessa's) come to us only via their incorporation into this academic text.

Similarly, in her work on how therapists reformulate what their clients actually say, Kathy Davis (1986) claims to reveal how therapists pathologize the clients' troubles, reformulating them as problems amenable to therapy. However, it is precisely through her own reformulations of the *therapist's* talk that Davis is able to 'show' the client to be a 'victim' of therapy. In doing so, she manages further to perpetuate an image of the subject as silenced and in need of the discourse analyst's insightful perspective. A less one-sided analysis might examine therapy as a *negotiated process* between therapist and client, rather than assuming 'power' to be a stable entity residing with the therapist. It is this assumption that, ironically, perpetuates rather than liberates the 'powerless voice' of the client.

The following text takes the form of various voices as a way of highlighting the ineluctable nature of authorship, exploring some of the tensions that arise when quoting and speaking for Others, and the way in which those voices are incorporated within academic texts. The three voices are nested one within another like Russian dolls, with the first voice, 'Katie MacMillan's', introducing and concluding this chapter. Nested within that is 'Netta Speaker', the research 'subject'. Within that, nestled in the centre of this work, is the third voice consisting of Speaker's quotation of, and comments on, a section from MacMillan's doctoral thesis, which purports to analyse an interview with Speaker. Note that the convention of rendering subjects anonymous, or pseudonymized, justified on ethical grounds, or often as their own choice, is also a means of rendering irrelevant, or of deleting, their personal identity. They speak to us not as the persons they are, but as the *kinds* of people the research makes relevant. Such indeed is the status of the anonymized 'Cynthia, Andrew and Vanessa', Tomm's therapeutic clients, while 'Karl' (Tomm), as therapist and academic author, speaks as himself.

According to Speaker, MacMillan's analysis represents MacMillan's concerns rather than hers. Stemming from this is the more general concern that the analyst *usurps* the subject's voice through the very process of offering it as part of an academic discussion. This may have the effect, ironically, of further subduing the subject to whom the analyst aims to 'give voice'. Jennifer Coates, citing the work of Shirley and Edwin Ardener (1975, 1978), discusses the way that dominant modes of expression prevail in all cultures. This means that if 'members of a "muted group" want to be heard, they are required to express themselves in dominant mode' (Coates, 1986: 35). However, it follows from this that if the 'muted group' speak in 'dominant mode', this may not be a representation of the minority so much as a representation of the dominant perspective speaking *about* the silenced group (Alcoff, 1994). Thus the authoritative voice of the majority is further warranted and reinforced.

In the following sequence Speaker's 'voice' questions the researcher's authority as analytic expert. It is important to bear in mind, however, that *this is a warrant for the author's argument* that 'authority' (in the authorial sense at least) is a textual accomplishment.

The Subject Takes Issue

On visits back to my home town, when I was in my early 20s, my mother would come shopping with me, and speak for me out of habit. 'She's looking for . . .', she'd say, or 'She wants half a pound of . . .', and I'd be subdued even before I'd opened my mouth. All that seems such a long time ago now, so it was with a sense of indignation that I read Katie MacMillan's analysis of *my* talk, and realized she was writing about me as though I didn't have a tongue in my head, as though I was some sort of *victim* (the term 'therapist's dope' springs to mind). Now, I had thought I would be perfectly comfortable as the 'subject' of discourse analysis, since I had assumed that my tape-recorded discussion with my friend Pam was for me to have my say on hypnosis. (I'd been to see a hypnotherapist some time ago, to see if hypnosis could help me to stop smoking.) What I hadn't realized was that the researcher (MacMillan) would use my talk to illustrate an argument about hypnosis that *she* has been working on, and that my taped conversation would supposedly show the way in which a client's (my own) behaviour can be pathologized by the therapist!

I extracted the following data from MacMillan's (draft) doctoral thesis, so that I could use this as an opportunity to present *my* discussion in a forum that may allow the 'subject' to speak for herself. In offering a sample of MacMillan's analysis, I intend to reveal it as one perspective among many. I do this in order to show that what any of this stuff offers is the author's creation of Netta Speaker – not the *real me*.

Anyway, back to the analysis: in the example below MacMillan has taken my description of a session with a hypnotist, in which I say why I know I can't be hypnotized. She then uses it to expose the therapist in the act of establishing his position of authority, at my expense.

The Thesis as Subject

In the following example Netta and Pam are discussing a therapy session, in which Netta had paid a therapist to get her to stop smoking, using hypnosis. After what would appear to have been an unsuccessful session, however, Netta relates that she is told, by the therapist, that she can never be hypnotized. As we shall see, the therapist uses the notion of 'resistance' as a means of converting a potential failure of therapeutic technique into a problem located within the client. In this way a situation he might otherwise be held accountable for – a session with a hypnotist in which the paying client doesn't get hypnotized – is transformed into one in which the client is at fault.

EXAMPLE 1

7	*Pam*:	Right, you were sa:ying ((*laughing softly*)) Netta, you can't
8		be hypnotized
9	*Netta*:	No I can't (1.0) E:h (.) I went there and I laid on this sort of
10		(0.2) *chair* reclining chair told me to look at this *black* piece
11		in the ceiling (0.5) *all* the time talking very soothingly (0.2)
12		'n then saying how heavy my eyes were (0.5) and then ah I
13		couldn't raise my fingers on my right hand
14	*Pam*:	mmm
15	*Netta*:	which I did
16	*Pam*:	((*laughing softly*)) ye:a:h
17	*Netta*:	then he continued a bit more and he went on and he said
18		'*now* you can't move your fingers on your right hand'
19		of course I could 'n he said 'well get down' he said 'A::h I
20		haven't hypnotized you.' So I said 'no I realised that.'
21		So he said 'it's *you* that's blocking it.' So I said 'no I *want* to be
22		hypnotized' I said 'I've come to give up smoking and I want to
23		be hypnotized.' He said 'yes, you might think you do but at
24		the back of your mind you're not, you're saying *no*.'

The psychoanalytic notion of 'resistance' (Freud, 1976) is widely available as a therapist's explanatory category. It can be used by the therapist to reformulate a 'failed' intervention as a stage of the therapeutic process in which it is understood that the client is unable to go into hypnosis because of unconscious fears (lines 23–4). In Netta's account of the hypnosis session she describes how the hypnotist tells her that certain things will happen but they don't (lines 12–19). This is a tricky situation for the hypnotist when, according to Netta, he has made suggestions that she can't raise the fingers on her right hand and she does, twice. The hypnotist responds to this apparent lack of compliance by accusing Netta of 'blocking it' (line 21) and preventing hypnosis from happening.

'Resistance', as a rhetorical resource, is a beautifully designed psychological category. It can be used by the therapist to show that, if therapy doesn't work, if trance doesn't occur, then the 'subject' didn't allow the expertise of the therapist to guide her towards the therapeutic outcome. The goal of psychotherapy, for the clinical hypnotherapist Milton Erickson, was to facilitate the 'breakdown of biases to allow objectivity and freedom of action' (Havens, 1985: 140). This reflects a familiar view of therapy that the client may know best (cf. Lietaer et al., 1990; Rogers, 1961), but the therapist knows even better. By asserting that it is frequently the client's 'resistance' that is blocking the way to better mental health and self-understanding, therapists can position themselves as experts who know, better than the client herself, what her best interests are. This rhetorically powerful device means that it is very difficult for the therapist to be seen to have failed (MacMillan, doctoral thesis in preparation).

Speaker Resumes

Now there is a vital flaw in MacMillan's analysis. She seems to have glossed over the importance of looking at the discussion as something that is occurring between myself and Pam, and that what went on between the therapist and myself was only what I *said* went on. She does not attend to its status as my description of the therapy session, and the fact that I'm not talking to the therapist, I'm talking *about him*. I wonder just how much of my own voice would have been retained, had MacMillan restricted herself more closely to analysing my talk, instead of championing this need to speak for me.

Where, for example, in my discussion with Pam, do I get bothered about this Freudian notion of 'resistance' and how the therapist establishes his position as an expert? It seems to me that this is MacMillan's concern, not mine. Despite speaking for the 'subject' (me) in what I am sure is a well-intentioned manner, MacMillan misses the irony of doing so – that her own analysis is in danger of perpetuating the very thing that she speaks out against, the 'disempowerment' of the 'subject'. By choosing to speak for another, MacMillan should recognize that the act of 'speaking for' carries with it the implication that the 'Other' cannot or does not speak adequately for herself. Now I resent that implication! I should be able to say what I want to say, when I want to say it, perfectly clearly, without any well-meaning discourse analyst jumping in and analysing things as she wants to see them, and not as they might have been intended.

In my talk, as far as I'm concerned, I was telling Pam about *my experiences* with the hypnotist, and that's what interested me – what had happened to me in that therapy session. But in MacMillan's hands all that gets packaged up and analysed as *discourse*, and recruited for a thesis on therapy talk, and on issues of empowerment. None of that is what I had in mind when I was describing my experience of hypnosis to Pam. What I'm doing, *I* think, is saying something about myself, in connection with hypnosis. When I tell Pam the bit about where I say to the hypnotist 'no I realized that' after he's said that he hasn't hypnotized me, I'm showing that I was responding to the hypnotist in a way that clearly defined me as nobody's fool. Not only am I someone who knows the difference between being in trance and not being in trance, I am also the sort of person who is able to tell a hypnotist that she is well aware that she hasn't been hypnotized. As such I show that I am not a stereotypical hypnotist's 'subject', that is – I'm not some compliant female who might be expected to respond like Svengali's Trilby!

Conclusion

In the same way that a predominantly male perspective has been perpetuated through its scientific descriptions of nature (Haraway, 1989; see also Griffin, 1978; Merchant, 1980), and different voices and gendered talk place value on particular ways of seeing the world (Gilligan, 1982; Tannen, 1991), so *all* texts construct their own authority, and one way of doing that is by having their 'subjects' speak directly to the reader. This device, as if by-passing the analyst/writer's intervention, works like science's 'inscription devices' (Latour and Woolgar, 1979), and 'empiricist repertoires' (Gilbert and Mulkay, 1984), in which the object under investigation seems to write its nature straight on to the page, without let or hindrance from the scientist–author.

In this study, Netta Speaker's presentation of a selected extract from Katie MacMillan's thesis claims that the analyst *used* the 'subject's' voice in order to promote her own research interests. This implicates analysis as a version cut and polished for an academic audience. However, the irony of offering Speaker's objection to MacMillan's analysis is that this is still an author's reformulation of Speaker's objection, in which personal protestation becomes generalized into an argument about analyst and subjects.

Netta Speaker, *as a fiction*, is the constructed voice which enables a decon-struction of Katie MacMillan's position of authority as an analyst, and illustrates the point that all texts construct their subjects (in both senses: topic and author). Had I invited the *real* Netta Speaker to speak on this topic, would there have been a personal issue she would want to voice in an academic journal? If so, how would it have to be presented? Would her comments have inevitably been recon-structed and generalized (by the researcher) into academic concerns moulded for journal requirements?

Finally, the construction you are reading now includes the device of present-ing 'Katie MacMillan' as the true author (the name below the title of this chapter), as if what you are reading now is my real voice (when the 'I' who writes the text is as much its artefact as Netta Speaker). An inevitable feature of any representation and 'speaking for' is a *usurping* of the 'subject's' voice, however benignly intentioned. However, by making explicit some of the 'moves' involved in constructing analysis, particularly that which represents 'the Other', the 'authority' of the analyst itself becomes available for analysis – as does, of course, this author's analysis of the analysis.

References

Alcoff, L. (1994) 'The Problem of Speaking for Others', in S.O. Weisser and J. Fleischner (eds) *Feminist Nightmares – Women at Odds: Feminism and the Problem of Sisterhood*, pp. 285–309. New York: New York University Press.

Ardener, S. (1975) *Perceiving Women*. London: Mallaby Press.

Ardener, S. (1978) 'The Nature of Women in Society', in S. Ardener (ed.) *Defining Females*, pp. 9–48. London: Croom Helm.

Coates, J. (1986) *Women, Men and Language*. London: Longman.

Davis, K. (1986) 'The Process of Problem (Re)formulation in Psychotherapy', *Sociology of Health and Illness* 8: 44–74.

Freud, S. (1976) *The Psychopathology of Everyday Life*. Harmondsworth: Pelican. First published 1901.

Gilbert, G.N. and Mulkay, M. (1984) *Opening Pandora's Box: A Sociological Analysis of Scientists' Discourse*. Cambridge: Cambridge University Press.

Gilligan, C. (1982) *In a Different Voice*. Cambridge, MA: Harvard University Press.

Griffin, S. (1978) *Women and Nature: The Roaring Inside Her*. New York: Harper and Row.

Haraway, D. (1989) *Primate Visions: Gender, Race and Nature in the World of Modern Science*. London: Routledge.

Havens, R.A. (1985) *The Wisdom of Milton H. Erickson*. New York: Irvington.

Latour, B. and Woolgar, S. (1979) *Laboratory Life: The Social Construction of Scientific Facts*. London: Sage.

Lietaer, G., Rombauts, K. and Van Balen, R. eds (1990) *Client-Centred and Experiential Psychotherapy in the Nineties*. Leuven, Belgium: Leuven University Press.

Merchant, C. (1980) *The Death of Nature: Women, Ecology and the Scientific Revolution*. San Francisco: Harper and Row.

Rogers, C. (1961) *On Becoming a Person*. Boston: Houghton Mifflin.

Tannen, D. (1991) *You Just Don't Understand*. New York: William Morrow.

Tomm, K. (as Karl, Cynthia, Andrew and Vanessa) (1992) 'Therapeutic Distinctions in an On-going Therapy', in S. McNamee and K.J. Gergen (eds) *Therapy as Social Construction*, pp. 116–35. London: Sage.

24

Across Differences of Age: Young Women Speaking of and with Old Women

Marian Titley and Becky Chasey

As two clinical psychologists working full time in the British National Health Service for older adults, our clients are mostly women in their 60s to 90s. We are routinely ascribed the authority to represent old women. Is our shared gender commonality enough to do this well or are age differences more salient? If we are to pay proper attention to good service delivery, then addressing this question is vital.

At the start of our work, we were enthused by curiosity and a desire to explore women's experiences throughout their lives. We shared a sense of frustration at the artificial separation of women below and above the age of 65 imposed by service organization. Expecting to draw on the commonality of shared gender, we were struck by the extent to which their gender and ours was disregarded. In so much of the literature and in clinical practice, the gendered process of growing older is presented as neutral, old people are seen as neutered and services for old people appear peculiarly bland. Increasingly, we have been struck by the question of why, when so many young women work for and with so many old women in specialist services, the issue of being women has been so little addressed.

An explicitly gendered analysis of the nature and bases of gender inequalities pertinent to old women is provided by Arber and Ginn (1991). This was important to us in rendering gender visible within academic discussion, providing a framework to begin examining our clinical practice. They detail the ways in which unequal access to the key resources promoting independence particularly disadvantage old women. Yet, in services, we tend to relate to old people as if those stratifications which so shaped and influenced them during their younger lives no longer have any significance. It helped us to make sense of what we were seeing and feeling about services for old women.

We became aware of the silence and absence of old women's voices. We realized how little is written by old women themselves about the experience of being old. Reading MacDonald and Rich's (1984) book, *Look Me in the Eye*, challenged our assumption that shared gender was commonality enough. With many decades between ourselves and our clients, and with clients facing multiple physical and mental health problems, the differences are stark. Working in this setting confronts us with a profound and obvious sense of old women as the Other.

This mix of 'sameness' and 'Otherness' raises a number of tensions and dilemmas. To avoid openly discussing old women protects us from the charge of 'wrongful representation', while seeming to credit us with acknowledging the limits of our professional and personal experience. However, by avoiding this risk we are complicit in the continued devaluing of old women's experiences. Both we and they are then silenced.

Our decision to represent old women's experiences and concerns emerged from considering what we know of the current realities of their lives. Firstly, not just old, they face the 'double jeopardy' of being old and female (Rodeheaver and Datan, 1988). Old women are targeted by negative, demeaning stereotypes which portray them as ugly, helpless, dependent and passive (Itzin, 1990; Sontag, 1977). Secondly, in our work we meet old women at particularly vulnerable points in their lives. They may be facing difficult decisions about options regarding their own care, while facing complex health problems. In the context of community care, they are likely to find themselves dependent on other people's assessment of the nature and priority of their own needs. Old women also receive formal care in a context in which the philosophy and practice of advocacy is poorly developed. As a group, they are recipients of a significant proportion of health and social care, yet are largely excluded from policy-making and service development (Women's National Commission, 1992). Against this backdrop, to be silent is tacitly to support this status quo. With few fora available to us to hear from old women collectively, we are hampered by the lack of direct feed-back to us about our portrayal of old women. Nevertheless, at present the challenge to us seems to be to articulate our experience as young women workers, while critically reflecting on this in the light of those old women's accounts available to us.

Research consistently shows that most old women do not fit the popular stereo-types, remaining fit and active throughout much of later life and living with relatively minor disability (Payne and Whittington, 1976). Indeed, much of the informal care that people receive is provided by old people (Qureshi and Walker, 1989). Yet, as specialist workers, we are aware that the women whom we meet reflect a small subgroup whose ill-health and dependency unwittingly confirm our stereotypes. This intensifies our experience of old women as Other. In addition, the old women we meet in hospital have undergone the transition from 'person' to 'patient'. The passivity and objectification of this process is well documented (Greene et al., 1986) and its impact on old women is particularly damaging since it reinforces the negative stereotypes that they already carry.

As Biggs (1989) points out, many helping professionals are more at ease with younger clients than with older people. Having not experienced old age for them-selves, empathy based on commonality is unavailable. Yet, in our work with old people, we are forced to know more about debilitating physical conditions as well as learning directly about old women's experiences of dementia. Witnessing this distress is hard to bear; we must also deal with the fear that our own old age might be similar; that their current reality might be our own future (Genevay and Katz, 1990). In drawing away in order to cope with this, we exaggerate the sense of Otherness.

Menzies (1970) has argued that this type of individual defence has been institutionalized in the medical context. While the recent emergence of social gerontology stands opposed to the entrenched medicalization of later life experience, medical explanations of later life experience predominate. To grow old is almost synonymous with becoming sick. Psychological and sociological analyses of old age remain relatively underdeveloped (Arber and Ginn, 1991) and consequently have relatively little impact in medical settings.

Changes in the terms used to refer to specialist services have attempted to redress the negative stereotyping of old age in formal care settings. 'Geriatric' has been replaced by 'elderly', to be superseded by 'older adults'. The importance of the choice of words used to represent Others has been recognized across all devalued client groups, with growing recognition of the unconscious dynamics of language choice (Lerner, 1976). However, the change of labels lays itself open to the charge of superficiality or tokenism. We have yet to witness a change in service delivery where old women are truly valued and respected; where ageism and sexism are consistently challenged.

We know from old women's accounts that the term 'old' is deeply problematic for many. 'Old' is a label that nobody wants to own. This is encapsulated in the title of Thompson et al.'s (1990) book, based on interviews with old people, *I Don't Feel Old*. Itzin (1990) examines how the use of the word 'old' by old people does not apply to any calendar age, but to a state of 'decrepitude and feebleness'. She argues that what old people are denying is not their age, but a derogatory stereotype of incapacity and encroaching senility in which they do not recognize themselves. Passing for 'young enough' is a common concern for women of many ages. Copper emphasises the divisive nature of this process:

> In our thirties we do not want to be mistaken for forty. In our forties we do not want anyone to assume we are fifty. Somewhere in the fifties anxieties about the increase in rejection and invisibility which old women face become critical. This is often a time when our trained inability to identify with women older than ourselves reaches its climax. (1988: 74)

Rich suggests that one common way of coping is to deny old age, such that becoming old is then a misfortune that befalls other people (MacDonald and Rich, 1984). She goes on to argue that this denial alienates an old woman both from herself and from others like herself. As de Beauvoir (1977: 316) points out, the attitude 'so long as you feel young you are young' shows a complete misunderstanding of the complex truth of old age. She comments on the way that old age is particularly difficult to assume because it is always regarded as something alien: 'Within me is the Other – that is to say the person I am for the outsider – who is old; and that Other is myself.'

Matthews (1979) raises a similar point from her interviews with old women, observing that old women must deal with others who see them as old even though they do not see themselves in this way. Whenever old women discover that aspects of their own behaviour conform to their own internalized and negative stereotypes of old age, this can be experienced as a threat to their images of themselves. As a consequence, a range of coping strategies must be developed to maintain a precarious self-identity.

Recent theoretical developments describe how self-identity is actively constituted and reconstituted in interpersonal communication (Jordan et al., 1991; Shotter and Gergen, 1989). In arguing for the importance of relational processes in the construction of identity, Coupland and Nussbaum (1993) emphasize the socially and politically constructed meanings of growing old. They illustrate the means by which the old woman's social context influences the way in which she attempts to retain a valued self-image. Their research is supported by Nikander (1995), who interviewed a group of women friends in their 70s. She was interested in describing the ways in which old women in this group setting continuously negotiated variable and momentary identities in their conversations with each other. Micro-analyses of the talk between older and younger women by Coupland and Coupland (1990) illustrate some important skews and distortions in both the way that old women represent themselves in conversation and in the perceptions that others make of them. With a peer, one old woman talked more about positive aspects of her life experience, but with a younger listener she emphasized her dependency and misfortune (Coupland et al., 1991).

What can we draw from this as young women practitioners? Clearly, it is insufficient to claim that commonality of gender is enough in itself to enable us to represent old women well. To acknowledge the salience of difference between old and young women is complex, but crucial. Resisting the tendency to simplify and categorize the diverse experiences of old women has become increasingly important to us. In writing this, we recognize that while we currently use the term 'old women', we are concerned to find better ways of speaking about women many decades older than ourselves. We continue to question the use of the category 'old women' in order to tease out the ageist assumptions behind this. We wonder, too, whether the issue of age difference is more salient to us as younger women, than to those with whom we work. For us, this highlights the one-sided nature of our reflections so far, since we have yet to debate these issues directly with old women. Although we have drawn on available accounts by old women, old women's views have yet to be well heard, both collectively and individually. Making ourselves more accountable to those we represent requires us to find more and better ways of speaking well, together with old women. As old women so clearly testify, the combined effect of ageism and sexism continues to render old women marginalized and invisible. Part of our task is actively and publicly to question their continued absence and silence.

References

Arber, S. and Ginn, J. (1991) *Gender and Later Life: A Sociological Analysis of Resources and Constraints*. London: Sage.

de Beauvoir, S. (1977) *Old Age*. London: Penguin.

Biggs, S. (1989) 'Professional Helpers and Resistances to Work with Older People', *Ageing and Society* 9: 43–60.

Copper, B. (1988) *Over the Hill: Reflections on Ageism between Women*. Freedom, CA: The Crossing Press.

Coupland, J., Coupland, N. and Grainger, K. (1991) 'Intergenerational Discourse: Contextual Versions of Ageing and Elderliness', *Ageing and Society* 11: 189–208.

Coupland, N. and Coupland, J. (1990) 'Language and Later Life: The Diachrony and Decrement Predicament', in H. Giles and W.P. Robinson (eds) *Handbook of Language and Social Psychology*, pp. 451–68. New York: Wiley.

Coupland, N. and Nussbaum, J.F. (eds) (1993) *Discourse and Lifespan Identity*. Newbury Park, CA: Sage.

Genevay, B. and Katz, R.S. (eds) (1990) *Countertransference and Older Clients*. London: Sage.

Greene, M.G., Adelman, R., Charon, R. and Hoffman, S. (1986) 'Ageism in the Medical Encounter: An Exploratory Study of Doctor–Elderly Patient Relationship', *Language and Communication* 6: 113–24.

Itzin, C. (1990) 'As Old as You Feel', in P. Thompson, C. Itzin and M. Abendstern (eds) *I Don't Feel Old: The Experience of Later Life*, pp. 107–36. Oxford: Oxford University Press.

Jordan, J.V., Caplan, A.G., Baker-Miller, J., Stiver, I.P. and Surrey, J.C. (1991) *Women's Growth in Connection: Writings from the Stone Center*. New York: Guilford Press.

Lerner, H.E. (1976) 'Girls, Ladies or Women? The Unconscious Dynamics of Language Choice', *Comprehensive Psychiatry* 17: 2.

MacDonald, B. and Rich, C. (1984) *Look Me in the Eye: Old Women, Ageing and Ageism*. London: The Women's Press.

Matthews, S. (1979) *The Social World of Old Women*. Beverley Hills, CA: Sage.

Menzies, I. (1970) *The Functioning of Social Systems as a Defence against Anxiety*. London: Tavistock Institute of Human Relations.

Nikander, P. (1995) 'Seventy-something: Women, Language and Self-identity', paper presented at the Women and Psychology Conference, 7–9 July 1995, Leeds, UK.

Payne, B. and Whittington, F. (1976) 'Older Women: An Examination of Popular Stereotypes and Research Evidence', *Social Problems* 23 (4): 448–504.

Qureshi, H. and Walker, A. (1989) *The Caring Relationship: Elderly People and their Families*. London: Macmillan.

Rodeheaver, D. and Datan, N. (1988) 'The Challenge of Double Jeopardy – Toward a Mental Health Agenda for Ageing', *American Psychologist* 43 (8): 648–54.

Shotter, J. and Gergen, K.J. (1989) *Texts of Identity*. London: Sage.

Sontag, S. (1977) 'The Double Standard of Ageing', in *Saturday Review of Society*, cited in B. Copper, *Over the Hill: Reflections on Ageism between Women*. Freedom, CA: The Crossing Press.

Thompson, P., Itzin, C. and Abendstern, M. (eds) (1990) *I Don't Feel Old: The Experience of Later Life*. Oxford: Oxford University Press.

Women's National Commission (1992) *Older Women: Myths and Strategies. An Agenda for Action*. Crown Copyright.

25

Responsibility and Advocacy: Representing Young Women

Anita Harris

This chapter offers some suggestions for the representation of young women in feminist research. Traditionally, young people have been placed as passive objects of research. They have often been identified only through their 'problems' or, in the case of young women, have been either ignored or had their issues subsumed or belittled by the prioritizing of those of young men. This problem, of course, has been substantially redressed over the past 20 years by the feminist rehauling of youth studies. In a broader sense, however, young women are not particularly prominent on the feminist agenda. There is a commonsense notion in Australia, at least, that young women consider feminism passé, or have developed a 'new' version of it, following the lead of Denfield (1995), Roiphe (1993) and others, that is fundamentally unfeminist in its rejection of the analysis of gender relations as power relations (Summers, 1995). While by no means seeking to 'blame the victim' myself, I am interested here in how feminism can work to encompass issues of relevance to young women and thereby represent them more adequately. Working out the process of this representation means tackling several practical and epistemological issues. By focusing on the notions of responsibility and advocacy, I hope here to tease out some of these issues and suggest some possibilities for fruitful and respectful representation.

Responsibility

The first task in the process of representing young women in feminist research is to establish where responsibility lies for this representation in the first place. It has been pointed out more recently in feminist writing that it is the responsibility of feminists who have status and authority in the public world to question their exclusionary practices, and it is not the responsibility of the excluded to start representing themselves in a way that can be recognized (Carby, 1982; Frye, 1983; Sykes, 1984). This is not to say that young women are helpless and passive and need someone else's interpretations of their experiences to override their own. There is a broader issue at stake in the question of representation, and that is, who counts? Young women are often very vocal and active; the problem is not with them not being vocal enough, or even not being vocal in ways that can be heard outside their milieux, but with a feminist platform that does not seek to incorporate their experiences.

There are two issues here. The first is that a lot of young women are engaged in feminist activity which is simply either not named as such, or not claimed by the broader Women's Movement. The Riot Grrrl movement in the United States of America, the shifts in education and youth work towards female peer education and counselling, the establishment of feminist media for and by young women such as Grot Grrrl in Australia, young women's involvement in self-defence, sport, lesbian relationships, unisex fashion, their own commitment to girls-only schools, are all important activities that are clearly significant to feminism, but have gone relatively unremarked upon in contemporary feminist theory and debate, except when focusing on young women as a special interest group. The second issue is that, as members of the political category 'women', young women must be represented by the political movement that speaks for that category. It is not only young women's unnamed feminist activities that need a place within feminism, but also their experiences of struggling with the constraints of patriarchy. The problem clearly is not how to make young women's issues fit with feminism, for by definition they already do, but how to make feminism include their experiences as a matter of course. There has been an important effort to make them count on the agenda of the sociology of youth, and this has been reasonably successful in shifting the 'youth' focus from white, working-class young men. While this is feminist work in itself, it seems quite likely that young women have more in common with older women than with young men, but remain for the most part stranded in youth studies. As an example, in an informal survey of *Australian Feminist Studies, Feminist Review, Women's Studies International Forum* and *Gender and Society*, I found only three pieces specifically about or inclusive of young women for the years 1989 to 1994. This needs to be addressed not only so that feminism can be more truly representative, but also so that the catchcry, 'I'm not a feminist, but . . .', will not be seen as such an accurate or desirable self-description for young women.

If we accept, then, that young women should 'belong', and that their membership depends on rethinking the agenda (the first part of representation, the responsibility), it is necessary to enquire how to represent them without speaking for them.

Advocacy

It seems quite evident that it is not possible to 'speak for' someone else without performing some form of appropriation. 'Speaking for' implies that the voice of those represented is invalid until mediated and presented in the correct forum, and that someone else may have a 'better' understanding of Others' experience than they do themselves. Equally, it is politically untenable to argue that one is not able to have an opinion about, and to locate on the feminist agenda, experiences that are not immediate to oneself (see hooks, 1991; Jones, 1993; Kitzinger, 1994; Scott, 1991; Yates, 1990). To designate these experiences as undiscussable is in some cases to allow the debate to take place free of any sort of feminist analysis, and to give up the notion that feminism should as a defining feature forge political links across the lives and oppressions of all women. Kitzinger argues that political usefulness rather than authenticity of experience should be the grounds on which theory is judged. She says, 'Experiential authority . . . prevents dialogue . . . and leads to silencing . . .' (1994: 6). In light of this, a 'solution' reached by many working in feminist epistemology and methodology is not to bow out of the debate if one has no personal experience of it, but to locate oneself, including either one's alternative or complete lack of experience, in the research. This means giving up the arrogance of scientific objectivity, the unchallengeable 'truth' of one's own perspective, the anonymity of the researcher, and instead acknowledging one's own 'place': background, expectations, reservations, shortcomings and *agenda*. This creates a way of doing research beyond immediate experience because it accepts that all work is inevitably bound by subjectivity. Consequently, the way one person experiences patriarchy will not be the same way that someone else does. It does not then need to be argued that it does not exist (which makes feminism meaningless). The basic feminist premise can be maintained that patriarchy, even while experienced in different forms, remains hegemonic and oppresses all women, without assuming that it is received and dealt with in identical ways. The researcher can therefore speak about the experiences of Others from their political as well as subjective position. The politics, rather than the experience, enables one to *advocate* for Others, that is, support or uphold their position, rather than speak in place of them.

What is also vital about this process of self-location and the strategy of advocacy is that it establishes *with the powerful* the responsibility of dealing with the power imbalance. It is a real alternative to the strategy of 'letting them speak for themselves', which denies the power implicit in *allowing* someone to speak in the first place, treats minority groups as homogenous, and proceeds as though they will have only one point of view and what they say is somehow untouched by social conditions and therefore more authentic. One of the biggest problems I have faced as a researcher is in dealing with the many contradictory stories and interpretations offered by young women of their experiences. They are not necessarily able to give me a convenient singular truth of their shared experiences because of the differences between them. Even if, in an attempt to avoid colonization, I were just to present their stories as they have formed them with no interpretation from me, the true and sole opinion of young women would not be self-evident. There are lots of differences between them. It makes the data messy. From the perspective of 'ask them and they will give you the answer' research, this is immensely frustrating. If you are prepared to locate yourself, however, and say, 'this is what I think is going on, here are the contradictions and complexities, from my point of view it could mean this,' fruitful outcomes can emerge. This stickier part of representation – to maintain that my analysis of someone else's circumstance is only one analysis, but nevertheless a legitimate one – is usefully handled with the principle of advocacy. Neither subjective knowledge nor the objective truth is required actively to espouse or support the causes of another. Advocacy is a strategy that takes a declared political analysis rather than experience or truth as its reference point. As a political strategy, it allows for the possibility that alternative interpretations of circumstances can exist, but that, politically, a strong case can be made for one's own.

Choosing not to represent young women has not left them uncolonized and free to speak for themselves. On the contrary, they feature most prominently as the targets for patriarchal ideologies enforcing feminine identities. As a consequence, their self-representations are often (unsurprisingly) celebrations of achieving images damaging to their health and autonomy. These expressions of identity could hardly be considered unmediated. It is necessary to allow young women to find other ways to speak about themselves than these, but this assumes a forum where they will be heard. It is crucial that work is done to make room on the current feminist agenda for them. Part of this work is taking their issues on as important to feminism even though these may differ from (although often dovetail with) what affects the lives of older women. Representation is therefore not about appropriation, or knowing better, or speaking for, but first about questioning for whom you should stand. This is the responsibility of those already on that agenda. The second part of representation, speaking *about* and advocating *for* young women, is not colonization. It establishes that they matter, and that there is a place for them, as women, within feminism. While work by members of a 'majority' group about members of a 'minority' group needs to acknowledge the power relation in this difference, this should not result in an abdication of responsibility to other women. The work is necessary because it makes connections across borders and it allows majority group feminists to acknowledge their role in maintaining these borders. We should not seek to replace the stories of Others with our own versions, but we do need to talk about them for feminism to be meaningful as a political movement representing all women.

References

Carby, Hazel (1982) 'White Woman Listen! Black Feminism and the Boundaries of Sisterhood', in The Centre for Contemporary Cultural Studies (eds) *The Empire Strikes Back: Race and Racism in 70s Britain*, pp. 212–35. London: Hutchinson.

Denfield, Rene (1995) *The New Victorians*. Sydney: Allen and Unwin.

Frye, Marilyn (1983) 'On Being White: Toward a Feminist Understanding of Race and Race Supremacy', in *The Politics of Reality*, pp. 110–27. Freedom, CA: The Crossing Press.

hooks, bell (1991) 'SISTERHOOD. Political Solidarity between Women', in Sneja Gunew (ed.) *Feminist Knowledge: Critique and Construct*, pp. 27–41. London: Routledge.

Jones, Allison (1993) 'Becoming a "Girl": Poststructuralist Suggestions for Educational Research', *Gender and Education* 5 (2): 157–66.

Kitzinger, Celia (1994) 'Experiential Authority and Heterosexuality', in Gabriele Griffin (ed.) *Changing Our Lives: Women in/to Women's Studies*. London: Pluto.

Roiphe, Katie (1993) *The Morning After*. Boston: Little, Brown.

Scott, Joan (1991) 'The Evidence of Experience', *Critical Inquiry* 17(4): 773–997.

Summers, Anne (1995) 'Shockwaves at the Revolution', *The Age Good Weekend*, 18 March.

Sykes, Bobbi, (1984) in Dale Spender (ed.) 'Women Who Do and Women Who Don't Join the Women's Movement', pp. 63–9. London: Routledge and Kegan Paul.

Yates, Lyn (1990) *Theory/Practice Dilemmas: Gender, Knowledge and Education*. Geelong: Deakin University Press.

26

Beside the Standpoint

Mike Gane

I remember, back in the 1960s, coming across some ethnography of socialist states of Eastern Europe in which it was recorded that when workers were asked for their views they would often hesitate. They would describe their own views as 'unscientific' and 'unsound', deferring to the party officials and their higher logic and truth. There is an enormous literature on this question in Marxism: the problem of the relation of theory to practice, of intellectuals to workers. It is difficult to imagine Marxism without its struggle over the proletarian position or 'standpoint' in theory. In fact, any movement which involves intellectuals and non-intellectuals inevitably has to confront the problem of how the oppressed (non-intellectuals) express their experience and the way this is represented and articulated by movement leaders. In Marxism, it gave rise to attempts to identify the 'correct' way to handle the relation, and 'deviations' from this: substitutionism, 'ouvrierism' or 'workerism', theoreticism, etc. In Maoism, of course, it was developed into a theory of 'from the people to the people'. If Marxism wanted to represent the oppressed, it had also to present the oppressors: to speak for also meant to speak against, yet it did not develop any practice of representing the class enemy in any other terms than outright war, or a last-resort tactical alliance.

The whole issue arises in a different way within the Women's Movement because this produces its own intellectuals from within itself. Yet there is a similarity. If women express any point of view that is on behalf of women, if they try to elaborate a 'feminist point of view,' inevitably they aim to express a common, collective position. And if men on behalf of women do this, it might well lead to the situation where the male voice is more objectively 'feminist' than that of the women collectively. This seems perfectly possible in theory, as does the situation where men criticize women from a 'feminist' standpoint. This ironically reproduces the dominant position of men in society which some men may be criticizing. Of course, if men do not criticize women on the grounds that this would indeed reproduce patriarchal relations, they can then be criticized for being patronizing. Obviously, the tangle here stems from the fact that a man is a member, whether he likes it or not, of the oppressor group. It was slightly different in communist practice, with Marx for example, because he was not directly involved in capitalist oppression (although Engels was).

I have tried to investigate some of the problems here by looking at some historical examples, where, of course, reconstructing the position of the Other has to be in many cases conjectural and in the last instance unconfirmable. A particular interest in my work was the relation of Marx and Engels to the women in their lives and to their gender politics (Gane, 1994). One is led to consider the relation between Jenny Marx, wife of Marx, on the one hand, and Mary Burns, unmarried partner of Engels, on the other. As far as I know, no letters or likenesses of Mary Burns are extant. She exists through representations given to her by Others. She was an illiterate Irish textile worker in Manchester, England. Engels lived with her (as Mr Boardman) and presented her as the new communist proletarian woman to the Communist League in London. At the League meeting, Jenny Marx, with German aristocratic connections (and related to the Duke of Argyle), refused to meet her and she was never allowed to visit the Marx home because of Jenny Marx's objections.

Marx devoted most of his intellectual work to trying to define the laws of class formation and struggle in the capitalist mode of production, and much of this analysis was taken up with the development of the textile industry in Lancashire and in Manchester in particular. Engels had presented much of the raw material for this analysis in his report on the condition of the working class in 1844. In that report he made it plain that about 80 per cent of the working class were women. However, when Marx wrote up his account of the formation of the working class somehow this class became a very masculine proletariat, rather like the heroic male communists in the League. A complex pattern was set up which formed the context for Marx's theorizing: (a) the model of the League (mainly craftsmen fighting mechanization), with its masculine model of revolution; (b) the influence of Jenny Marx (educated, proudly married and against sexual experimentation); and (c) the position of Engels (promoting the proletarian communist woman and true 'sex-love'). What was Marx's own way out? It was to avoid all reference to women: it was Engels who wrote on gender, marriage and sexual relations. It was Engels who 'represented' Mary Burns. But Engels' social position was as complicated as that of Marx, since he was a member of the factory-owning class. Was he, in fact, acting as a patriarch in presenting and idealizing Mary Burns as the communist woman? Was he, even though trying to frame a theory of oppression and a politics of emancipation, simply writing a voice-over part for her? And what of Marx? The influence of Jenny Marx seems to have been enough to have inhibited any thesis of the proletarian woman from his pen: he followed Engels when it came to its theoretical formulation.

In trying to think about what Marx and Engels wrote about the oppression of women, I have set the issue in a wider framework of other writers (Gane, 1994). In each of the cases I chose, there was a man speaking for women by selecting his own partner as exemplar. Of course, the particular exemplar verified and exemplified the man's own thesis on gender. And, in many cases, the man was speaking for women as a group, and trying to work out a politics of gender by identifying the future social position and role of women. Often this conjecture was achieved in direct dialogue with a particular woman, who acted as informant and advisor as well as model. In some cases, the death of the woman formed a situation where powerful emotions were unleashed, giving rise to something akin to religious worship of the lost partner. Idealization in many cases was supported by selective publications of poetry, letters and other writings of the woman concerned, as indications of her purported extraordinary virtues and sensitivity.

How is the situation different today? In the work I am currently doing I am trying to ascertain, through the work of women theorists themselves, what they think of both men and women. There is a vast amount of autobiographical writing to draw upon, so the problem of the unrepresented nature of intellectual women in the nineteenth century has to a large measure disappeared. In contemporary writing, it is clear that women have no difficulty in representing men to themselves and in defining their own 'idealization' of men. In this process there is not so much an attempt to represent the oppressed Other so much as to identify, on the one hand, a lack (or weakness) in men, and, on the other, the operation of intimate individual practices of patriarchy. It is through or against such representation of them that men have felt the need to reassess (or consciously reject a reassessment of) their own nature, their own ideal of their own nature. In this research, then, I am not so much examining male representations of women as an oppressed group, as women's changing representation of their relation to men as Other. Discovering how the representation of the Other's view is achieved in this way is one route to understanding the diversity of responses in the men's movements.

At present, there is a considerable amount of writing (much of it influenced by French philosophers) by men who want to become women, or to become more feminine than feminine, and to argue at the same time that 'woman' does not exist. But to want to become the Other is always just as much an impossible dream as wanting to deny the Other's existence. A way to rethink this is to pose the question more politically, to identify common problems, objectives, allies, enemies. In this way there can be alliances against sexism, racism, and other oppressions, without trying to reduce and eliminate differences within the progressively aligned groups or movements. From this perspective, men have the choice to define themselves as anti- or pro-feminist; and, rather than tell women what to do, to identify and work against common enemies. A 'standpoint' does not mean adherence to a doctrine defined in the space of an imaginary subject – and one which can be possessed, even put under copyright, as some French feminists once tried to do. It means working towards a common alignment to a problem to be solved. It very quickly becomes clear in 'reading feminism' that it is not a single entity with a single voice. As feminisms become more effective, so men are confronted with many different images of themselves in a complex, contradictory context of patriarchal and anti-patriarchal strategies.

Reference

Gane, M. (1994) *Harmless Lovers*. London: Routledge.

27

'Some of This Seems to Me Straight *Feminist* Stuff': Representing the Other in Discursive Psychotherapy Research

Anna Madill

This chapter examines issues surrounding 'representing the Other' raised through taking a discourse analytic approach (Potter and Wetherell, 1987) to my research on psychotherapy change processes. All the material for my research was drawn from the therapies of female clients presenting with a major depressive episode. In one of these cases, the client introduced some of her problems in terms of her situation as mother and wife. In response, the therapist suggested that some of these issues seemed 'straight *feminist* stuff'. So, in exploring issues of representation, I shall also make a reflexive move and consider whether or not my research on psychotherapy too could be considered feminist.

But first, what is meant by 'representing the Other'? Lee (1994) suggests two pertinent meanings of the verb 'to represent': to speak for and to speak about. However, the nature of the correspondence between the object represented and the meaning it is awarded is not straightforward and depends on one's epistemological stance. For example, realist positions, supposing a knowable reality independent of experience, maintain the possibility of representing the world in a more or less direct way. Issues surrounding representing the Other would therefore hinge on how accurately research presents those studied. On the other hand, relativist positions consider representations to be versions of the world; constitutive *of* reality, culturally bounded and contextually variable. Thus, there would be considered no objective truth one can attempt to reflect, only plausible and useful accounts that may be offered.

Feminist research takes many forms and may be conducted from differing epistemological standpoints (e.g. Olesen, 1994). Here, I want to explore issues surrounding whether or not I might coherently work from an explicitly feminist standpoint (as I would like to) while conducting *relativist* discursive research. This question arises from a basic tension between feminism and discursive psychology (see, for example, Wilkinson and Kitzinger, 1995). This tension is apparent in the relation between feminism's political commitment and the seeming neutrality that a relativist position may require (see Edwards et al., 1995 and Gill, 1995, for discussion). It is also apparent in the way in which 'experience', of fundamental importance in feminism (e.g. Griffin, 1995), is problematized in discursive psychology.

Couched in terms of group membership, the call for contributions on the topic of 'Representing the Other' asked: (1) How are we to represent members of groups to which we do not ourselves belong? (2) Do the problems become particularly acute when members of a 'majority' group attempt to represent members of a 'minority' group? From a relativist discursive position, group membership is not regard as an either/or matter but as a discursive achievement (Widdicombe and Wooffitt, 1990). Hence, even if membership can be considered physically bounded (e.g. 'women'), discursive approaches demonstrate the ways in which that understanding (that groups consist of people of a particular *kind*) is linguistically managed (Wetherell and Potter, 1992). Moreover, regarding human understanding as constructed in and through sociocultural discourses, experience and identity are no longer regarded as the property of individuals. In representing the Other, one is understood to draw on a reservoir of impersonal, linguistic resources; functional, local and revisable, just as the Other does in producing a representation of her/himself. So, from a relativist or discursive position, the notion that group membership has the potential to problematize representation is challenged in two ways. First, the possibility of providing a true or false representation of the group disappears as in its place are found only ever-changing fragments of borrowed discourses. Second, personal experience and identity (possibly as a member of a group) are considered functionally constructed from impersonal, sociocultural discourses and awarded no privileged status (see Potter, 1988).

Let me ground this theory in my own research. Material for my research was drawn from the therapies of three women presenting with depression. As such, there may be a potential to represent such women with regard to their treatment in psychotherapy. However, in doing so, could I be considered to be representing a group of which I was a member? Like them, I am female, white, middle class and in professional employment. However, unlike them, I do not have children, am not in my 40s, have not been in individual therapy nor had a clinical diagnosis of depression. But what characteristics should I take into account when considering if I am, in fact, studying a group, or in considering whether it is one of which I have membership? Moreover, even if I defined my study group in terms of 'women treated psychotherapeutically for depression', I could still argue this need not exclude me from membership. I could negotiate the boundaries of this definition and present a claim to membership in terms of having had experience as a client in therapeutic groups and of being depressed in my own life. However, in discursive psychology, the researcher's account of her/his own subjectivity would not be considered immune from analytic procedures. For example, such descriptions could be deconstructed in terms of the implications made available about the prima facie legitimacy of the research (Madill and Doherty, 1994). On the other hand, though, my research *would* be understood as informed by cultural discourses and by understandings of psychotherapy and depression – as is the subjectivity and experience of the women I study. This is so, whether or not I might plausibly claim membership of the same 'group'.

Positioning subjectivity and experience in discourse has drawbacks but also important benefits. A disturbing drawback is that regarding subjectivity as textually and socially constructed can undermine claims to personal knowing and so potentially disempower those we study. A contrasting alternative is to view subjectivity in an individualistic way; that is, as deriving from essential features of the person her/himself. However, this too is potentially disempowering. An individualistic stance can make the implication available that differentially valued distinctions between people are of a natural kind. An important political benefit of a discursive perspective, therefore, is that in viewing such distinctions as linguistically managed it becomes possible to challenge their naturalness and thus the legitimacy of the practices they sustain.

Even if one accepts that representations are forged from impersonal, cultural resources, may there still not be some, perhaps critical, differences between representation of oneself and representation of Others? Individuals might be thought to have differential access to ways of understanding themselves and the world. Furthermore, the circumstances of people's lives might be considered to provide differential expertise in the mobilization of cultural meanings. Such issues are implicitly addressed in discursive psychology. In analysing text, one does not attempt to recover true meaning but to explicate how participants manage their concerns during interaction (e.g. Edwards and Potter, 1992). In this way, my research has examined how participants have themselves represented the Other. Thus, one study included an exploration of how a client characterized her mother during therapy and demonstrated how this description functioned to provide an account of the client's depression (Madill and Barkham, 1993). Another examined sequences in which a therapist's representation of a client, in terms of offering an account of her problems, was subject to disconfirmation by her (Madill et al., 1993).

Hence, in its relativist stance, discursive psychology does not purport to represent the Other in terms of 'speaking for' or attempting to present a veridical account of the subjectivity or experience of those studied. Rather, a discursive analysis seeks to explicate the rhetorical detail and functional implications of the variable descriptions offered by participants. In doing so, however, discourse analysis has been described by one of its main exponents as 'fundamentally an interpretative exercise which offers up readings of texts for scrutiny' (Potter, 1988: 51). And it is when one orients to the interpretative elements of discursive analysis that issues surrounding representing the Other, in terms of 'speaking about' participants' interaction, emerge.

If there is some interpretative leeway in discourse analysis, how might this effect the researcher's representation of interaction? It is my own observation and that of some of my colleagues that, in psychotherapy research, 'lay' researchers appear to be particularly sympathetic towards clients' accounts (Field, Harper, personal communications). Harper suggests, though, that she has developed an appreciation of the therapist's standpoint, possibly through becoming more familiar with the therapy protocol, listening to therapists reflect on their interventions, and through her own experience of being a client. Moreover, as a therapist involved in psychotherapy research, Stiles (personal communication) suggests that his client-centred orientation allows him readily to engage with the client's perspective in his research. Exploring researchers' descriptions of their experience does appear to offer some insight into the process of representation in psychotherapy research. However, as suggested above, from the standpoint of discursive psychology, a reflexive move must be made and deconstructive analytic procedures applied to researchers' accounts of their work. Although necessary in terms of theoretical and epistemological coherence, this can be a frustrating aspect of discursive research and may be experienced as undermining the sincerity and potential usefulness of researchers' reflections on their own process.

In a strong statement, Parker similarly suggests that it is perhaps unhelpful to 'write off experience as just another social construction' (Parker, 1994: 240). And, if discourse analysis is acknowledged to have some interpretative elements, surely it is legitimate to enquire in what the researcher's representation of the Other is grounded? Discursive psychology focuses on how participants' concerns are managed by them during interaction. This may be understood as, or indeed have the effect of, claiming that analysis merely emerges from the text. Such implied empiricism, though, might suggest the possibility of objectivity incompatible with discursive psychology's relativist epistemology (Doherty, 1994). Potter (1988) has challenged this view. He suggests that, in making the process of interpretation as explicit as possible within the presented analysis, discursive psychology allows an audience to contest the offered representation and to assess its value.

This, however, still sidesteps the issue of what discursive analysis is grounded in. In this regard, relativist and *critical* realist positions have been contrasted. Advocating a critical realist discourse analysis, Parker (e.g. 1992) argues that an analysis sensitive to the power of discourse must be grounded in the assumption that there is a reality outside the text. However, this too is where a relativist discursive analysis may be understood to be rooted. That is, even in taking a relativist stance, one must utilize cultural knowledge in producing an analysis of text (e.g., Wetherell and Potter, 1992). Critical realism accepts and prioritizes the notion that material conditions and social structures are the preconditions of discursive formulations. Relativism, on the other hand, accepts some things as *provisionally* real in conducting analysis but maintains the possibility of deconstructing its own analytic assumptions and research findings (Edwards et al., 1995). So, in principle, the two positions can be differentiated. However, there is a question regarding the possibility of sustaining this difference in practice. That is, unless one is explicitly deconstructing one's own assumptions during analysis, a relativist stance itself can be understood as a claim which obscures the perspective of the researcher. In a relativist framework, though, the researcher is regarded in the same way as the text studied. Fragmented, s/he is not assumed to occupy a stable position with regard to the work.

So, how is it that I have addressed issues surrounding representing the Other in my own discursive psychotherapy research? Taking a relativist stance, I do not purport to represent in terms of 'speaking for' those I study, as there is no stable position from which the Other speaks, no truth to be veridically represented. But, in producing an analysis, I represent in terms of 'speaking about' the Other. I produce an account of the interaction between client and therapist which is always open to challenge and subject to the validity criteria of coherence, plausibility and usefulness.

To return directly to the issue of feminism, though, where does this leave me in terms of being political in my discursive research? Although positioning oneself as a feminist may be problematic in relativist discourse analysis, my own personal feminism has been temporarily placated by the understanding that this does not mean that my research may not have feminist *implications* (see also Doherty, 1994). For example, one study focused on how a therapist's interventions had the effect of transforming a client's account of problems located in her domestic circumstances to problems considered internal to her (Madill et al., 1993) – thus demonstrating how problems may be positioned within clients and exclude sociocultural accounts. This indicates how research from a relativist stance may also be at least the basis of 'straight *feminist* stuff'.

Note

This research was supported by a Medical Research Council training award.

I am indebted to the Clinic Team of the MRC/ESRC Social and Applied Psychology Unit, University of Sheffield (now the Psychological Therapies Research Centre, University of Leeds) for providing the psychotherapy archive (Shapiro et al., 1990) from which the research material was drawn.

I would also like to express my gratitude to Heather Harper, Researcher with the Sainsbury's Centre for Mental Health, for her invaluable comments on earlier drafts of this chapter; to Susan Field, Department of Clinical Psychology, University of Leeds, for helping me clarify my thoughts in discussion with her; and to William B. Stiles, Department of Psychology, Miami University, USA. I would like to express my appreciation to Kathy Doherty, Department of Communication Studies, Sheffield Hallam University, with whom I have had many informal discussions on the implications of discursive psychology. Finally, I would like to thank the reviewers of the original article for helping me develop my understanding of this area.

References

Doherty, K. (1994) 'Subjectivity, Reflexivity and the Analysis of Discourse', paper presented at the British Psychological Society London Conference as the introductory paper in the symposium 'Do subjects matter? Qualitative approaches to the psychology of women'.

Edwards, D. and Potter, J. (1992) *Discursive Psychology*. London: Sage.

Edwards, D., Ashmore, M. and Potter, J. (1995) 'Death and Furniture: The Rhetoric, Politics, and Theology of Bottom Line Arguments against Relativism', *History of the Human Sciences* 8: 25–49.

Gill, R. (1995) 'Relativism, Reflexivity and Politics: Interrogating Discourse Analysis from a Feminist Perspective', in S. Wilkinson and C. Kitzinger (eds) *Feminism and Discourse: Psychological Perspectives*. London: Sage.

Griffin, C. (1995) 'Feminism, Social Psychology and Qualitative Research', *The Psychologist* 8: 119–21.

Lee, N. (1994). 'Child Protection Investigations: Discourse Analysis and the Management of Incommensurability', *Journal of Community and Applied Social Psychology* 4: 275–86.

Madill, A. and Barkham, M. (1993). 'Subject Position and Discursive Processes of Change in a Successful Psychodynamic–Interpersonal Psychotherapy', MRC/ESRC Social and Applied Psychology Unit Memo 1469, Department of Psychology, University of Sheffield.

Madill, A. and Doherty, K. (1994) '"So You Did What You Wanted Then": Discourse Analysis,

Personal Agency, and Psychotherapy', *Journal of Community and Applied Social Psychology* 4: 261–73.

Madill, A., Widdicombe, S., Barkham, M. and Shapiro, D.A. (1993) 'Problem (Re)formulation in Psychodynamic–Interpersonal Psychotherapy: Discursive Analysis of Client Disconfirmations', MRC/ESRC Social and Applied Psychology Unit Memo 1439, Department of Psychology, University of Sheffield.

Olesen, V. (1994) 'Feminisms and Models of Qualitative Research', in N.K. Denzin and Y.S. Lincoln (eds) *Handbook of Qualitative Research*, pp. 158–74. London: Sage.

Parker, I. (1992) *Discourse Dynamics: Critical Analysis for Social and Individual Psychology*. London: Routledge.

Parker, I. (1994) 'Reflexive Research and the Grounding of Analysis: Social Psychology and the Psy-complex', *Journal of Community and Applied Social Psychology* 4: 239–52.

Potter, J. (1988) 'What is Reflexive about Discourse Analysis? The Case of Reading Readings', in S. Woolgar (ed.) *Knowledge and Reflexivity: New Frontiers in the Sociology of Knowledge*. London: Sage.

Potter, J. and Wetherell, M. (1987) *Discourse and Social Psychology: Beyond Attitudes and Behaviour*. London: Sage.

Shapiro, D.A., Barkham, M., Hardy, G.E. and Morrison, L.A. (1990) 'The Second Sheffield Psychotherapy Project: Rationale, Design and Preliminary Outcome Data', *British Journal of Medical Psychology* 63: 97–108.

Wetherell, M. and Potter, J. (1992) *Mapping the Language of Racism: Discourse and the Legitimation of Exploitation*. London: Harvester Wheatsheaf.

Widdicombe, S. and Wooffitt, R. (1990) '"Being" versus "Doing" Punk: On Achieving Authenticity as a Member', *Journal of Language and Social Psychology* 9: 257–77.

Wilkinson, S. and Kitzinger, C. (eds) (1995) *Feminism and Discourse: Psychological Perspectives*. London: Sage.

28

Questioning Representing the Other

Jean Carabine

Central to much feminist research and writing is a concern to address issues of difference: 'Other' is given the dictionary definition of 'not the same, different' and 'Otherness' as 'the state of being other or different' (*Longman Concise English Dictionary*, 1985), suggesting that difference and Otherness are identical. The purpose of this chapter is to argue that it is not helpful to merge difference and Other because to do so blurs the interdependent relationship between the two and risks masking the power relations at issue.

Significantly, Other and difference have differential outcomes in terms of power effects. I will demonstrate, first, that being 'Othered' has social signifi-cance, while difference is socially significant only in certain situations. Second, the Other is generally a feature of power relations, effected by context, time and space in ways that do not always apply to difference. Third, the process of Othering has specific outcomes and implications for how we understand power relations in ways that difference on its own does not. Finally, I consider the impli-cations of this argument for feminists concerned with representing Others and difference.

The centrality of difference to feminist research and writing is well established (see, for example, Barrett and Phillips, 1992; Brah, 1992; Gunew and Yeatman, 1993; de Lauretis, 1986; Martin, 1994; Sawicki, 1991; Williams, 1995). Similarly, there are various explanations and analyses of Othering (see, for example, de Beauvoir, 1972: 192; Foucault, 1979; Hill Collins, 1991: 40; Smith, 1988). Writing about difference often entails addressing the experiences and processes of Othering and sometimes the two are conflated. I want to disentangle them here, looking first at the question of their relative social significance.

We understand difference in a variety of ways and not all differences are the same. Brah (1992) suggests that we can understand difference in four ways: as experience, social relations, identity and as subjectivity. Williams (1995) offers three political understandings of difference: difference as diversity, division, and as difference. In particular, not all differences are socially significant (as in the colour of our hair), nor do all differences necessarily imply a hierarchical relation of power as with difference as diversity. Difference as diversity is claimed on the basis of a specific shared experience but 'not *necessarily* associated with a sub-ordinated or unequal subject position – a shared language, nationality . . . age, generation, sexual identity and marital status' (Williams 1995: 12).

In contrast, I would maintain that Other is generally imbued with social significance. Particular meanings are embedded in the notion of Other along with a set of power relations. 'Other' is not transparent, to be accepted simply as it is, as a word, it is deeply implicated in power relations (Said, 1978). Often the word 'Other' only ever applies to those outside of, or subordinate to, the unspecified taken-for-granted group of people who constitute the not-Others, or the group that I will refer to as the 'Same'. In practice, the positioning of Other is not usually positive. It suggests a positioning where the subject becomes the object and is de-humanized.

Other is attributed a negative value and that which is Same a positive value as in woman/man, black/white, homosexual/heterosexual, and so on. Although difference may give rise to a negative positioning of individuals and groups that results in their subordination on the grounds of gender, sexuality, religion, ethnicity and disability, it can also give rise to a positive positioning as in 'different but equal' and some equal rights claims. Equal rights approaches have focused on obtaining the same privileges as the dominant group. However, Phelan (1994: 2) suggests that arguing that lesbians and gay men are equal, or potentially the same as, heterosexuals fails to challenge heterosexuality. Another use of a positive positioning of difference is what Williams (1995) describes as difference as division. Here a shared experience of difference is translated into a form of domination: being white, British, heterosexual and male forms an identity which protects a privileged position.

Second, embedded in the notion of Other, and in the process of Othering, there is inevitably a set of power relations (see, for example, de Beauvoir, 1972; Brittan and Maynard, 1984; Hill Collins, 1991; Said, 1978), often expressed in terms of dichotomies such as male/female, white/black, heterosexual/homosexual, able-bodied/disabled, and so on. Other does not generally signify *diversity* but rather difference as *opposition*. For Patricia Hill Collins (1991: 42) 'the construct of dichotomous oppositional difference may be a philosophical lynchpin in systems of race, class and gender oppression.'

The understanding of Other as *oppositional* difference is also central to the construction of Sameness in a way that difference as *diversity* is not. '"Heterosexuality", for example, has meaning only in relation to "homosexuality"; the coherence of the former is built on the exclusion, repression and repudiation of the latter' (Seidman, 1994: 130; see also Wilkinson and Kitzinger, 1993; Carabine, 1996). Other and Same are hierarchically interdependent whereas diversity is not.

The negative positioning and coupling of Other to its Same does not mean that the Other is fixed and cannot be subverted. Often the experience of being Othered acts as a catalyst for individuals and groups to transform a negative positioning as Other into a positive political identity, as with black, woman, gay, lesbian and disabled. It is the experience of being Othered rather than difference per se that results in individuals and groups claiming a positive identity out of a negative categorization. In this way, political identity is constructed out of and through the experience of oppression. Here, Other is closest to Williams' (1995: 12) definition of difference as 'a situation where a shared collective experience/identity . . . forms the basis for resistance against the positioning of that identity as subordinate.' However, this positive identity and positioning has meaning only through the assertion of the Other and the existence of its related Same. In claiming Other as a positive identity, individuals and groups may also redefine it, creating what Foucault (1979) refers to as new discourses and new relations of power through resistance.

The positive claiming of Other has been criticized, on the one hand, for reinforcing and reproducing existing hierarchical relations (Seidman, 1994: 130–1) rather than undermining them. Moreover, a politics based on a 'fixed identity position privileges those for whom that position is the primary or only marked identity' (Duggan, 1994: 4), which in lesbian and gay politics usually means white, middle class and male, and within feminism usually means white, heterosexual and female. The positive claiming of Other can also be criticized for its assertions of universalism and for failing to acknowledge the differences *among* those claiming Other as a positive identity (Williams, 1995: 8): for example, the Women's Movement's attempts to transform a negative positioning of women in relation to men into a positive political identity, but one which only has meaning as a result of the binary dichotomous construct 'men/women' which it reproduces and reinforces. Additionally, this transformation was initially at the cost of failing to recognize the differences amongst women (Bhavnani and Coulson, 1986; Carby, 1982; Hill Collins, 1991).

Third, individuals may experience being Other in some, but not in all, contexts – at some times and not others. A black Nigerian man is likely to experience being Othered for being black in a British context but not in a Nigerian context. An Asian woman from India is likely to experience being Othered in the context of Britain because she is black and a woman but within the context of her country she is more likely to be Othered for being a woman and possibly for her caste than because she is Asian. The experience of Other and its social significance is therefore effected by context, space and time in a way that difference as diversity is not.

I would suggest, therefore, that the use of Other is problematic precisely because it is embedded within a set of assumptions and reflects relations of power. However, this begs the question: are there alternative uses/meanings of Other? Feminists, in our concern with difference, have sought to use Other in ways which challenge and differentiate power relations. However, it seems to me that a relationship of power is always implicit in the use of Other, no matter what Other is being written about. Can the male be Other to the woman, or white be Other to black, or heterosexual Other to lesbian/homosexual? There is a danger in thinking that conducting research on powerful groups reverses or undermines the Othering dynamic. I do not believe it necessarily does. We may be presenting representations of these powerful groups and individuals but it is a representation of difference as different *from* us. To argue that this is representing the Other is to run the risk of masking the power relations at issue. My research on powerful men (Carabine, 1992, 1995) may result in challenging and even undermining power relations and/or knowledge but does not result in men being subordinated, oppressed or Othered, nor would I want it to. Similarly, conducting my research from the position of a working-class lesbian does not mean that the heterosexual men and women I interview are Othered as a result (unless, of course, they are, for example, black or disabled and I ignore the power dimensions of race and disability).

Admittedly, this discussion is a rather dualist and binary fixing of the question but it reflects my concern that the placing of Other tends to take place along a binary plane which mirrors sets of power relations, usually expressed in terms of dichotomies: male/female, white/black, heterosexual/lesbian, non-disabled/disabled, and so on. This is one outcome of focusing on Other rather than on a broader notion of difference which encompasses but goes beyond the concept of Other. Adopting the term 'Other' risks restricting our thinking to the boundaries of the Other/Same coupling and to the power relations arising out of that relationship. A focus on Other is problematic because it tends to shift the debate back to a preoccupation with binary oppositions and runs the risk of locking 'differences . . . up in the oppositional categories of oppressor and oppressed' (Trinh, in Gunew and Yeatman, 1993: xix). At the same time, the categorization of Other can suggest an essential and natural quality, making black and lesbian into fixed, distinct and uniform groups presenting category members as homogenous and obscuring the differences both within and between each of them. It also often results in the Other as singularity and fixedness rather than recognizing Others as multiple and shifting identities. Similarly, a focus only on Other may also mean that we end up ignoring the commonalities that we share and the potential for other points of resistance.

In sum, I have argued that difference and Other are distinct in significant ways. Other is generally a socially significant negative positioning within hierarchical power relations and differentially effected by context, time and space. Difference, by contrast, may or may not be socially significant in that it does not always imply an unequal or subordinated subject position and can result in either a positive or negative positioning. Implicit in my argument is the claim that Other is not simply difference and neither is difference necessarily Other. The process of being Other and the dynamic of difference are interdependent in specific and particular ways, as when unequal hierarchical power relations are a central feature of difference. Difference does not necessarily or inevitably imply Other, but within specific circumstances of subordination and domination it supports Otherness – and this, of course, makes difference a difficult concept for feminists.

In the preceding paragraphs I have tended to focus on Other and difference as though they were separate and distinct. To some, my argument might seem crude, but my aim is primarily to illustrate that the relationship between Other and difference is complex and to emphasize that our understanding of Other has important implications for how we understand difference. Unless we are aware of the political and ideological assumptions embedded in terms like 'Other' and 'difference', we run the risk of simply reproducing precisely those power relations we want to undermine, through their unquestioned incorporation in our work.

References

Barrett, M. and Phillips, A. (eds) (1992) *Destabilizing Theory, Contemporary Feminist Debates.* Cambridge: Polity Press.

de Beauvoir, S. (1972) *The Second Sex.* Hardmondsworth: Penguin.

Bhavnani, K.-K. and Coulson, M. (1986) 'Transforming Socialist–Feminist theory' *Feminist Review* 23: 81–92.

Brah, A. (1992) 'Difference, Diversity and Differentiation', in P. Braham and P. Skellington (eds) *Racism and Anti-Racism.* London: Sage/Open University Press.

Brittan, A. and Maynard, M. (1984) *Sexism, Racism and Oppression.* Oxford: Basil Blackwell.

Carabine, J. (1992) 'Constructing Women: Sexuality and Social Policy', unpublished PhD thesis, University of Sheffield.

Carabine, J. (1995) 'Invisible Sexualities: Sexuality, Politics and Influencing Policy-making', in A. Wilson (ed.) *A Simple Matter of Justice?* London: Cassell.

Carabine, J. (1996) 'Heterosexuality and Social Policy', in D. Richardson (ed.) *Theorising Heterosexuality.* Milton Keynes: Open University Press.

Carby, H. (1982) 'White Woman Listen! Black Feminism and the Boundaries of Sisterhood', in Centre for Contemporary Cultural Studies (ed.) *The Empire Strikes Back: Race and Racism in 70s Britain.* London: Hutchinson.

Duggan, L. (1994) 'Queering the State', *Social Text* 39: 1–14.

Foucault, M. (1979) *Discipline and Punish.* London: Penguin. (First published 1975.)

Gunew, S. and Yeatman, A. (eds) (1993) *Feminisms and the Politics of Difference.* St Leonards, Australia: Allen and Unwin.

Hill Collins, P. (1991) 'Learning from the Outsider Within: The Sociological Significance of Black Feminist Thought', in M.M. Fonow and J.A. Cook (eds) *Beyond Methodology: Feminist Scholarship as Lived Research*, pp. 35–59. Bloomington, IN: Indiana University Press.

de Lauretis, T. (ed.) (1986) *Feminist Studies/Critical Studies.* Basingstoke: Macmillan.

Martin, J. Roland (1994) 'Methodological Essentialism, False Difference and Other Dangerous Traps', *Signs* 19(3): 630–56.

Phelan, S. (1994) *Getting Specific.* Minneapolis, MN: University of Minnesota Press.

Said, E. (1978) *Orientalism.* London: Penguin.

Sawicki, J. (1991) *Disciplining Foucault: Feminism, Power and the Body.* New York: Routledge.

Seidman, S. (1994) 'Identity and Politics in a "Postmodern" Gay Culture: Some Historical and Conceptual Notes', in M. Warner (ed.) *Fear of a Queer Planet: Queer Politics and Social Theory.* Minneapolis, MN: University of Minnesota Press.

Smith, D.E. (1988) *The Everyday World as Problematic.* Milton Keynes: Open University Press.

Wilkinson, S. and Kitzinger, C. (eds) (1993) *Heterosexuality: A Feminism & Psychology Reader.* London: Sage.

Williams, F. (1995) 'Postmodernism, Feminism and the Question of Difference', in N. Parton (ed.) *Social Work Theory and Social Change.* London: Routledge.

29

Issues of Power and Conflict Resolution in Representing Others

Gabriele Griffin

Insisting on Difference

the beginning woman of color is invisible both in the white male mainstream world and in the white women's feminist world, though in the latter this is gradually changing. The *lesbian* of color is not only invisible, she doesn't even exist. (Anzaldúa, 1983: 165)

[Betty Friedan] made her plight and the plight of white women like herself synonymous with a condition affecting all American women. (hooks, 1984: 2)

But what kind of an argument is it to say that the subaltern's 'voice' can be found in the *ambivalence* of the imperialist's speech? (Chow, 1993: 35)

Feminism (and I shall ignore the issue of such a homogenizing term for a moment) has a history of problematic relationships with Others – whether these be men, women from diverse ethnic backgrounds, lesbians or other Others. That's what all the quotations above are about. The issue has been one of identity and identification, borders that we draw.

- *Scenario 1*: 'I am not a feminist but I am interested in women's issues'
  (an absolutely standard position taken by women wanting to do women's studies)
- *Scenario 2*: 'You're a man-hater'
  (typical standpoint of threatened males responding to perceptions of 'feminist tendencies' in a woman)
- *Scenario 3*: 'We're all women here'
  (the answer to the request to give space to lesbians' perspectives in a mixed hetero/lesbian women's group)

Feminism has been accused of three failings in its relationship with those whom we/it have/has Othered:

1 *Exclusion*: The failure to include certain groups of women within 'feminism', to promote some kinds of separatism, to privilege certain standpoints and ignore others. This accusation, dating back to the beginnings of feminism, whether we see these as the 1970s, the early twentieth century, the nineteenth century, the late eighteenth century or earlier, has been one of the major catalysts in promoting change in feminist thinking and theorizing.

2. *Subsumption*: The failure to allow or encourage diverse women to raise *their*

own voices, subsuming these instead in a position which takes a certain commonality for granted. For some, this has amounted to a false inclusion in which the notion that 'we mean you too' when we speak/act has seemed to exonerate women from the accusation of exclusion or, indeed, subsumption, while at the same time not really offering those spoken for a space of their own on equal terms.

3. *Assumption*: The failure to recognize that it may not be possible or appropriate for one group of women to speak on behalf of another, or to assume that those who speak have the knowledge and right to do so in the interests of those spoken for.

All three notions of failure are underpinned by the idea of an incontrovertible difference which determines groups of people and differentiates them clearly from each other. Such positivist thinking informs not only the views of those who attack particular 'brands' of feminism for their failings, but also many feminist perspectives which operate from the basis that an essential difference or specificity separates women from men and is at the bottom of the discrimination to which women have been subjected. Hence statements such as 'A lesbian is the rage of *all* women condensed to the point of explosion'. (Radicalesbians, 1969/1988: 17; my emphasis) become possible. There is thus a congruence between the basis on which diverse feminisms have been constructed *and* the assumption of incontrovertible difference which informs accusations levelled at feminism for being exclusionary, including both silencing and/or elitist. Both work from a materialist position which privileges the idea of specific categories linked to some essential feature such as sexual orientation or racial identity as the ground on which group identity is founded.

But Where Are the Boundaries?

The idea of representing the Other assumes certain boundaries and categories which supposedly ensure that Otherness is recognizable and identifiable. These boundaries are established and maintained through a variety of sign systems such as language. Yet every day shows the breakdown of such boundaries. In fact, a certain kind of news industry, predicated upon such breakdown as its chief source of news, is based on the idea of incongruity arising out of the collapse of such boundaries: the incongruity of a 20-*stone* woman running an aerobics class; the incongruity of a *mother* killing her children; the incongruity of a *woman* sexually abusing other women. The highlighting of such incongruity serves, of course, both to reinforce the supposed extraordinariness of what is presented and simultaneously to reinscribe social, cultural and other norms which inform our expectations and assumptions of boundaries and categories in daily life.

While we negotiate between boundaries and slippage in our everyday lives, a whole range of theoretical frameworks from psychoanalysis to deconstruction have taught us not to confuse appearance with essence, indeed to question the notion of essence. And, contrary to what popular parlance and wisdom might suggest, our daily lives are thoroughly informed by an understanding of the provisionality of appearance, the instability of categories. Virtually all women's magazines, for example, propound in one way or another the possibility of trans-formation, usually in the direction of supposed (self-)improvement – a different hairstyle, slimmer figure, enticing lingerie, change in cooking etc. can – and *will!* – move you into a different category. Between the affirmation of the specificity of what it means to be in a particular category and the possibility of *you too* getting into a different one or moving beyond, provisionality – one mainstay of late capitalism – is played out alongside an idea of an absolute truth of 'the real you'. The point is that the contradiction between a position of a 'true self' and the mobility and transformability of that self is one which endlessly informs our daily lives. If we can change ourselves, we can be different, an Other.

On Others' Behalves or for Their Own Good?

The idea of representing Others is therefore not foreign to us. It is on one level the basis for living in formations larger than very small communities. In the former, temporary absence need not necessarily be filled, in the latter, transfer (of authority) to act on someone else's behalf becomes essential to sustain the idea of the unity of a particular society or group of people or to further a particular struggle. This is what Rigoberta Menchú writes about the relationship of Indians and *ladinos* in Guatemala:

> if we call a strike, it's for all workers. If we call an assembly, we listen to the views of all the masses. It was my job to sound out the views of all the *compañeros* . . . and send them to the regional coordinating body . . . the example of my *compañero ladino* made me really understand the barrier which has been put up between the Indian and the *ladino*, and that because of this same system which tries to divide us, we haven't under-stood that *ladinos* also live in terrible conditions, the same as we do. (1984: 165)

The issue, then, is not so much about representing Others as such but rather about the contexts which decide the limits of such representations and which lead 'us' to make representations about 'them'. After all, the reason why representing Others is a concern at all is that there are situations when such a move becomes problematic.

These situations are bound up with issues of power and vested interests. The question that needs to be asked is why some situations of representing Others are more problematic than others. The examples listed in the Call for Papers on Representing Others – for example, white women commenting on black women's work, women with no experience of madness representing Others who have had that experience, childless women presuming to speak on behalf of mothers, etc. – all seem to me to imply a power structure where, as regards current western culture, the first term tends to be positively valued, so to speak, and the second term negatively. Those who represent have – by that very fact – more power than those who are represented. It is the issue of subject and object, of agency. We may resent someone whom we see as more powerful than ourselves representing us, purely because this act is an expression of their power relative to our power-lessness. However, this resentment will be augmented a hundredfold if we per-ceive those who represent us as not acting *in our interests* and as not consulting with us. In a recent interview (in Griffin, 1995: 81), Hannana Siddiqui of Southall Black Sisters made the point that white feminists' desire for single-sex schools, arising from a sense that women achieve more educationally in a sex-segregated environment, does not necessarily serve Asian women's needs for whom co-educational schools can be one way of preventing these women from being '[cut] off from other [than fundamentalist] influences and possibilities available in coeducational schools'. There can thus be a real difficulty when legitimate but contradictory interests of different (groups of) women converge on one issue which both groups seek to address and for which they have different solutions. This is the context in which Chantal Mouffe (1993) calls for a 'radical and plural democracy' to allow the articulation and enactment of diversity, a political scenario which does not encourage the atomization currently in train everywhere but instead seeks interaction, consultation and mutual empowerment.

Resentments about power differentials among women are coupled with a particular kind of validation of experience expressed in the assumption that only experience enables you to access the 'truth' of a situation. White women cannot know what it means to be black. Childless women cannot know what it means to be a mother. Clearly, in some respects this is the case. But the answer is not necessarily that whereof we have no experience, thereof we cannot speak. There may be good strategic reasons to allow and indeed encourage our (whatever such an 'our' refers to) representation by people not of the same group or experience. What is at stake is not so much the representation of Others in itself but the uses to which such action is put. The point of protest about being represented by someone else usually marks a recognition of disempowerment, a sense of usurpation by those who speak on our behalf who thus confirm us in our place at the bottom of some hierarchy, outside the place of participation. Protests by bell hooks (1994) about the treatments of blacks by whites are about such exclusions and not predominantly about the impossibility of representing Others as such. After all, she speaks, assumes to speak, in the name of more than her self when she says, for example, *a propos* a white woman protesting that she cannot understand what a black woman is going through: 'understanding comes from our capacity to empty out the self and identify with that person whom we normally make the Other' (hooks, 1994: 219). Easier said than done – partly because the ability to do what hooks suggests has to entail an understanding of the power structures which make Othering possible.

Doing It for Ourselves – Again

It is in this context that I wish to draw attention to the work of Italian feminists, specifically that of the Milan Bookstore Collective, which is interestingly and tellingly completely neglected within Anglo-American feminist thinking. I think it is neglected because it speaks of power, not in the backlash sort of way typical of the 'superstars' of North American feminism such as Naomi Wolf, but of how differential power among women, a fact still flatly denied by many, can be utilized *for* women. Within much contemporary western feminism, power is still conceived either as an issue for women in relation to men or as an individual thing a woman either has or does not have (for example, in terms of powerful women such as Shirley Conran's 'superwoman' or Maggie Thatcher). Such conceptions of power ignore the power 'ordinary' women have in their everyday lives and ignore the possibility of making that power explicit and, most importantly, utilizing it for the empowerment not only of oneself but of others. This is precisely the arena within which discussions have been held among Italian feminists who have proposed both an explicit recognition of power differences among women and the establishment of a social contract between women for the purposes of the empowerment of the woman who is in a disadvantaged situation. The women from the Milan Bookstore Collective (1990: 112) describe this as 'gendered mediation'. As they suggest:

> Without gendered mediation, the wealth possessed by one woman may be resented by another as something stolen from her. The symbolic mother puts an end to this sad state of poverty. Because of her, disparity, made recognizable and usable, becomes a means of enrichment. (Milan Bookstore Collective, 1990: 113)

Many feminist activists, in fact, work in this way. They campaign on behalf of women less powerful than themselves, meaning less able (for whatever reason) to access the resources and lobby the relevant bodies to change their situation. But such feminist activism still often operates within *unacknowledged* hierarchies, with counsellors and clients, for example, being seen as occupying positions of difference but that difference never being openly acknowledged. Let me be quite clear here: I think there are real and material differences among women. These should not be denied but should be openly acknowledged. The usefulness of these differences for women is diminished when they are not acknowledged and when it is not understood that these differences are to be used to empower women. Such acknowledgement might also help to reduce the sense of unease which always exists when unacknowledged differences are felt to be present. It is only through the acknowledgement of difference, and the impetus to use that difference in favour of other women, that representing Others can become a tool for change.

References

Anzaldúa, Gloria (1983) 'Speaking in Tongues: A Letter To Third World Women Writers', in C. Moraga and G. Anzaldúa (eds) *This Bridge Called My Back: Writings by Radical Women of Color*, pp. 165–74. New York: Kitchen Table Women of Color.

Chow, Rey (1993) 'Where Have All the Natives Gone?', in *Writing Diaspora: Tactics of Intervention in Contemporary Cultural Studies*, pp. 27–54. Bloomington, IN: Indiana University Press.

Griffin, Gabriele (1995) 'The Struggle Continues – An Interview with Hannana Siddiqui', in G. Griffin (ed.) *Feminist Activism in the 1990s*, pp. 79–89. London: Taylor and Francis.

hooks, bell (1984) *Feminist Theory: From Margin to Center*. Boston: South End Press.

hooks, bell (1994) *Outlaw Culture: Resisting Representations*. London: Routledge.

Menchú, Rigoberta (1984) *I Rigoberta Menchú: An Indian Woman in Guatemala*, ed. E. Burgos-Debray. London: Verso.

Milan Bookstore Collective (1990) *Sexual Difference: A Theory of Social-Symbolic Practice*. Bloomington, IN: Indiana University Press.

Mouffe, Chantal (1993) *The Return of the Political*. London: Verso.

Radicalesbians (1969/88) 'The Woman-Identified Woman', reprinted in S.L. Hoagland and J. Penelope (eds) *For Lesbians Only. A Separatist Anthology*. London: Onlywomen Press.

PART III
THE SPOKEN WORD

30

Speaking of Representing the Other

Celia Kitzinger *in conversation with* Manjit Bola,
Amparo Bonilla Campos, Jean Carabine, Kathy Doherty,
Hannah Frith, Ann McNulty, Jackie Reilly and Jan Winn

Because of the overwhelming response to the Call for Papers for the Special Feature on Representing the Other, the Editorial Group of *Feminism & Psychology* agreed to extend the discussion through inviting a small group of feminists with interests in this area (mainly PhD students or new academics) to meet at Loughborough University[1] to discuss our own experiences of 'representing the Other' in the light of our reading of the previously circulated copies of pieces from the Special Feature.[2] As coordinator of this Spoken Word, I took responsibility for inviting the participants, organizing the day (beginning with lunch at a local pub!), and pre-circulating the papers and some 'key questions' for discussion. These included: 'Who is the Other and how do we represent the Other?'; 'Who are "we" and how do we represent ourselves?'; 'What are the benefits and problems for us, as feminists, in representing the Other?'; 'What strategies have we developed for dealing with the problems and how successful are they?' What follows is my edited version (checked and approved by all the participants) of a transcript of a 2½ hour discussion, during which we covered a wide range of provocative and challenging topics. While the reader will find little by way of agreement or resolution in this Spoken Word, it certainly illustrates the sheer diversity of views and the various multiple readings which can be brought to bear on each of the contributions to this volume. As coordinator of this piece, I would point out that, although all contributors are happy with the way in which they are represented (or represent themselves) in this Spoken Word, the text produced here is very much one which has been orchestrated, selected and edited with particular kinds of representational goals in mind and should not, of course, be read as a 'transparent' text.[3] We began with short introductions, in which each of us in turn said a little about her own interests or research area, and raised questions or concerns that she hoped to discuss with the group.

Celia Kitzinger

Spoken Word Participants — Loughborough, 1995

Standing (left to right): Jean Carabine, Celia Kitzinger, Manjit Bola, Kathy Doherty, Ann McNulty. Sitting (left to right): Jan Winn, Jackie Reilly, Amparo Bonilla Campos, Hannah Frith. Photograph by Sue Wilkinson.

Introductions

Hannah: The research I'm doing for my PhD is on young women's sexuality and in particular, saying 'no' to sex. So I'm representing the experience of some young women who are a lot younger than me, and I've been interested in how I position myself as at times similar, and at times different from them – and also how they do that to me as well, and what that means for the way that the conversation goes.

Kathy: I've been interested in questions of agency, gender, subjectivity, reflexivity and representation for several years in a theoretical sense, through my PhD work in discursive psychology.[4] Now these are about to translate into practical concerns. I'm going to be interviewing women who have experience of domestic violence and I *don't* have experience of domestic violence. There are going to be all sorts of differences between me and them, and I'm interested in how, as Hannah said, they're going to represent themselves to me – as different or as the same. How they're going to maybe reject me as being completely unable to understand them and their lives.

Manjit: My PhD research is on white women's experience of pregnancy, so in my own research, really, the tables have been turned. I'm the minority investigating the majority – and right from the beginning the question arose: should I research the majority group when other minorities aren't being investigated? At the beginning of my research I was on the receiving end of a lot of hatred. I was described as a coconut – you know, brown on the outside, but with white identifications. I wondered: 'Is that true? Is that what I'll end up as if I do investigate whites?' But other black women said, 'yes, it's about time the tables were turned: why don't you go and investigate *them*, the way they do us?' – although that sounded a bit like revenge, which wasn't what I wanted either really. Doing the research raised a lot of questions about power in the research process [see Chapter 19].

Amparo: For my PhD, I'm researching career choices, and how gender is constructed at that particular moment in young people's lives when they choose their university subject. I've also been thinking about 'representing the Other' in terms of equal opportunities policies – about how the Other is represented, and about how 'difference' is constructed, by these policies.

Celia: I'm interested in this topic partly as a result of having read too many papers which end up saying: 'Of course, these subjects were all white, middle-class, 18–21-year-old, heterosexual students and things are probably different for black women, working-class women, older women, lesbians, etc.' Full stop. End of paper. This tells you which women are the 'norm' and which are Others, and the experience of the norm is never investigated. One of our interests in editing the material on heterosexuality[5] was to ask questions of the norm: what is it like to be heterosexual? And we recognized quite quickly that we were in the position of Othering heterosexual women, and they told us so in no uncertain terms.[6] To treat 'heterosexual' as Other is apparently not acceptable – which is interesting because, of course, lesbians have been Othered for a very long time.

Ann: I've engaged in 'representing the Other' through my work with the Northern Initiative on Women and Eating,[7] which was set up to support women experiencing eating distress. That's involved listening to about 700 women, over the telephone and in groups, talking about ways of using food which they describe as damaging and painful. My present position as coordinator of the project involves talking about the work, and so representing the women who are using the service in lots of different places – to other workers, to the media. I don't have a research background, and I have to say that I feel 'Othered' in this context, even here in a discussion among women who are in many ways the 'same' as me – i.e. women representing women in some capacity. It's difficult when I am not able to understand terminology because of not having a background in research, and I think it's very important to consider the representer's *choice of words* in writing or speaking about the experience of Others.

Jean: My research is on sexuality and social policy.[8] My interest in the topic of this discussion arises out of my belief that one of the main projects of feminism is acknowledging difference, and saying that difference is important. My question is: 'How can we do that without actually placing women in a position that is Other?' The whole notion of the 'Other' is problematic for me because it reflects a whole set of power relations. Being 'Other' is not usually a positive thing; it's very often imbued with a negative value. So I'm interested in thinking about how, as feminists, we can represent women without placing them in the position of Others.

Jan: I'm doing my PhD research on media representations of female multiple murderers, so I am starting off in a dodgy position, because I'm representing representations – I'm not going to interview these women. I've found that I've got a lot in common with these women. It's actually started getting to the point that I see more commonalities than differences – and this freaks me out because, you know, we're talking about murderers here, and these women are consistently represented as Other in relation to non-murdering women like me. The fact that I, as a feminist, have fallen prey to this idea (to some extent) highlights the power and importance of representation and the effect this has on the individual's image of themselves and Others.

Jackie: When I first saw the call for papers for Representing the Other I wasn't going to bother to write a piece at all because I didn't really think I was representing the Other. I'm doing my PhD research on PMS and a few years back I would have said that I had PMS, and I identified quite strongly with the women I was interviewing. But it nagged away at the back of my mind for a few days, and the more I thought about it, the more I really couldn't get to grips with this whole idea of categorizing people as 'the Other' on the basis of the one single thing that you're researching. There are always commonalities as well as differences, and as Hannah said, even in the course of one interview you can feel very strongly identified with a woman on one issue but feel very strongly different and separate and Other on another issue. You can't decide 'I'm only going to look at people who are the same as me', because that's going to leave a whole load of people with no representation. In an ideal world, every group would have a researcher from their group doing research on them, but that's not how it is now, and you can't really leave whole groups unrepresented.

Who is the Other?

Jan: It seems to me that there's this presumption that the Other is always someone who has nothing better to do than be included in research. The Other is someone who isn't as important as you.

Amparo: So the Other suffers the violence of being made the object of the positivist method.

Celia: That's true of a lot of research, but not all. I've done some research which involved interviewing a lot of men,[9] some of them important men at the head of various organizations, and they certainly have better things to do than be interviewed by me. They tell me so! These are men who are Other to me, but – though I'm the researcher – the power dynamic seems more complicated than you've represented it.

Jean: There are different levels of Other. There's Other in individual terms – there are lots of individuals who are not the same as me; and there's Other in terms of social structure and clear relations of power. Yes, I would agree that men might be Other in the first sense, but in terms of patriarchal society, it is, as Simone de Beauvoir[10] states, *women* who are positioned as Other: man is the norm and woman is the Other in relation to him.

Jackie: Nobody is Other, and everybody is Other. Even if you define yourself as the same as the participants in your research on the basis of one variable, there are going to be other experiences you've had, and categories you belong to, that are going to differentially affect your own personal experience of that one variable.

Ann: I think as a researcher or representative of Others, you have to be honest about the power you have in doing that. There is a risk that the object of the research is subordinate and that the voice of the researcher is more powerful, and doesn't acknowledge the sharing involved in any research or representation. As researchers or representers, we should be aware of the power we have as the named agents in a piece of representational work.

Jan: But in saying that you're erasing the power of the research participant. There is power there – you can't just ignore it.[11]

Manjit: In the papers we've read, most writers assumed that the *researcher* was
in the powerful position, that the research participant was the Other, and that
strategies for representing the Other could be chosen by the researcher at will. I
think that assumption needs questioning. It's true that the researcher is always the
one with power in the sense that the researcher is the one doing the research, but
in other ways they can be less powerful than the participant, and there doesn't
seem to be much written about the dynamics of moving in and out of power.

Hannah: I think that came out in some of the papers where people talked about
the ways in which their research participants had Othered them. Ros Edwards
[Chapter 11], for example, was made powerless, at least in her role as researcher,
by her participants' refusal to participate in her research. As researchers we
don't just define who our participants are and what we are interested in. They
define themselves and their own interests and they define us too. With my own
participants, sometimes they will say 'we' meaning all of them and me too, and
at other times they'll say, 'but it's different for you', and in that way they Other
me. I'm still in the powerful position as researcher, but they're not passive
participants – they're doing something too.

Jean: I quite liked the idea that Magdalene Ang-Lygate [Chapter 5] raised about
how a group first excluded her because they thought she was Scottish, and then
they included her because she was Chinese, and then she goes on to talk about the
differences between Hong Kong, Malaysian and Nonya women and how her
Chineseness alone could not automatically be assumed to be a source of commonality. [*Reads from text*] 'Still', she says, 'it was upon this premise that I
gained access to a group which would otherwise have excluded me.' And, this is
the bit I like: 'In this case, the imaginary boundary that demarcated Otherness
was shifted by her to let me in. Since that time, more imaginary lines based on
sexuality, class, religion, and politics have indeed been drawn and I have been
routinely excluded or included depending on the circumstances.' I wonder
whether it is helpful to stop thinking about all this as though it's something *fixed*
– seeing instead that these are imaginary boundaries which can be shifted and that
we *are* shifting between them at different times.

Manjit: This word 'imaginary' – so many of the positions that we're in are *not*
imaginary.

Jean: They're socially constructed.

Amparo: But they *matter*. They are socially constructed for *reasons* and they have
real effects in the world.

Hannah: I think this is a problem to do with power. When feminists have talked
about power in the research process they've talked about strategies like feeding
back your research results to your participants and things like this which I don't
think get to the root of the problem. A lot of these papers have been *so* caught up
with the idea of fluid identities, and shifting identifications, and asking 'in what

ways are we similar and in what ways are we different?', without really thinking about what differences are *important* – and some differences are more important than others. Differences are not all equal. Differences are structured along lines of power and powerlessness and I was a bit disappointed that power was not more central to the discussions.

Who are 'We'?

Hannah: I suppose in this context that 'we' are feminists, but I have found it quite difficult to identify with feminism, as a young woman.[12] There's all this discussion about how feminism isn't what it used to be, and if you were around in the 1960s and 1970s everything was much more strident and we were out on the streets . . . So young women are sort of pushed out by older feminists, and there's all this discussion about how young women aren't feminist – which if you *are* or you're trying to be, makes things very difficult. It's taken me quite a long time to call myself a feminist.

Jan: Who's a good enough feminist?

Amparo: I haven't been told I'm not a feminist because I wasn't around in 1970s feminism, but I don't feel close to 1970s feminism: it feels very distant. Sometimes I find it so difficult to say 'we', 'we, feminists' – joining *all* the other feminists.

Manjit: This is to do with the theme of diversity and difference *within* any category.

Amparo: One of my personal experiences of constructing a 'we' was when I came out as a lesbian, and began to move into a lesbian social world; then I moved from feeling very isolated and apart from other people to seeing myself as the same kind of person as other lesbians are. So I can talk about 'we' as 'we the lesbians', because I realize that it is being lesbian that has isolated me for so many years. At the same time, I don't think I'm exactly the same as other lesbians and I feel different from many lesbians in different ways and as though I don't qualify sometimes.

Celia: Have 'we' been represented by other feminists and felt they've done it well?

Jan: Yes, that paper at the Women's Studies conference on working-class women.[13] That was a really emotional experience for me. It struck a chord. My experience of education is that my sexuality and my gender are, these days, covered from all sorts of diverse perspectives, but what wasn't was class, and I hadn't realized how important class was. I think there's a lack of representation of class.

Kathy: I wasn't at that conference but I think the only time I've ever come away from a paper and thought, 'yes, she's really talking about *me*', is when I heard

Valerie Walkerdine speak about her experiences as a working-class academic.[14] I identified really strongly with that.

Manjit: I suppose I identified with the disability paper [Deborah Marks, Chapter 7], and that's why I liked it so much, because of having poor health but still staying in education. I remember as an undergraduate, the hospital was right opposite the university and I used to send my papers over from my bed. I liked the way in which the disability paper stressed autonomy and that we're not the pathetic little individuals that we often get portrayed as.

Jean: I agree with a lot of this. I haven't been represented in any way that really, down deep, felt like it was me. I've stopped expecting to find that now. I just hope that there's something there, some aspect I can recognize. I went into education very late and continually felt Other about being academic, about being working class, about being discovered for the fool I really was . . . [*laughter*] But you *can* make being Other positive.

Jan: Yes, a lot of life experiences that I've had are presented as very debilitating and very . . . I'm supposed to be sitting in a corner somewhere sobbing. But actually I've found strength through some of those experiences. I feel very angry about being offered a victim status that I don't actually want.

Manjit: It was difficult to identify with some of these papers because you do go with a mixed baggage to reading each paper. Like, the weight one [Joan C. Chrisler, Chapter 13], I read that thinking: 'well, this is a white, middle-class view anyway, that weight is a problem' – that's the way it came across to me. It's the opposite for me. A lot of mature black women come up to me and say 'eat!' and you can see that for them, being bigger is better. And when I have put a bit of weight on they'll come up to me and say 'you look much better.'

Excluding the Other

Jan: Malestream research traditionally *excluded* all sorts of groups, but we've got to a stage in feminist research where it seems we've got to include everything and everyone. It's 'validity through inclusion'. I think sometimes it can be better to reflect on the different categories and then *exclude* some of them. Exclusion isn't that much of a problem for me. What's a problem is if the same people are getting excluded time and time again.

Jackie: A lot of people who would call themselves feminists are quite sure that PMS is purely and simply a psychological problem. They reckon that if everyone would only get their heads straight, nobody would have PMS. How anyone can say that something that hundreds of thousands of women suffer from, and spend a fortune on remedies that aren't shown to be helpful and can actually be harmful, and have their lives upset by . . . For those women that's a real experience. You can't just say that PMS doesn't exist. You can't exclude the experience of other women just because it's not *your* experience.

Celia: *Feminism & Psychology* has published articles which explicitly say that PMS is a dangerous political construct and that it's not useful for feminists.[15]

Jackie: Just because it might be dangerous politically is no reason not to examine it. I don't think you can say that because you don't like the implications of what you might find, you should just stick it in a corner and tell everyone who's complaining that it's in their imagination. I don't think that's a very feminist attitude actually. I think women should be open to the suggestion that other women *do* have different experiences, and be genuinely interested, and take the responsibility of looking at it. And if it turns out that they don't like what they find, well, they have to take the responsibility of facing up to that too.

Celia: Although Diana Russell [Chapter 12], concerned about the possible political implications of her research with black women, decided not to do it.

Jackie: I disagree with Diana Russell. I'd have gone ahead and done that research on everybody, because – as Ros Edwards [Chapter 11] says – how can you deliberately leave certain people out when you're doing research? Certainly you're going to be guided by your own personal interests and background, but I don't think you can make a conscious decision and say 'right, I don't like the political implications of that so not only am *I* not going to research it, but I'm going to say that it's politically dangerous, and nobody else should research it either.'

Jean: Are you saying, then, that all kinds of research are alright?

Celia: Research on genetic causes of homosexuality, race differences in IQ, research leading to the abortion of disabled foetuses . . . ?

Jackie: This all boils down to moral judgements and everyone has to decide that for themselves. I don't think I am doing anything in my research that is contrary to feminism. What I am trying to do is give some sort of representation to women who say that they are suffering. I feel privileged in having a forum in which I can speak and be heard by academics who wouldn't listen to the personal testimony of these women. If a woman says, 'I have PMS', someone who is familiar with the literature is going to say, 'ah, well, she's under stress; her husband doesn't help out with the kids, she's powerless . . .' and they're not going to believe her. But if I do my research sensitively, and don't attempt to speak for them, but attempt to represent them, and deliberately adopt the stance of the Other, then their voices might be heard. I don't think these voices should be deliberately excluded.

Kathy: Exclusion is a problem, but I think Diana Russell makes a very strong argument. She started off wanting a representative sample, and then engaged in what I think is an extremely useful political analysis of what the outcomes of this would be, and she made the decision *not* to include black women in her sample, because of the possible political ramifications of that.

Hannah: I think similar points were made by Chris Griffin [Chapter 14] in terms of interpretations that are made about researchers' representations. She asks us to think about the responsibility we have to think through all the different ways in which our research might be used. She points out that we need to be accountable for our research, and says that we need to make that accountability integral to doing the research, so as to try to exclude certain interpretations which we wouldn't want made.

Jean: And it's still a problem in Diana Russell's research because black women could say they're still being ignored even if the reason given for ignoring them is different. They're being abused and their abuse is not researched, not recognized.

Amparo: And she was still accused of racism anyway!

Jackie: Sometimes whatever you do as a researcher you're going to get criticized.

Kathy: That's why her article is called 'Between a Rock and a Hard Place'![16]

[*General laughter*]

Jackie: If a black woman had been researching black incest survivors, would that have had different political implications? I mean, would she have done the research any differently, and would the results have been any different? Would the political implications of the results have been affected by the fact that it was a black researcher rather than a white researcher?

Manjit: I don't see why Diana Russell went for total exclusion of black women. With something as salient as sexual abuse, why couldn't she say 'let's look at the commonalities'? There are cases in which that can be dangerous, but in *this* research I think it would have been useful to show that this is something that can happen across cultures, that this is a significant commonality.

Jean: I agree with you entirely about representing commonalities, but there may also be significant differences.

Manjit: But given the political implications, it's surely the commonalities which are important. It wasn't as though the only choices were representative sampling or total exclusion. She could have gone for half black and half white women, and not made race a particular issue.

Getting it Wrong

Kathy: There seems to be a great fear that we're going to misrepresent, that we're not going to get it right, that we're not going to be accurate enough.

Manjit: But that fear is justified. We shouldn't lose that fear. I thought Anna Livia's [Chapter 2] paper was atrocious. She was putting herself on a pedestal and although she was trying to claim that you can and should identify with Others, she doesn't actually do that in her own work. She talks about Jews and their dress, and she says, 'well when I asked Jewish people what they thought, I got mixed responses, and I made the mistake of paying attention to what they said.' So she's saying, 'No, you shouldn't listen to the so-called experts' at that point. What she calls a 'mistake', I think is an admirable strategy. And then at another point, when she starts critically looking at the way in which lesbians have been represented in certain texts, she puts herself in the role of the expert. So she's acting as the expert on lesbians because she belongs to that group, while rejecting the expertise of Jews, a group she doesn't belong to. I don't think it makes so much difference that it's fiction: her characters aren't entirely fictitious – they're not aliens. She's writing about people in our world, people we can all see or have the same stereotypes about.

Kathy: I think there's a problem with the 'exoticization' of Others.

Manjit: If I were one of the black women subjects that Ros Edwards [Chapter 11] was approaching, I'd say 'on your bike', you know. I can totally understand the response she got. It's not so much that white women *shouldn't* research black women. It's that they must take account of the historical processes through which black women have been excluded and misrepresented, and not perpetuate that.

Kathy: I totally agree, and I think part of the problem is that she underplayed the importance of the hierarchical relationship. I can almost imagine her walking in there with her suit and briefcase and saying 'can I do some research on you?', and it would be like, 'on your bike', as you say. And then she's expressing surprise, 'oh well, if I got involved in their social networks that's okay.'

Jackie: But, looking on the bright side, if you do a *bad* job of representing Others, then it stirs people to respond. Christine Griffin [Chapter 14] was referring to the Nava article: even a poor attempt gives the people you're attempting to represent a voice, in that it stirs people to speak back. I don't think fear of getting it wrong should stop you from attempting to speak.

Jan: Yes, too much sitting around and thinking about these issues can be absolutely paralysing. You end up thinking, 'oh my god, I'm going home and never doing any research again.'

Silence, Challenge and Disagreement

Ann: Women say that they're not able to speak on their own behalf, because it feels risky or whatever. When you take up the task of speaking on their behalf, it's important to think carefully about when that may no longer be appropriate. I suppose the whole Initiative on Women and Eating is about supporting women in finding their own words. It's also about not continuing to speak on someone else's behalf after it's ceased to be useful.

Celia: Has anyone else got any specific examples of a time when they thought 'now I will *not* speak on behalf of the Other'; 'now the Other can speak for herself using her own words'; 'now I have to shut up'. When have we shut up?

Manjit: I think I have in the way in which I'm trying to do the analysis of my accounts because I used a diary method, so they've actually put their words in writing, and although, obviously, I've got a role in directing what they've said in these diaries, compared with the direct interaction of an interview, there's been far less intervention. So I've tried to stick with their words. And my interpretations, I've tried to keep entirely separate. Obviously I am making choices by which themes I'm pulling out, and how I'm structuring these themes and choosing the extracts. But they do speak for themselves. I provide another voice on top of them – my own interpretation and analysis – but you can read them as they are and make your own interpretations.

Jean: Is it a mistake to envisage this whole notion of representing the Other as a question of speaking or not speaking, and of finding the right moment to switch off? And is that not a bit patronizing anyway, that the researcher should claim to find the right moment to shut up? You know: 'I got that right – pat on the back'! When I was interviewing powerful people, there were certainly times I shut up, when to have intervened would have stopped them from talking about things I wanted to know, about how sexuality issues get on the agenda.[17] And that's a very different kind of shutting up. And there are other situations where . . . when I was interviewing a black woman who felt very very strongly about feminism – about what she perceived as white feminism – and I was terrified, you know. I was thinking: 'Oh, god, why's she speaking to me then? She feels so strongly . . .'. And also I felt miffed because I was thinking, 'well, *I* don't belong in that category.' So in some ways I felt then that it *was* appropriate to shut up and not to challenge that, not to say, 'well, not all white feminists are like that.' I did say at the end of the interview, however, 'well, I am interested to know why you agreed to be interviewed given that I am a white woman.' And she made it very clear to me that black women were very rarely included in research, and she didn't want black women to be presented as women who are weak or without any kind of agency.[18]

Celia: But what happens if, in your opinion, the words women find are not the 'right' words politically? I think this is the problem for Joan Chrisler [Chapter

13]: that the women's words are not right and so she still needs to go on speaking 'over' them.

Ann: Joan Chrisler's paper on weight was one of the papers – I could say this of several papers – where the researcher is actually privileging herself and saying 'my views are the right views and your views are wrong.'

Hannah: As in, 'you might think differently from me, but I know what's best for you!' which I thought was outrageous. But people *do* disagree with your analysis and your representation of them, and how on earth do you deal with that?

Ann: I think the problem is that she's suggesting that her position is informed by having listened to fat women, so she justifies her position as right by saying that she's listened to them, but it doesn't always feel as though she *has* listened.

Hannah: I thought it was very interesting how she justified her position, because she positions herself in contrast to a former self who was doing a nasty horrible patriarchal thing of advising women on weight control. So she was saying, 'look how much better I am now.' I actually didn't think she was that much better now.

Manjit: Can I come back to this point of your feeling, Jean, as though you were being challenged and yet you couldn't identify with this challenge personally. In a couple of these papers there's mention of how black feminists have challenged the researcher and again I felt as though what we were getting here was an attack on that challenge. It's almost as though they're saying, 'how dare you challenge me? And right now I've got the power to put in print that you challenged me and this is how I think you're *wrong* in your challenge.' And there's no come-back. There are dangers when you start representing the challenge because you haven't got the other side, the Other, to come back and challenge *you*.

Jean: The question, then, is, should I take a passive role in any challenges that are made to me by black women in my research? Or is that in itself disempowering? Is that in itself silencing women? And does that mean that people then get fixed, so that you know, black women get fixed, lesbians get fixed, and we just have single identities? And the point you were making earlier about searching for commonality . . . it stops us engaging in some kind of way. Also, harking back to what Hannah was saying, sometimes there will be people whom you research who you *don't* agree with, and you don't *want* to agree with, you know . . . and they *are* the Other . . .

Amparo: And you have to give an explanation about this disagreement between you and them. In my research on young people choosing their careers, what the figures show is that this is a social thing, that career choice is clearly structured by social class and by gender. But young people represent themselves as making individual choices. So they dismiss equal opportunity policies as not being important at all, because for them, there isn't a problem, and, obviously, I disagree with them.

Jean: So they think they're making strong individual choices, and you're coming along and saying, 'it's social structure'?

Amparo: Yes. I think these disagreements happen all the time. For example in this paper on women's weight [Joan C. Chrisler, Chapter 13], she is talking about weight as a *social* problem for women, so she is criticizing the 'experts', meaning the women themselves, who say that it is an *individual* problem. The difference I think between this paper on women's weight, and the paper on disability [Deborah Marks, Chapter 7], is that women working on disability have already constructed a very clear idea of disability as a *social* problem and as a *political* concern. In the paper on women's weight, the women are individualistic, they don't have this social and political understanding, although the researcher does. I wouldn't expect that my interpretations would be the same as my participants' point of view because mostly my participants aren't feminists. You just have to realize that sometimes the people you are researching are not going to agree with you, and what you need to do is give an explanation of how the oppression of patriarchy is hidden from the oppressed, how it works, how it reproduces itself without people realizing that's what's happening.

Jean: It's difficult though, isn't it, because you run straight into the notion of 'false consciousness', and the problems inherent in that?

Amparo: That's certainly something I don't intend. I don't agree with the notion of 'false consciousness'.

Hannah: One way people have attempted to get around the problem of false consciousness is not to say 'I'm right and they're wrong' but by saying instead 'here's *my* interpretation and here's my *participants'* interpretation – you make up your mind.' And I don't think it's as easy as that, because some interpretations are more heavily weighted than others.

Amparo: Christine Griffin [Chapter 14] says that we should say where we are starting from, state our standpoint and whose interests we are serving in doing our research.

Hannah: I think that can be a bit dishonest though, because it's alright when you're writing up your theory to say that stuff, but when you meet your participants you probably don't start by saying, 'I'm a feminist and this is what I think, and this is the framework with which I'm going to be writing up your experiences.' To what extent is that deception?

Jean: There's no reason why you can't make that information available. You could make it explicit, you could give them a sheet with the information on. But it's about more than simply saying 'this is who I am' and leaving it at that. It's about saying 'well, who *am* I?' and questioning that, and questioning how it impacts on the research and positioning yourself and your identities. The authors of that 'sameness' paper [Tracey L. Hurd and Alice McIntyre, Chapter 10] did that, questioned the assumptions they made about understanding something, challenging themselves.

Kathy: I think that's very important because otherwise you do run the risk of using the statement of who you are and what you stand for as a rhetorical stance to warrant your research. I think your own account of who and what you are has to be open to reflexive analysis in and of itself in terms of what it's trying to achieve. I would say, though, that certain types of research are encouraged and others are actively undermined in academia – from the gatekeeping process right through to funding, time limits, and all the rest of it. And some of the solutions that we've been talking about (like feeding our data and analysis back to our participants) which, as feminists, we can't afford, perhaps, *not* to take, are extremely time-consuming – and we'll be penalized for that.

Creating Social Change?

Celia: We've talked a lot about the *problems* of representing Others. Given the risks, why as feminists do we go on doing it? What are the *benefits* of representing Others? Why would one do it? Why is it important?

Manjit: It's to do with building bridges really, isn't it? You've got to get some level of understanding from different positions. There are things we can learn from each other.

Hannah: One of the main ideas that came out from the papers was this idea of advocacy. I was a bit unsure about that – whether it was just a nifty linguistic way of justifying what you're doing, but . . . People who, for want of a better phrase, can't speak for themselves . . . The benefit put forward by several of the authors is that if *we* don't talk about it, no one else is going to.

Jan: Or, if we don't talk about it, someone else *might*, which could also be a problem.

Ann: Yes, not only because other people *might*, but also because they already *are*, and we want to introduce other perspectives. The debate about eating disorders has been appropriated by the medical profession and they've established the language and the framework for thinking about this. We want to challenge their ownership of this area and think about different ways of representing eating distress.

Kathy: And although, on occasion, we may find our attempts at advocacy firmly rejected, that's something that seemed constantly there – the question 'to what extent will this piece of research that I am doing contribute to some notion of social change?' I think we've thought a lot today about the risks of doing research on and representing Others, but I think we need to ask ourselves about the risks of *not* doing it, as well.

Jean: I have real problems with this notion of advocacy because it puts us in the position of identifying ourselves as the advocates and the Others as not the advocates. Maybe we have to ask, what does it mean that in this work, this person is represented as Other to me? What processes of representation are at work? To what extent is that relationship of Otherness fixed and to what extent is it possible to change that?

Kathy: I think what's become clear is that there are many ambiguities in talking about this issue but I think that overall, in terms of how this discussion has gone . . . I am just surrounded by so many mainstream psychologists who just never question their right to describe what they've come up with as 'the hard facts' of other people's lives – and who have no qualms at all about publishing them. Although we've come up with more questions than answers, it's obvious that these are very important questions and that, as feminists and social scientists, we should really be discussing them more.

Notes

1 Thank you to Sue Wilkinson for her help on the day.

2 Thank you to the authors of these for permission to circulate pre-publication copies of their contributions. It should be noted that, due to pressures on time, most of these were circulated *before* authors had revised their pieces in line with suggestions from reviewers and from the Editor. This means that there are some differences between the pieces as they were read by the Spoken Word participants, and as they were finally published in the journal. The circulated pieces were those by Magdalene Ang-Lygate, Joan C. Chrisler, Rosalind Edwards, Christine Griffin, Tracey L. Hurd and Alice McIntyre, Anna Livia, Deborah Marks, and Diana E.H. Russell.

3 My thanks to Erica Burman for insisting on this point.

4 See Anna Madill and Kathy Doherty (1994) '"So You Did What You Wanted Then": Discourse Analysis, Personal Agency and Psychotherapy', *Journal of Community and Applied Social Psychology* 4 (4): 261–73.

5 Celia Kitzinger, Sue Wilkinson and Rachel Perkins (1993) Special Issue of *Feminism & Psychology* on Heterosexuality, 2 (3). Later expanded into a book: Sue Wilkinson and Celia Kitzinger (eds) (1993) *Heterosexuality: A 'Feminism & Psychology' Reader*. London: Sage.

6 See Celia Kitzinger and Sue Wilkinson (1994) 'Re-viewing Heterosexuality', *Feminism & Psychology* 4 (2): 330–6.

7 The Northern Initiative on Women and Eating (NIWE) was founded in 1988 in Newcastle upon Tyne, UK, in response to women asking for support around eating distress. NIWE has also developed group support for women experiencing eating problems, and training sessions for other workers. Its work has been recognized as an example of innovative and significant good practice in working with women by Good Practices in Mental Health (see Caroline Harding and Jan Sherlock, 1994 *Women and Mental Health: An Information Pack of Mental Health Services for Women in the UK*. London: Good Practices in Mental Health).

8 See Jean Carabine (1992) 'Constructing Women: Women, Sexuality and Social Policy', *Critical Social Policy* 34: 24–37; Jean Carabine (1996) 'Heterosexuality and Social Policy', in Diane Richardson (ed.) *Theorising Heterosexuality*. Milton Keynes: Open University Press; Jean Carabine (1996) *Women, Sexuality and Social Policy*. London: Macmillan.

9 In two contexts: on sexual harassment, Alison Thomas and Celia Kitzinger (1994) '"It's Just

Something that Happens"': The Invisibility of Sexual Harassment in the Workplace', *Gender, Work, and Organisation* 1 (3): 151–61; and on understandings of human rights, Rex Stainton Rogers and Celia Kitzinger (1995) 'A Decalogue of Human Rights: What Happens When You Let the People Speak', *Social Science Information* 34 (1): 87–106.

10 Simone de Beauvoir (1972) *The Second Sex*. Harmondsworth: Penguin.

11 Ann's comment on reading through the transcript: 'Certainly, one of the aims of NIWE is to challenge the representation of women experiencing eating problems as "sufferers", i.e. women without any kind of agency. The way they are using food is what they happen to be doing at a particular point to communicate what it doesn't feel possible, just yet, to verbalize.'

12 See Hannah Frith (1994) 'Turning Us Off', *Feminism & Psychology* 4 (2): 315–16.

13 Christine Zmroczek (1995) 'Rough Ideas: Working Class Women, Class and Women's Studies', paper presented at the Women's Studies Network (UK) Conference, Stirling, Scotland.

14 Valerie Walkerdine (1993) 'Psychology, Postmodernity and the Popular', paper presented at the British Psychological Society London Conference, London, December. See also the Special Issue of *Feminism & Psychology* on social class, edited by Valerie Walkerdine (1996) 6 (3).

15 See Paula J. Caplan, Joan McCurdy-Myers and Maureen Gans (1992) 'Should "Premenstrual Syndrome" be Called a Psychiatric Abnormality?' *Feminism & Psychology* 2 (1): 27–44; Mary Brown Parlee (1992) 'On PMS and Psychiatric Abnormality', *Feminism & Psychology* 2 (1): 105–8; Paula J. Caplan, Joan McCurdy-Myers and Maureen Gans (1992) 'Reply to Mary Brown Parlee's Commentary on PMS and Psychiatric Anomaly', *Feminism & Psychology* 2 (1): 109.

16 This was also the title of Barbara Smith's (1988) essay on relations between black and Jewish women in the USA, in *Yours in Struggle: Three Feminist Perspectives in Antisemitism and Racism*. New York: Firebrand Books.

17 See Jean Carabine (1995) 'Sexuality, Politics and Policy Making', in Angelia Wilson (ed.) *A Simple Matter of Justice*. London: Cassell.

18 Jean's comment on reading the transcript: 'I feel uneasy about what I said here, because I can see that the way I have expressed it is in itself problematic and that many black feminists would be angry that I didn't challenge them and would see that as a kind of racism. However, in the context of this particular research project, I wanted to know black women's views about a particular campaign which had resulted in a serious split between black and white feminists who had previously been working together.' For further details, see J. Carabine (1992) 'Constructing Women: Women's Sexuality and Social Policy', unpublished PhD thesis, University of Sheffield, UK.

Index